BY THE SMOKE
& THE SMELL

THAD VOGLER

BY THE SMOKE
& THE SMELL

MY SEARCH FOR THE RARE & SUBLIME
ON THE SPIRITS TRAIL

TEN SPEED PRESS
California | New York

All rights reserved.
Published in the United States by Ten Speed Press,
an imprint of the Crown Publishing Group,
a division of Penguin Random House LLC, New York.
www.crownpublishing.com
www.tenspeed.com

The names and identifying characteristics of some of the people
portrayed in this book have been changed to protect their privacy.

Ten Speed Press and the Ten Speed Press colophon are registered
trademarks of Penguin Random House LLC.

Library of Congress Cataloging-in-Publication Data
Names: Vogler, Thaddeus, author.
Title: By the smoke and the smell : my search for the rare and
sublime on the spirits trail / Thaddeus Vogler.
Description: First edition. | California : Ten Speed Press, [2017]
Identifiers: LCCN 2017016196
Subjects: LCSH: Liquors. | Distillation. | Distilling industries.
Classification: LCC TP597 .V64 2017 | DDC 663/.16–dc23
LC record available at https://lccn.loc.gov/2017016196

Hardcover ISBN: 978-0-399-57860-1
eBook ISBN: 978-0-399-57861-8

Printed in the United States of America

Design by Angelina Cheney
Cover illustration by Martin Azambuja

10 9 8 7 6 5 4 3 2 1

First Edition

TO KATHERINE,

FOR ALL THOSE TIMES YOU COULDN'T BE THERE

At the foot of the hill there's a neat little still,
Where the smoke curls up to the sky,
By the smoke and the smell you can plainly tell
That there's poitin brewin' nearby.

—"Rare Old Mountain Dew," traditional folk song

BY THE SMOKE
& THE SMELL

CONTENTS

PART ONE   1

A category of human experience is
becoming extinct and it is cause for tears

    3   Chapter One
        CALVADOS: The right way to be French

   28   Chapter Two
        COGNAC: They'll hire the guy who fucked your wife

   48   Chapter Three
        ARMAGNAC: All those moments are lost in time,
        like tears in rain

PART TWO   79

Ammunition?! This is no time for ammunition!

   81   Chapter Four
        CUBA, Part I: The reality of cultural capital

  108   Chapter Five
        CUBA, Part II: Unbutton your trousers . . .
        this is how we do it, man

PART THREE   135

Gin a body meet a body / comin thro' the grain

137   Chapter Six
      SCOTLAND, Part I: Haloo, Grigalach!

159   Chapter Seven
      NORTHERN IRELAND: But I was young and foolish

171   Chapter Eight
      SCOTLAND, Part II: Gin a body kiss a body / need
      a body cry?

PART FOUR   207

A category of human experience is becoming extinct
and it is cause for celebration

209   Chapter Nine
      OAXACA, Part I: A stop on the Hippie Highway

236   Chapter Ten
      OAXACA, Part II: Pinche teachers

266   Chapter Eleven
      KENTUCKY: The rare old mountain dew

289   Acknowledgments

291   About the Author

PART ONE

A CATEGORY OF HUMAN EXPERIENCE
IS BECOMING EXTINCT
AND IT IS CAUSE FOR TEARS

Chapter One

CALVADOS

THE RIGHT WAY TO BE FRENCH

Each time Craig, Eric, and I connect with Charles Neal in France, it's at the McDonald's in the American Terminal at Charles de Gaulle Airport (CDG) in Paris. Nowhere are cultural differences more palpable and exciting than beneath the golden arches in a foreign country. The smooth, manufactured surfaces with their familiar palette of cantaloupe and tangerine are grounding, but the menu bears unfamiliar tidings: Le Menu Maxi! Nos Steak Haché! We see our own culture reflected in a funhouse mirror. We drink *café crème* from stenciled, eight-ounce Styrofoam cups and use the free Wi-Fi while we wait for Charles. He will be late this morning. Once we're in his care, we will be late to every appointment and every tasting for the next week.

Craig, our head barman at Bar Agricole, sits alone with a half-finished cup of coffee and bent over his phone in a familiar posture; I know he is preparing playlists for our trip. He is dressed in many layers today, like a big-game photographer, wearing two thick, collared shirts over a turtleneck with a warm flannel coat encompassing the whole ensemble. Craig is a sweet man with whom I've worked for fifteen years in numerous places. He is lean, handsome, and fashionable; a devout indie rocker, he always dresses the part. Despite a restless youthfulness, middle age is imminent, evident in his discreetly thinning hair and a less visible assortment of skin and abdominal maladies that become apparent as you spend more time with him. He was at my wedding. For two years around the time he was getting divorced, after each of our shifts together, I'd stay up and talk with him until two in the morning. That he works for me is probably my most impressive credential as a bar owner. He is an artist and music enthusiast who has found real meaning in our work at the bar. Devoted to the craft, Craig works harder than anyone I know to make this job something we can feel proud of as we move from our forties toward our fifties. Our parents used to wonder what we were thinking when it came to this bar stuff; we had spent tens of thousands of dollars on liberal arts degrees that were not being put to use at all. We were underachievers; now we get mentioned in the *New York Times.* Craig has a beautiful softness to him, and he's also a little bit of a lush in the best sense of the word. On a given night, he might go a little too far, speak a little too freely. You wouldn't think he's an asshole—just a bit careless in how he speaks. At these times, there's always a sorrow to Craig; he can fall into despair. Craig and I are glad to see each other. We shake hands, '70s style, locking together the way you would if you were helping up someone who'd fallen over.

If Craig is here, Eric can't be far away. On these trips he is always the curious child, wandering at the periphery or falling behind, where a cat or an old photograph has caught his attention. Eric is my business partner in Bar Agricole as well as Trou Normand, our second place, named for the brandies we taste on this annual trip around France. He put his life savings, including the money his father left him upon his death when Eric was very young, into our first place. Eric arrives right on cue, carrying two-liter bottles of Badoit mineral water, one of which he tosses to me with a smile. I can see a baguette sandwich emerging from his windbreaker pocket. The jacket fits him snugly and complements his winter scarf, adeptly folded in half then draped in half again over his neck, the twin tails pulled snugly through the loop end; this scarfmanship is something he learned when he lived in Belgium as a younger man. Eric, like Craig, is slim, maintaining a European gauntness that aids him in his passion of motorcycle track racing. He is a devout vegetarian and benefits from that flattering kind of male pattern balding. You may see him in a belted leather jacket enjoying a coffee and feel certain he is Italian or French. He is unilaterally positive and, to my great approval, actually once attended a Tony Robbins seminar.

I'm off to the counter of McCafé, adjacent to the McDonald's proper, to order my first *café crème* of the trip. McCafé is a still greater departure from our domestic McDonald's, with its macarons and elevated pastry offerings. Walking to the counter I'm keeping an eye out for two more from our party whom we haven't met, two representatives from Marx Importers, a wine wholesaler in Los Angeles.

Returning to our table with my coffee in hand, I see my guys have found the Marx Importers contingent. I arrive just in time to finish out the round-robin of handshakes. The first of them is the nephew of the owner and appears to be twenty-one or twenty-two. He wears a sinister beard. I've never met him before, but I don't trust him. This probably tells you more about me than him; I can be inhospitable. He is young, and moments after shaking hands at the airport McDonald's, he is gracelessly working shoptalk into our first conversations.

The other is in his mid-thirties and is called Leon. He's a likeable guy with a lot of tattoos. From the tattoos and the full Victorian beard, you can tell right away that he's a bar guy. His hair is messy, and he has a soft, kind quality that reminds me of my stepfather.

Our party complete, now all there is to do is wait for Charles Neal, owner of Charles Neal Selections. I have been buying his spirits for years, and of late we have grown our relationship to the point where Charles and I travel to France each year to choose barrels of grower-producer brandies—spirits that Eric, Craig, and I will use in mixed drinks in our bars in the coming year.

I am a restaurateur. I own two bars that serve food and have pretentious French names. My colleagues and I are in France to buy brandies that will furnish these locations. Our bars participate in the Bay Area tradition of meticulous sourcing. We are known for mixed drinks and they are good because we source our base spirits very carefully, not because we are particularly inventive or talented. Our goal on this trip is to select and purchase single-barrel and blended selections of calvados, armagnac, and cognac. These bottlings will keep us in business for the next year until, if we are lucky and Charles will have us, we repeat the drill. For me, this trip is the high point of the year. Craig and Eric claim to feel the same.

At my places, Trou Normand and Bar Agricole, we use these French brandies as the foundation for as many of the drinks we serve as possible. We scour the thousand-and-one drinks books of the late nineteenth and early twentieth centuries for recipes featuring brandy in its various forms. I suppose brandy is one of our few specialties because these liquids have real provenance. Sadly, spirits with this sense of identity are available in only a few places around the world. These brandies are crops, grown and harvested by the same farmers who ferment them and distill them. They are not well-known spirits and they are not affordable, but we love them dearly and they give our work, our lives even, meaning.

So here we begin, exhausted in a French McDonald's in the early morning. Exhausted and late. Kermit Lynch has already written elegantly about the work of tasting trips in *Adventures on the Wine Route*. People who have read that book or hear what I do for a living never believe me when I tell them this is work; they joke that they wish they had our job. They're not wrong; our job is great, but this will be work—we're running from the moment we begin.

At last, it's Charles. Giddily, we watch him move confidently through the crowd of the airport mall. Taller than most of the people he passes, he pulls an expertly packed, wheeled carry-on behind him like an expensive dog on a leash. This single piece of luggage is as much as he ever brings on these trips. He's the coolest person we know. A novelist, music critic, essayist, importer, and father of two admirable teenage girls. Today he is dressed perfectly Euro in narrow boots, an Adidas hat, boot-cut jeans, and a bright-colored windbreaker, and when he strides into our McDonald's the air in the room changes. "What's up, fuckers?" is his greeting. I think Charles looks a little like a young Warren Oates, with his thin, nearly imperceptible beard and his youthfully dark rock-and-roll hair that he wears collar-length. My first tasting with Charles was at his home in the Richmond, a quiet and diverse residential neighborhood that lines the San Francisco artery, Geary Street, as it winds toward Ocean Beach. His home is intellectually decorated with framed posters from Fassbinder films on his walls. To feed Charles's guests at the tasting, his French wife, Nathalie, warmed up half a leftover roast chicken from the previous night's dinner. I had found my role model. Here and now, at CDG, Charles is moving things along: "Everybody has met each other? Excellent. Okay, are you ready to *do* this?"

As we hurry through the airport, working to keep up with Charles—some of us trying the conveyor-belt walkways, others moving more freely without mechanical assistance—I fail to convince Leon from Marx Importers that this trip might turn out to be a little grueling. Only a few days later, at three in the morning in the barrel room of a viscount who produces armagnac, Leon would turn to me and tell me I had been right.

We arrive at the rental car lot where Charles has already secured our vehicle. As we approach the van across the frozen lot, Charles points proudly. "I think that's it." Our future is visible on the horizon, white and unremarkable. Equipped with two rows of seats in addition to the front driver and passenger seats, technically the passenger van could fit nine; for our crew of six, this van will be just enough space with its merciless gray upholstery, dispiriting microfibers that will absorb all categories of filth in the ensuing miles, windows that don't open, and hard-contoured surfaces. This is home.

We climb in and assume what will become permanent positions: Charles is in the driver's seat with Eric as copilot. The Los Angeles contingent take the center row and Craig and I sit on opposite ends of the longer back bench seat. The weather is shitty as we get underway. Driving through suburban industrial Paris, it's hard to believe we're bound for idyllic, pastoral moments: fresh goat cheese at dusk as we look out over a valley; beautiful breeds of cow like the Blonde d'Aquitaine and the Vache Normande; sharp-peaked pear trees mixed with plump, shorter apple trees. These moments are always in juxtaposition with the hell-bent pace at which we drive and the noisy playlist curated by Charles, usually comprising genre bands I don't know or perfectly chosen indie rock from every era. Among the books he's written is a collection of interviews conducted at the height of New Wave, featuring conversations with the likes of Ian Curtis. Currently, we are being assaulted by *Lulu*, a rock opera and collaboration with Lou Reed and Metallica. It is dissonant and awful, and over the din Charles explains, "Lou Reed brought these demos to the recording to take the shit to the next level." Lou Reed speaks characteristically over Metallica's soundtrack in an attempt to recapture the turgidity of his youth. "They recorded it live, just sitting there looking at each other," Charles says. "Apparently Lou Reed challenged Lars Ulrich to a street fight."

The first drive is a few hours from CDG to Normandy. We stop for lunch at a bistro in Rouen, one of the larger towns in the region. We order whole wheat bread and duck rillettes: our first meal in

France. I have beef tartare, and so does Charles. I finish Marx's nephew's healthy slice of country paté and cornichon. I can tell he doesn't really like to eat. He moves his food around on the plate without putting it in his mouth.

(At the end of this trip, in the airport hotel where I've arrived in time to sleep four hours before our flight home, I will find bright red blood in my toilet bowl after passing an enormous jagged, scarring brick of digested animal protein and fat from every part of every kind of animal in France. My wife, the nurse, assures me the bright red quality is a good sign.)

Now we are in Normandy, the northwestern coast of France, just across the Channel from England. Normandy, named for the Vikings who once colonized this region, is the home of calvados, one of our sentimental favorites. As simply as possible, calvados is an heirloom apple or apple and pear brandy named for the eponymous region, which is part of Normandy. Like whiskey or vodka, it is generally bottled in the vicinity of 40 percent alcohol by volume (ABV). Unlike a clear eau de vie, calvados is aged in oak, giving it the warm autumn tones we are accustomed to in scotch or aged rum. While apple brandy can and has been made in a similar fashion around the world, calvados can only be produced here, where it adheres to the rules of the Calvados appellation that monitors the agriculture, fermentation, and distillation. In general, Normandy is known for apples, which are also featured in the ciders of the region, but we are here for the calvados.

The Normans have produced this rare brandy here for centuries and, while it does not enjoy the notoriety of cognac, the famous grape-based brandy, this rustic, simply made liquor has a cult following. Calvados is also the foundation of *le trou normand*, or "the Norman hole," one of the few great traditions that pairs spirits with food. This is a small drink of calvados taken between courses in a very long meal, sometimes with apple or pear sorbet, supposedly to reawaken the appetite. This detail is worth mentioning because we named our second bar Trou Normand, where occasionally French tourists will drop in and explain to us that we have no idea what *le trou normand* is. We love the French.

After lunch, we visit our first producer, Domaine de Montreuil, which is a good first stop because it is the first property we encounter on our road, geographically, but also for more intangible reasons. We crest a large, soft hill crowned with skeletal winter apple trees, gaunt against the gray January afternoon sky, and descend toward the farmhouse and distillery of Montreuil, progressing down a softly undulating slope. Apple trees populate every level patch of grass. Our visits here are uncomplicated, and we've sold a ton of Montreuil over the years. The proprietor, Patrice, bottles an affordable blend of younger vintages for us that we use a great deal. Zealots or purists might hesitate at the notion of mixing farmstead spirits like these in drinks. I understand; we definitely cherish the older bottlings that we share with our friends, families, and paying guests, but we've found an appealing hollow of younger spirits that show the bright, lively characteristics of the base material—in this case, apples. Sometimes we will blend a little bit of an older barrel with the greater quantity of the young spirit to give more depth to the spirit while it retains its youthful vigor. Drinks mixed with young calvados shine with malic acidity, reminding us of what we'll never forget: good spirits are grown first. At times, using grower-producer stuff in cocktails feels sacrilegious, but it is young and the producer is happy to sell it. The real artists, in our opinion, are not the bartenders but the distillers, the people who make the ingredients with which we work, and our distillers are generally farmers. Maybe we're a little like Sting or Metallica in their later careers, when they wanted to work with classical or jazz musicians. We've gone as far as we can mixing drinks, so why not associate ourselves with true artists?

Patrice's style is simple and shows nice bright fruit in the mid-palate. This can be a pleasing aspect of young calvados; instead of the baked, caramelized, oxidized apple of those aged longer in the barrel, these can taste fresh and young, like a bite of green apple or a sip of acidic apple cider.

Patrice always wears a one-piece coverall that looks like a mechanic's suit. On the plane, I'd watched Truffaut's *Fahrenheit 451*, the 1966 vision of a future in which firemen, wearing helmets like the kaiser, drive through the English countryside in anachronistic fire engines, pausing periodically to burn books. Like Truffaut's firemen, our host and his workers wear utilitarian jumpsuits as they move through the scape of apple trees and winter fields. He has just bought a new bladder press, an imposing stainless steel device in which a large elastic balloon expands, gently extracting the juice from the apples as they are forced against the walls of the press, and he is proud to show it to us. I politely take a picture with my phone, wishing to myself that these producers would do a better job of honoring my Sturbridge Village fantasy and lose the technology. They should insist on living in the nineteenth century, here with their stone structures amid haunted fruit trees dwarfed by enormous winter skies, and heirloom cheeses in every corner shop. Patrice should receive visitors in costume and character. He doesn't even understand how to be French.

This prejudice of mine reminds me of a story I once heard about Francis Ford Coppola when I was consulting on his two resort properties in Belize. One of them is a beachfront lodge, at which he imagined a small, primitive place where you'd sit and eat grilled fish. "Feet in the sand" is the phrase my collaborator used to describe the mood of the place. Apparently Francis, as they call him when he's elsewhere, came to inspect the fruits of his imagination. The fish hit the table adorned with the clichéd decorative garnish of a bed of lettuce. Francis scowled at the presentation before tossing it in the sand and condemning it furiously, "So fucking third world." While less scornful, I am similarly judgmental when I mourn the arrival of Patrice's bladder press, nostalgic for an imaginary time I never experienced.

Patrice is modest and quiet. We efficiently taste some vintages, ranging five to twenty years old. As I've said, we'll be selling a blend of younger stuff from Patrice, but it's always good to stand and talk and taste. We'll remember these smells and sensations when we taste Patrice's stuff back home. There's a nice piece of cheese on an old table, and as we taste from barrels we tentatively eat more and more of the cheese, as if we were deer who'd become bold after seeing one of the herd safely eat from a human hand. The cheese is a Livarot, one of the three primary cheeses of Normandy. We'll have it several times before we leave the area. The others are Pont l'Évêque and the most-famous Camembert. I love the Livarot. It is a soft, strong-smelling, raw cow's-milk cheese. We've heard, and will hear again, the Vache Normande spoken of with reverence. Cows are a big part of the Norman economy, which explains the three beautiful, fresh, raw cow's-milk cheeses of the region. They taste like earth and grass and shit.

And this is why we came here: cold, January country air; the cellar; our first taste of cheese. Eric, Craig, and I look at each other quietly, steam coming out of our noses and we nod conspiratorially, like kids who have all taken acid or ecstasy and it is beginning to come on. Charles will often interject at a moment like this, saying something like "Breathe it in, lads. In a week, you'll be back in San Francisco, honking at a guy who's texting at a green light."

The French have worked to protect a sense of place. The synergy between the smell of the earth, the cheese, and the spirits is no accident. The government and the citizens are committed to it. This is the beauty of the appellation system. You will hear farmers and producers bitch about the bureaucracy at times—allowing certain grapes, not allowing certain grapes, changing the nomenclature so it does not favor a certain growth any longer—but these regulations are why some of our favorite spirits come from this part of the world. How they are produced and what they are produced from are ordained and protected. Sadly, in most of the world, there is no such governance, and categories of spirit that once evinced place and history are disappearing before our eyes.

Even with the supervision of the appellation, though, we also are watching this kind of spirit diminish in France. Mass production and economies of scale price true artisans out of the market. True grower-producers may one day no longer find it worth the trouble. We may be aging; we may be nostalgic; it may be like saying they used to sell Coca-Cola in a proper wooden box. Nonetheless, we love these ideal moments all the more because they are fleeting and harder to find.

We sell spirits for a living. I got stuck in this trade because I lacked self-esteem and ambition. When I was at Yale, I worked for three years at Robert Henry's, which was voted best restaurant in Connecticut several years in a row (by whom I don't remember). As a busboy, I was not allowed in the kitchen and I was not permitted to speak unless spoken to. No women were allowed to work at the restaurant. The French chef was a literal fascist. The maître d', Larry, was a sweet guy in his early thirties, which seemed middle-aged to me then. He embodied his title admirably. He behaved as the mother of the house, intermittently soothing and disciplining the employees. Larry took me on a number of edifying field trips in the time I worked for him, the most memorable of which was my first excursion to the Cloisters, where I admired Renaissance tapestries depicting the hunt of the unicorn. We drove silently down I-95 from New Haven to New York, my first experience of Enya ringing out portentously from the cassette deck. Sometimes after work we would end up at Larry's apartment drinking pink gins while listening to Winchester Cathedral, my first experience of a true vintage mixed drink. Larry presided over and forgave two of my greatest gaffes in the restaurant business. The first was when I dropped a heavy, sterling service tray, which struck the brick floor of the kitchen atrium and produced a tremendous noise, much like a Chinese gong, startling the patrician clientele. Larry was quiet for a pregnant moment then pronounced, "Dinner is served" in a stilted English accent. The other occasion involved another of these same silver trays, which held our massive sterling coffee urn. At Robert Henry's the busboy would perform the entire coffee service on one trip, moving the demitasse, then the cream and sugar from the tray to the table before grabbing the full coffee pot and filling the delicate cups. When serving a large table, this operation was grueling, particularly because the urn was all the more full to accommodate all eight guests. I was finishing laying the table with the coffee service and had to reach a bit to place the last demitasse spoon in front of a somber, gray-haired man who was of an average age and demeanor for the table. As I leaned to put down the spoon I was unaware that the tray in my left hand was tilting. The linen napkin beneath the giant urn slid against the smooth surface of the silver tray and allowed the brimming coffee pot to collide with the lip of the tray and leap into the center of the large, linen-covered table and explode all over its occupants who were covered with scalding coffee. Some of them endured second-degree burns and, needless to say, the dinner was on the restaurant. For some reason Larry didn't fire me. There was something devotional and loving about how he worked, which is why I was not surprised when he told me he'd applied to the Catholic Church, particularly as he lived asexually as far as I could see. Sadly, the church rejected his application. I heard from Larry recently, thirty years later, and I'm excited to see him in New York and get caught up with him and his new (to me) partner.

He is one of those people who brought me into this business and whose compassion influences me still today.

At Robert Henry's each evening I would work for one waiter who had a tiny section of three or four tables. Everything was sterling silver service. If a finished cigarette butt was left in an ashtray, I was in trouble. If someone lit his or her own cigarette, I was in trouble. I always had a couple of china ashtrays in my back pocket. Hot plates always hit the table simultaneously before the maître d' and servers would pull the ornamented porcelain domes from the plates at exactly the same moment. Steam would escape and mingle over the table, along with the smells of each plate. I was enmeshed in a psychosexual relationship with the waiter for whom I bussed. I would please him for weeks at a time, then disappoint him; and he would ask to work with another boy, leaving me heartbroken as I began working with a new waiter. What had I done? I was hooked on this industry.

I graduated from Yale and moved to San Francisco where I worked more as a busboy, then a food runner, and then an expeditor. I had been voted the most valuable employee for the year 1993 of One Market Restaurant. I was so proud. Other people in my class were finishing law and medical school. This award gave me the capital to move to the most prestigious part of the restaurant, the bar. I started bar-backing for Terry, Paul, Roger, and Gyorgi, who all used me mercilessly. Nothing, however, would be as sweet as those first daddies at Robert Henry's in New Haven, Connecticut!

I never made it out of bars. I bartended, then managed, then consulted, then opened my own places. All of this happened in San Francisco, though I traveled and worked abroad for years at a time. As I worked in San Francisco, I was gradually captivated by one cultural strain of the restaurants there: the Northern Californian, ingredient-driven cooking of Alice Waters, Judy Rodgers, and Russell Moore, from whom I learned more than I can explain.

I will always remember my collaboration with Russ and my friend Allison, his wife, to create a bar at their restaurant Camino. It prefigured and always surpassed my own places in its beauty, simplicity, and focus. These chefs, and others like them, were cooking with *the kind*. If you aren't, or never were, a stoner, "the kind" is a dated epithet for good weed.

I smoked a lot of dope then, and when it came to this vice, I was always looking for the best plant matter I could find. Not surprisingly, cuisine borne of that same impetus excited me, too.

The mentor who ultimately gave me my biggest break was Charles Phan, a Vietnamese immigrant who has gone on to become a titan in the Bay Area. I once asked Charles how he dealt with the stress of the restaurant business. He answered that a restaurant isn't stressful, a bomb blowing up outside your living room in Saigon is stressful. I was hired when his restaurant, the Slanted Door, obtained its first liquor license. I had been working in more old-school restaurants where service was arguably more of a priority than the quality of ingredients. I loved the money and precision and the fucked-up, classist tradition of restaurants. From *Down and Out in Paris and London* to *Kitchen Confidential*, I was a fan of the archetypal restaurant where people deal drugs and eat food off plates in the scullery. I liked my post at the façade of the bar, where I could use my Ivy League education to speak elegantly about food and booze. I was an apologist, shielding the guests from my own dysfunction and that of the staff who were all screwing each other, the raging chef, or whatever.

The Slanted Door was a family restaurant in that all of Charles's family worked there. The restaurant class system was destroyed because you never knew who you were talking to. The guy bringing in produce could be the brother-in-law of one of the owners; the morning prep cook could be a cousin. This dynamic forced me to encounter my own racism and classism, and I loved it. Charles was and is a genius. He effortlessly straddles three or four cultures, and draws from his U.C. Berkeley education as effortlessly as he does from his war-torn childhood in Vietnam. He has been building a family for years now, and I learned so much from being a part of it for five years.

He offered me a chance to run my first bar. We agreed that we wanted the quality of ingredient in the bar to match that of the kitchen. Charles was making ingredient-driven Vietnamese food (not fusion), and as I looked over the inventory of the bar he'd bought on Brannan Street, I found it strange that there was something like Seagram's 7 at a place that insisted on crediting farms on its menu, a practice that nowadays we're all a little tired of, but at the time was exciting. So I started a process that's never stopped. I asked myself, *Why would I sell this? Does this bottle share the aspirations of the kitchen next door? Does it share my aspirations?*

Historically, bars were always seen as an appendage to the restaurant, a kind of holding pen the guests occupied before dining. The promise of the restaurant bar, like that of the great hotel bars, is that one can always order the same thing: whatever is familiar, makes you comfortable, makes you feel at home. In a fine-dining or unfamiliarly ethnic restaurant, someone might be nervous before dinner. Restaurants reek of class and cultural difference. People are self-conscious, frightened of being judged, frightened of not getting it. A mentor of mine, Michael Musil, once explained that he wanted to put a drink in the customer's hand, wherever he's from, that makes him relax and get excited to have dinner: maybe it's a Cutty and water, maybe it's a blended piña colada, just something to help him—or her—feel more at ease.

At the Slanted Door I had another mentor, the wine director Mark Ellenbogen. A grumpy, dogmatic, and loveable man, Mark wrote the wine list—but he was also the agricultural conscience of the restaurant, and changed the way I thought about this business more than anyone I've known. His wine list at the Slanted Door was a Sutra, governed by a spiritual agenda that ensured low-alcohol and food-friendly wines of agricultural integrity. I loved to watch him police the contents of the walk-in or irascibly turn away wine vendors who did not share his conviction that wine was, first and foremost, a crop. It was at the Slanted Door that I decided that I wanted to connect guests to something beautiful, to a supply chain that wasn't actively destroying the things we all claimed to be celebrating in this cultural moment: stuff like love, quality, relaxation, different cultures, and sexuality. I stayed away from spirits made in factories, owned by multinationals, with added flavors and colors, or being sold by monopolistic distributors. Why would we want to put that in our bodies? For me, the issue isn't political; it's spiritual. This book is not polemic argument; it's a love letter or a treasure map, guiding you to some of the most beautiful liquids this world has to offer. So at the Slanted Door I started to get rid of the bad shit and started to go after the kind. And I've been doing it ever since.

Which is why we're eating cheese with Patrice in Normandy in January: we want the real article so we can make great drinks, and we prefer it right from the source because, to be honest, those who make and sell booze are prone to dishonesty and known to mislead us about what they sell.

Patrice has been selling us a young, functional calvados with shining acidity and the pleasant qualities of baked apple for a couple of years now. Maybe we'll pick up a bottle or two of a particular vintage if it's remarkable, but this is largely a social call to strengthen our business relationship. Near the end of the visit, we are joined by Patrice's wife, a moon-faced woman who smiles beneath a short, androgynous haircut. Her hips are as wide as she is tall. Their daughter, stolid like her mother, follows and we all smile at each other for a bit. Some speak French genially. Some eat cheese. All are happy.

Soon enough, we're back in the van and off to Calvados Adrien Camut. From one perspective, this is a gentle day: some driving, a lunch, and only two producers, but jet lag is upon us. Eric's head is bent forward dramatically, as if it is on a hinge; it rises and falls gently in accordance with the rhythmic movement of the van. I scan left to be sure that Charles is awake, and he is, bolt upright. As part of an unspoken agreement, one of us will try to be talking to Charles at all times. On this trip, he will log thousands of miles on only a few hours of sleep a night. I was terrified much of the time on our first trip with Charles four years ago, so tired that I just *had* to sleep, but if I fell asleep I would stop talking, and if I stopped talking, Charles could fall asleep at the wheel, and I'd end up awakening to my own death.

The van falls silent as we slow and catch a glimpse of the stone gate to the Camut estate; we who have been there before know we are home, and the others, here for the first time, are gripped by an appropriate deference, as Camut calvados is the shit. We're a couple of hours late and the light is fading. Always working, Charles wants to be sure Marx's nephew and Leon have a good look at the property before dark. I try not to be the guy who's been here before, explaining things, taking credit for any of this. The entrance to the estate is marked by a sign you wouldn't notice. You enter by a long dirt drive that borders a large shambling orchard comprised of quite a few different species of apple trees. You arrive at a large, circular dirt-and-gravel drive in front of a kind of château. The Camuts are not nobility and their house is not necessarily "grand," but it is striking. Built by hand in the eighteenth century from stone, it stands out against the twilight.

The Camut brothers are Vikings, literally. They are lumbering, huge descendants of the northern invaders who came centuries ago. Jean Gabrielle is almost my size, and I'm six foot eight and well over two hundred fifty pounds. Emanuelle is also far from tiny.

This is the time in France—here, now, with the towering Camuts—when I feel most at home. We hug each other mightily. They wear boots, broad-brimmed hats tipped at great, French angles, perfect winter coats. A small, handsome dog is always within arm's reach. They show us around the estate: a Napoleonic farmhouse with a fireplace big enough to stand in is at the center of several other eighteenth-century structures, which include a couple of caves and the stillroom. The Camuts maintain all of their own equipment, unlike many grower-producers who might need to share a press or traveling still with others in the community.

These fellows are French in the way I want them to be. They smoke and wear watches, but they are also farmers. A charming mixture of urbane and rustic, they both have traveled much more than most farmer-producers in this part of the world. They are diffident and would never comprehend that we actually see them as celebrities.

The brothers take turns leading the quick tour. One remembers he needs to grab bread for dinner. He leaves and returns; then the other goes to get tobacco. Then one is off to start dinner.

The property is in perfect disarray, which is to say that each room looks like a junk shop. The pot still is a hundred years old and is encased in brick. There's clutter on every surface. Old wrenches. Ancient tools I can't recognize, in pieces. Calendars. A pot of wax solidified in the cold. This is that quality exhibited by the French restaurateur: nothing is wasted, every carrot top needs to be used. Someone, after all, will pay for it. Everything has value, everything can be made tasty. In a place like the Camut estate, I feel lazy and wasteful. After all, I'm the kind of person who never takes the time to take something apart once it's broken. I lease new cars for three years at a time. I put a cheap, engineered wood floor in our more recent bar.

The cult of the new holds no fascination for the Camut brothers. Is this why their calvados is one of the best spirits in the world? They grow apples. They pick them up off the ground and make a naturally fermented cider that they distill in an ancient pot still. The only thing they add to any stage of this process is fire, which is used to heat the still that converts cider into clear, new make spirit—meaning, unaged or right off of the still—that will be aged in oak barrels before honoring our glasses. Wine can happen accidentally, but it takes humans to make spirits; that said, the Camuts intervene as little as possible. It is unrealistic to expect that everyone will make spirits in this way, but it was once more standard.

The other area where the Camuts excel is inventory, which is to say that they hold on to their stuff. They are in no hurry to sell because their well-made spirit will only increase in value as it ages. The great producers are like this. Holding on to inventory is the best way of betting on one's self. This is probably why it's taken us years to get them to sell us some young calvados to put in mixed drinks. Last year, they agreed to bottle some three-year-old calvados. For us, it was like having Bob Dylan agree to perform at our birthday party.

We pass forty-five minutes tasting really old barrels from the cave—thirty, forty, fifty, sixty, seventy years old. The family has been making calvados since the 1800s. The pleasure of tasting these older vintages isn't so much in the prestige of the old spirit as it is in growing your intimacy with this great producer. Like great age-worthy wines, these brandies retain bright acidity and good tannic structure. With each older vintage you enjoy the greater interaction with the oak barrel and fungus of the *cave*, the cellar where their brandies are aged; the more you enjoy the changes with age, though, the more you come to grasp what's at the heart of this flavor: the trees, the earth, and the still that are unique to this square mile. They don't break out the hundred-year-old calvados this trip, though we did get to taste it last time. My fantasy is they've withheld the most valuable stuff because we brought these new guys along.

Finished with the tour, we get back in the van and drive five minutes to a *chambre d'hote* (bed and breakfast) nearby, where Charles gives us fifteen minutes to drop our stuff in our room and take a shit or have a very quick shower. On these trips, you are constantly exhausted. Your whole body cries out for just twenty minutes of sleep. You look at your bed, maybe lie down and close your eyes for five minutes, and then you have to go.

Back at Camut, they are cooking a comically French meal. A leg of lamb on a little manual spit that sits amongst the coals in the enormous Napoleonic fireplace. A pot of flageolet. A simple endive salad and a scallop appetizer. Normandy is the north coast, so seafood figures heavily, as well as the Vache Normand. The famous Belon oyster is harvested in this part of the world. The cheese is already out, tempering. It looks as if we're going to get each of the big three cheeses.

Charles insists that we try to make cocktails for the brothers. This is always our least favorite part of the trip. Eric and I make Craig do it because technically he is our employee, which is a little shitty, but it is just a drag to be put on display as a barman—particularly because in most of the world the celebrity barman conjures the image of the flair bartender clad in tight trousers, flipping and tossing and catching. Flair, for those who don't know, is the style of bartending popularized by Brian Cox and Tom Cruise in the film *Cocktail*, a work that has caused our trade great embarrassment. Sadly, many imagine this performance art is what we mean when we describe ourselves as career bartenders. Craig opens the leather kit and earnestly tries to produce a few simple drinks. We have no good ice, which means to get things to temperature you have to overdilute them, so nothing tastes great. For citrus, we are using a pasteurized room-temperature bottle of shelf-stable lemon juice. Not ideal. The Camuts politely taste each one. None of them is even as good as their spirit served neat.

During the aperitif, we get our first glimpse of andouillette this trip. This charcuterie is a cold cut made from pig's colon. It is literally fetid. It smells and tastes like shit. We are hungry and standing in front of a Napoleonic hearth, and we are wearing boots against the cold, so we of course eat it. I have convinced myself I love it, as has Craig. Eric is a vegetarian. Marx's nephew politely tries it, and Leon from Marx Importers has a bit. The first three trips we made to France, Craig spent the morning after the Camut dinner vomiting. Eric and I are rooting for him this trip, and we all study him wondering and theorizing what he'll consume that will lead to his almost inevitable illness. The andouillette is everyone's first and best guess. Other possibilities are the rustic, unpasteurized cider the Camut brothers make for their own consumption. Of course, Craig will drink a great deal of calvados as well. And we are all vastly dehydrated from a day and a night of travel. Strangely, one of my more pleasant memories of any of these brandy trips is of the previous year when we'd stopped for Craig to vomit. It was mid-morning on a bright, sunny January day; we'd paused on a narrow road that split a huge field. Light bounced from the dew on the long blades of meadow grass as we listened to Craig puking discreetly. We couldn't see him, only hear. Between spasms he said, "The cool air feels nice." It was true.

One of the most lovely, and at times maddening qualities of most of our hosts on these trips is that they insist upon an extended aperitif. The term "aperitif" refers not only to the category of beverage—vermouth, sherry, sparkling wine, dry cocktails—with which we're familiar; it also delineates the period of time when we relax and have a drink before dinner. It generally lasts an hour or so and usually there are snacks on the table. At its best, this time allows you to leave behind the stress of the day and clean the mind and palate before dining. Americans do it, too: it's the time standing around the kitchen with a glass of wine while your friend finishes chopping or braising something.

The brothers offer calvados and Schweppes, probably our favorite discovery from these trips, which is simply room-temperature apple brandy and tonic. Shit sausage and room-temp highballs with Vikings: life is good. The aperitif can be misery when you are subject to three in a day. Two hours late for your next tasting and a producer is holding you hostage with reheated frozen snacks and their *pommeau* (rhymes with "homo"), which is simply apple juice from the region fortified with calvados. Producers each have their own, just as each generally makes their own cider. The most hellish aperitifs we've passed were at the inn of Charles's brother-in-law, who sadistically makes you wait until midnight before feeding you. (Bernard, with his gout and his insults, waits for us at the end of the trip. He is a complete bastard and deserves greater description, which will come.)

The meal is great. After the scallops, the endive, and the aperitif, we pause for *le trou normand*, our palate cleanser before the meat course. Rather than what some call the more conventional marriage of sorbet and calvados, the Camut brothers pour a large glass of very old calvados for each of the dinner's participants. Seventy year, the first time. This time, they share their bottled blend of brandies that average around thirty-five years.

The previous year, Emanuelle's ten-year-old daughter joined us. She was the only female guest, and she was very welcome. Now that I'm in my forties, I'm not enchanted by extended periods of time only in the company of men, and this is only worsened by protracted bouts of van travel. I worry Emanuelle's young daughter didn't enjoy our company the year before; maybe that's why we're getting younger calvados.

That last visit, we made great strides in our relationship with the Camut brothers. We were treated to tours of two additional facilities. As though their flawlessly curated calvados production weren't enough, Emanuelle has been in development on an apple balsamic vinegar cellar for about ten years. He is accumulating inventory, which is as essential for balsamic as it is for the successful sale of spirits. The cellar for the balsamic is above ground and stuns us: hundreds of small casks, perfectly old and charming, in a lovely order. We taste many vintages of the vinegar and beg to buy it, but it won't be ready for sale for years. They tease you, the Camuts. Taste this and that, but we probably won't sell it to you. We learned later that there is some contention with regard to the Camut estate. Other absent siblings are sharing in the revenue while Emanuelle and Jean-Gab do all the work. As a result, they seem to be selling the minimum to stay afloat while they reposition themselves.

This year we see the garage, which gratifies Eric, my partner, who is obsessed with engines. After I'd known him for years, he let it slip that after graduating from Bard College, he'd driven eighteen-wheelers for a couple of years. I hang back and work on my cigar, a Romeo y Julieta robusto, a habit I indulge when I am outside the United States. Engines roar. Eric and Emanuelle drive off for a bit. I see the end of memory in Craig's eyes. His body continues on affably, but he may not have great recollection of these last moments. This is probably true of several of us. I avoid being drunk because when I am my personality shifts dramatically and terribly. Fortunately, all my travel companions remain themselves. Charles jokes and shouts in unintelligible French. Marx's nephew corners Jean-Gab and questions him with bearded intensity about the different vintages poured at dinner. Everyone is engaged.

The wonder of this evening, which is always the best of the trip, says more of the place than it does of the participants: the food, the sleeping winter fruit trees, the laughter, the dog under the old table, the medieval hearth, the Viking brothers, the brandies. This is all in the bottle. And when we pour calvados, especially Camut, we are connected to all this. This is the supply chain in which we want to be a link. For years, buying spirits was limited to visits from distributors. They would present bottles to you, always drawing attention to the appearance of the bottle and how lovely it would appear on your back bar. This is one of the large distillers' key forms of marketing, placement in view of the guest. The distributor lets you taste and answers what questions he or she can. Maybe they've visited the producer, maybe not. You taste in a vacuum, with no understanding of a broader context, relying on one person rather than on an experience of where it was made, who made it, what they made it from. If you believe tasting is an objective experience then this may be fine, but I believe that this process of selection could not be more subjective. I don't want to be an expert; I want to be an enthusiast. With each bottle I choose, I am building community, connecting myself to people for whom I advocate every time I open one of their bottles to pour for a guest, like bringing a friend to a party at another friend's home. I need to be sure of my companion's character before subjecting the host to it.

I've given up worrying about Charles driving after hours on black French country roads. He gets us to the *chambre d'hote* by about 2:30 a.m. He'll be back in five hours. He drives back to the Camuts, where he'll probably drink some wine and maybe smoke a joint with the Vikings before getting a couple of hours of sleep and collecting us.

I am glad to see my bed. I force myself to shower because I haven't bathed in close to forty-eight hours and I want the experience of clean skin on new sheets. I close my eyes and wake four and half hours later. This is the jet lag waking me, but it's perfect because the alarm will sound in about five minutes. I dress and head downstairs to check my email and drink coffee while we wait for Charles. Even eighteenth-century French B&B's have Wi-Fi.

Charles is about a half hour late and Marx's nephew is still not downstairs. Charles can be late, but not us. If it had been Eric or Craig or myself who had been late, one of us would have his balls broken, but Charles is strangely sweet and patient with Marx's nephew, who is (I reflect) actually young enough to be my son. I resolve to take the same position. These trips are hard. Being so close to people, you lose perspective, seeing a person's worst qualities, and this myopia can lead to tension and conflict.

During our drive later today, the landscape will shift from a lush, open, agricultural landscape to the stonier, more barren region of Cognac. The architecture will become more mercantile. Cognac is farther from Paris geographically, but it feels closer; it is more urbane and commercial. We leave Calvados more convinced than ever that we have found our niche in this business. We will miss it for the year we are away.

Chapter Two

COGNAC

THEY'LL HIRE THE GUY WHO FUCKED YOUR WIFE

Some years ago, for a few months in San Francisco, a large billboard advertising Hennessy cognac flanked Harrison Street facing east, on the border of the Mission and SOMA neighborhoods. The star of the billboard was a black-and-white, sepia-toned John Leguizamo, who advised, "GREAT ACTING IS BEING ABLE TO CREATE A CHARACTER, GREAT CHARACTER IS BEING ABLE TO BE YOURSELF." Superimposed on the lower right of the image were the words "Pure Character."

Hennessy sells more cognac than anyone in the world, fifty million bottles a year, or 40 percent of the global supply. At this scale, Hennessy transcends its category, cognac. Hennessy is Hennessy. I don't find that most consumers are even aware that cognac is a category of brandy, which is such a loose term, inclusive of the sweetest, colored cordials like peach brandy as well as the most subtle, dry eau de vies like the famous Poire Williams pear brandy.

Richard Hennessy, an Irish merchant, began the brand in 1765. A *négociant* (merchant bottler), Hennessy bought brandies from producers in Cognac, aged them, blended them, and sold them to customers under his own label. His clientele grew to respect and rely on his taste and the Hennessy "house style." Today Hennessy is one of a group of only four companies that sell more than 90 percent of cognac around the globe.

Hennessy's strategy is similar to that of other major spirits brands, from Bacardi to Jack Daniel's: maintain consistent product, and through marketing, cultivate a larger and larger following around the world.

In France, the government has strict rules about what can be classified as "cognac," which, simply put, is a French brandy, distilled twice, and made from wine using grapes grown in the region. Over the centuries, merchants found that an easy way to control their product while maintaining the approval of the appellation was to encourage producers to make their brandy with Ugni Blanc, which is one of the more neutral-tasting grapes grown in the area. Double-distillation, dictated by the appellation, is another tactic; it can increase the alcohol by volume, which results in a more neutral flavor (the higher the proportion of alcohol, the more a cognac tastes of alcohol rather than the organic material from which it was made). Also, this pot distillation, as opposed to the single-column distillation in armagnac, allows for more precise cuts, eliminating esters that might obfuscate the clean spirit. I'm not saying this purity is categorically bad, but it does give these companies more latitude to mitigate their product with caramel color and flavor, which are also allowed by the appellation. The least charitable way to put this would be that these massive companies buy oceans of bland brandy from the distilling populace and hammer it with caramel before spending tens of millions of dollars to brand it and distribute it as widely as imaginable. Or to characterize it more generously, they use the tricks of the trade to maintain quality and excellence.

John Leguizamo's billboard extolled the great paradox of large liquor companies, and really that of large advertising brands in general: "Express your independence by drinking this brandy we would have absolutely everyone in the world consume if we had our way."

Spirits are food. They come from materials that grow in the ground (in the case of cognac, grapes). At its heart, spirits making is just another way to put leftover produce to use before it spoils. If a farmer had too many pears at the end of the fall, she could ferment them and distill them rather than wasting fruit she'd spent a year cultivating. Like a bottle of vintage wine or a jar of pickles, a well-made spirit honors a certain time and place. The distillers I love share something with the best apple growers, dairy farmers, and cheese makers: they are makers, not scientists aspiring to a perfect consistency of flavor over millions of bottles that will be distributed over all seven continents.

If we really love the sensuous experience of eating, why would we want to put something in our bodies that can be found at any time of day, in any part of the world, and that always tastes the same? Self-described "foodies" avoid food and wine that fits this description, yet rely on brands of liquor that never vary in flavor and are available in any bar. The beauty of good tomatoes is that no two are identical; imagine if one farmer supplied 40 percent of all the tomatoes consumed in the world. You wouldn't expect your chef always to have Del Monte peaches and Heinz baked beans in the kitchen. Why do you strain your eyes looking over your bartender's shoulder to see what brands he carries?

The distillates I love vary from year to year, from barrel to barrel, even from bottle to bottle. When I was a boy, I loved McDonald's and its assortment of sandwiches that tasted identical wherever I ordered them. Today I enjoy the opposite—the more varied a product each time I try it, the more interested I am, as the flavors are more closely tied to the rhythms and variety of the natural world, and we are assured that this is made by humans.

Cognac has some big players, owned by bigger players, and I've been tempted to vilify them; I suppose subtextually I do. But there are two good things about these large brands. First, they support all the small, family distillers in the region who sell their brandies to the big houses. Small cognac distillers enjoy enviable financial stability compared to operators of an equivalent scale in other parts of the world, even as close as Armagnac or Normandy. Second, each bottle of cognac sold strengthens the appellation, ensuring all the grapes used in spirits with cognac on the label are grown in the region of Cognac in one of the six designated *crus,* or growths. (In this context, "growth" refers to a specific plot of agricultural land that receives its designation from the government.) So, by definition, cognac, even Hennessy, is an agricultural product of sorts, though the large producers work hard to eradicate the happy accident of agriculture at every stage of the process, culminating with the addition of caramel and the uniform dilution with water of every bottle. But sometimes you want a Big Mac and sometimes you want a Hennessy and Coke.

The drive to Cognac from Normandy is around six hours, which makes our dinner date with a producer at eight improbable. Of course, Charles will drive the whole way with less sleep and more to drink than the rest of us, and once we get there, he will shoulder the lion's share of the work, translating conversations with producers, soliciting relevant information, avoiding every lull in conversation with his boundless social energy. He is a juggernaut. Really, our business now depends largely on Charles and his inclusion of us in his community. We are selling amazing grower-producer spirits in our cocktail bars. Literally no one else can boast the same.

For us, this trip is the opposite of a blind tasting. We look for as much context as possible, as much of a sense of place and person as we can assimilate. We surrender to subjectivity, willingly manipulated by the smell of the property, the charm of the children, how the cattle are cared for, the cheese they serve us. The blind tasting enslaves you to a myth of objectivity and expertise, the science of flavor. Almost inevitably, when tasting spirits blind, participants choose what's sweetest, which is understandable, at least biologi-cally, since rich flavors typically signify more calories, and calories are how we survive.

I believe the mind and all the senses must participate. One's soul must participate. The more you study wine or spirits, the more you understand that you will never know it all. We do not strive to be experts, only enthusiasts, and we let passion and impulse guide our selections as much as possible. I do know people who are prolific tasters and give more thorough accounts of the distillers of each region. My friend David publishes a tasting journal that is exhaustive and nicely augments his travel in a number of producing regions. When I was younger, I would spend Sundays at the record store, plowing through white labels until one caught my attention. Tasting spirits is similar for me to choosing music; arriving at a decision is a bit of a mystical process.

The producers in Cognac are relatively sophisticated because of the commerce and success of the region. They travel in the off-season. Their children may leave the region for university, due in part to the financial security offered by the big blending houses: as I've mentioned, the cognac producer can always sell her brandy to Courvoisier, Rémy Martin, or Hennessy. The brandies are twice distilled in a pot and rendered relatively neutral, which lends itself to the barrel aging and blending that characterize the spirit inter-nationally. The aforementioned huge sellers of cognac are famous for using additives to maintain consistent house styles. Most cognac enjoys a degree of adulteration that mindful eaters would forgo in their food. We are lucky to find grower-producers who sell their own unmolested brandies.

One such producer is the Dudognon family, which has been producing cognac in the heart of the renowned Grand Champagne region (not to be confused with the Champagne region in north-ern France) near the town of Lignières-Sonneville in southwestern

France, since the year of US emancipation from Great Britain. Notably, after the Second World War, Raymond Dudognon took the helm at the distillery and elevated the reputation of the domain with thoughtfully made brandies that endured less human intervention. While continuing to sell brandies to merchant bottlers (*négociants*), in 1950, Raymond started bottling under his own Dudognon label. In 1990, one of Raymond's estate cognacs won the gold medal at the International Spirits Show. The award-winning spirit, a blend of his first two vintages from 1948 and 1949, was humbly named Resérve des Ancêtres. For the rest of his career as a grower-producer, Raymond fought for the success of Dudognon and, perhaps unwittingly, for the future of small, independent cognac.

At the end of the 1990s, Raymond retired and divided his property, as is the law in France, evenly among his three daughters. He chose his daughter Claudine to succeed him as the head of operations. Raymond died in 2002, leaving the legacy of Dudognon in the capable hands of Claudine and her husband, Gerald Buraud. Now, twenty years later, the Dodognon-Burauds continue to distill by hand, relying on taste and smell rather than technology to separate the heads and tails, or as they're called in France the "têtes and queues," from the heart of the distillate. During the first distillation, the producer mindfully observes by smell and taste for the entire run. The first spirits out of the still, the têtes, contain such high levels of impurities that they are generally discarded. The majority of the distillation, called the *brouillis,* or hearts, is saved. What's left in the end, queues, or tails, is flavorless and undesirable and generally tossed out as well.

The potable liquid, *brouillis,* is put through a second distillation known as the *bonne chauffe,* which leaves the still between 67 and 72 percent alcohol by volume. It goes straight into barrels made of either Limousin or Tronçais oak, generally around 350 liters in size. The Dudognon-Burauds produce only one hundred barrels of cognac a year from grapes they grow themselves in nitrate- and chemical-free soil. Next year, 2017, will be the first of their organic certification. The wood for their barrels is dry aged for five years. As they add nothing but water to their spirits, the resulting brandies are pale and clear compared to the vast majority of cognac bottled and sold in the region.

To say Gerald and Claudine are youthful is understatement. Both are in their sixties but move like a man and woman in their twenties or early thirties wearing unconvincing gray wigs. Gerald is small and confident like a rooster in his black turtleneck. He is sure to make contact with each of us and has a wonderful story of the time one of the large houses rejected his distillate because it smelled of sulfur. This strategy is common according to a number of small producers we've met. The large house will manufacture a reason the brandy is inferior so they can reject it on a down year or negotiate a more favorable price. Full of Gallic pride, the next year Gerald sent a sample bottle he'd saturated with sulfur, causing it to smell worse than old deviled eggs. Gerald laughs and shrugs with his lower lip thrust out, very French, and continues to explain that they bought the whole lot. He never sold to any of the big houses again.

Most years, we've eaten at the Dudognon property. Claudine is a terrible cook. She generally serves at least one item truly raw and what's cooked to temperature isn't good. Dinner had been scheduled for eight and we arrive at ten. I imagine arriving two hours late had its effect. The braised chicken has been cooked to the consistency of paste. The canapés are cold and rubbery. Everyone is in good cheer, though, and after dinner we go to the property to taste in the cellar. Dudognon is our house cognac at the restaurants, and we are grateful they sell us barrels.

The stillroom is peaceful; a beautiful Charente still, painted a deep rust, runs within arm's reach of the table and keeps us all very warm on this cold January evening. The sound of cutlery on plates is soothing mixed with the music of natural French being spoken.

Charles hates conversation to turn political with his producers, and as chief translator he often insulates them from my pedantic questions. Tonight, though, he translates relatively transparently.

"Do people ever rely on someone like Hennessy and then have the rug pulled out from under them one year when Hennessy doesn't buy the brandies?"

"Absolutely," says Gerald. "And it's never the producer's fault. The large *négociant* will taste a sample and say that this year the quality is not right rather than admit they haven't grown the market or have fallen short in some other way." Gerald and Claudine talk while they eat, nodding emphatically with the fork in the left hand and the knife in the right. They make any number of mellow French noises for emphasis, sometimes with their mouths full.

Charles comments, "I think you're going to hear many of the small producers criticize the big houses for manipulating the brandies, but you're not going to hear them do that very loud. Here, in Cognac, you do see the spirit of all for one and one for all. Most of the producers see themselves as farmers who don't have the resources to market the brandies. They are happy to let the region do it." Charles pauses and tosses his head backward to get some hair out of his eyes. He is listening to the portable radio in the still-room that's been providing the evening's soundtrack. "Let's go back in time, to the city by the bay. The falsetto tones of Steve Perry. I hate this band. Fuck this band. Fuck REO Speedwagon. And Styx was the worst of this category . . ."

"I loved all those bands," I counter. "I was thirteen. And still . . . I miss the sincerity."

Charles's laughter interrupts me. "Yeah, right. I'll take five million dollars and twenty-five pounds of cocaine and go into that studio for a fucking year . . ." The conversation degrades into an argument about classic rock for a while, with Charles insisting that anything commercial is shit. Our hosts serve the main plate, a totally bizarre seafood *choucroute garnie*.

"It's really getting interesting with the sauerkraut and the cream," Charles observes dryly, relying on our hosts' lack of English. No one even eats a third of their portion. Claudine clears without ceremony, dumping a great deal of uneaten food in the trash; this is clearly not the first time she's done so. Charles turns his attention to their son, who appears to be in his early twenties: "So, if your father died tonight and his last words were 'I need you to take over the still,' could you handle that?"

"Of course," Gerald answers for him, then opens another bottle of wine loudly and begins to pour. There had been some confusion as to white or red with the main course.

I ask (and Charles repeats the question in slower English, giving the son a chance to show his parents the value of his education): "Do the positive aspects of the large houses outweigh the negative?" The son and heir answers in capable though halting English.

"Cognac offers a large economy with many ways to earn a living: the cardboard boxes. The bottles. The barrels. The drivers. Of course, the growers sell to the *négociants*. All of this is work that the strength of the region provides. But these are the industrial workers. We operate outside of this, though, for the most part. These big companies harm the purity of the spirit. They compromise its beauty."

"Some of these producers will sell to *négociants* other than the big four," Charles prompts, "like Otard or Camus."

"Otard makes the Jay-Z cognac," Craig inserts. "Would Dudognon like to work with Jay-Z?" This turns us to a conversation about Kanye, with Charles asking if the group liked his music. Charles has heard none. We resolve to listen to the *Yeezus* record in the van the next day.

We are in bed around 3:00 a.m., and we need to be up at 7:00. In the moments before the inevitable pull to sleep, I think about the Dudognon-Burauds. These visits pass so quickly as we move through the trip, inspiring the concern that we may not be honoring our hosts sufficiently. Each year we mean to bring gifts and we generally forget. Dudognon is a feather in our cap: a small family producer with more than a century of tradition that makes an elegant, additive-free spirit that is distilled from organically farmed estate fruit. And it's cheaper than a 750-ml bottle of Rémy Martin XO.

Breakfast is coffee and bread. Charles energetically collects us from our *chambre d'hote*; he'd spent the night at the Dudognon estate a couple of minutes away. We begin the day at an organic brewer. A couple of the beers are good, but their labels have that awful microbrew feel. Bright colors and clever puns. They use a lot of Pacific hops, too, which I don't like because they taste like Pine-Sol.

We have lunch in the town of Cognac and buy some cigars. I have a true *choucroute garnie*, which is served in a chafing dish. It is enormous. Pounds of cured meat and an equal amount of sauerkraut. The acidity of the vinegar immediately begins to sooth my stomach, which is already overwhelmed by the base quality of animal fat and bread.

From Cognac, we'll drive about twenty-five minutes to Cherves-Richemont, in the Borderies region, where our charming friend François Giboin lives and works. He is waiting for us on the gravel drive of his estate, which rests in the midst of an expansive flat valley. Giboin stands at attention as we climb bunglingly from the van. His right hand touches his chin, as though he's holding his head aloft, and his left hand props the elbow of the right arm. "Ah, Charles," he says, "you have arrived with your brigade!" To me, François is the picture of France. Slender, in practical trousers, a

Breton sweater, obligatory beret, and a neckerchief, he has ardent yet melancholic eyes with dark circles beneath them that are transformed when he smiles. He is the archetypal subject of a joke we often tell in France when someone walks by, looking particularly French. We will point discreetly at a fellow wearing a scarf and beret with two baguettes under his arm, holding a hand-rolled cigarette in his free hand and whisper excitedly to each other, "I think that guy might be French!"

We've never seen François *not* in a beret, though Charles claims to have spied him through the window once sans beret. He believed he might have seen Giboin wearing a yarmulke, which, true or not, dovetails with an interesting detail of the Giboin property: the family long maintained a secret shelf, sheathed in plaster, where some vintages were hidden from the Third Reich.

We all know the joke of how the French would speak German if were not for the intervention of the United States, and our group likes to deploy the metaversion of the joke where we mock those who tell the original, usually while we're in Normandy. I am relieved for Giboin, though, that his property remains the dominion of his family, and I can only imagine the barbarity of an occupying army of genocidal murderers drinking and eating all that is best in the French countryside. The Nazis, in part, were such exquisite villains because of their taste, their appropriation of the finest from each country they annexed. It was a rape of the land, which was particularly rough as France takes such pride in its agricultural goods.

Today at Giboin we are all about business. After a cursory review of the grounds and the *chai*, pronounced "shay," which is what they call the *cave* or cellar in these parts, we settle in his reception area to do some tasting.

"Would anybody like a coffee before or after ze tasting?" François offers kindly.

"You wanna coffee before or after?" Charles echoes, seeming to forget that the offer was made in English.

"After," we say. Coffee's bitter flavors would complicate the tasting. Better to have it later.

"Okay, after," answers François as he covers the tiny table with tasting glasses. They clink peacefully as they touch each other.

"With a very old Pineau des Charantes," Charles adds, to which Craig replies archly, "A capital idea," in a faux British accent. Pineau des Charantes (PDC) is grape juice fortified with young brandy, produced only in Cognac. It makes perfect sense when you are in a salon with a man wearing a beret, but, however excited we are sipping on it in this pastoral setting, when we get the PDC back to our bars in the United States our guests are not particularly interested; the stuff is a little sweet and inconsequential, and we end up giving it away.

"Here is your selection from last year," François says, arriving with some cognac in an unmarked bottle. "I will pour it right away because it is still a little cold." We all hold our glasses by the bell between our palms to warm the liquid within, as cold spirits have very little aroma.

It is soothing to slow to this pace of business, like lowering myself into hot water. I live in perpetual anxiety in San Francisco, waking without an alarm at 6:00 a.m. In that purgatorial combination of the simultaneous desire and inability to sleep, I create scenarios of failure and step out of bed positive that I am a failure. A businessman like François seems mindful of this; his family has been doing this business for a hundred years, and he shares the stress of our trade: the narrow margins, the seasonality, the never-ending stress of cash flow. As if trying to relax us, he proceeds at a doleful, deliberate pace, reassuring us wordlessly that none of us need to be anywhere else.

In Cognac, Armagnac, and Normandy, we always taste with the standard cognac glass, not a snifter, which is appropriate on a bearskin rug but not in a *chai* or tasting room. The ubiquitous cognac-tasting glass is shaped more like a wine glass, with straight sides tapering gradually inward. This structure focuses the aroma. With spirits, you are always protecting your sense of smell, swirling the spirit in the base of the glass and holding it as far from your nose as possible, then guiding it slowly toward the nose until you first become aware of the aromas. If you bury your nose in a glass of cognac as you might a glass of wine, you will completely anesthetize your sense of smell, which has much to do with your sense of taste. Working with spirits, you protect yourself from the numbing qualities of the liquid, which also explains why spirits are not necessarily best with food.

After tasting last year's selection, we try an older brandy Charles is bringing in to sell through his spirits distributor; though exceptional, it's not something we will use. Too expensive. We hold the glass up to the light, smell it from a distance as not to scorch the olfactory senses. In cognac, you are always wondering about caramel. Odds are it's in there, but is it enough to mar the brandy? Producers can't risk a spirit that lacks the commanding hue of teak or mahogany associated with prestige. In this case, it's a negligible amount; the fruit of the spirit is still evident with its golden, chalky acidity.

The Borderies are the smallest *cru*, or growing region, in Cognac. The soils are composed of decaying limestone that yields flint stones and clay, the consequence of which can be nutty brandies with hints of cocoa and striking floral aromas. This glass is a distinctive example of the *cru*, and we don't blame Charles for importing it. He asks how the label for this bottling is coming. François shows us a version of the label, which is a little ornate, a little "ye olde," but we all nod appreciatively and make positive noises or remarks.

Ultimately, we settle on a blend of 2005 and 2011 brandies. We have another twenty cases of the previous lot, a similar blend, to sell. François is concerned that the new selection will not match the last, which is typical of cognac where the "house style" of the large houses is fiercely maintained. Hennessy is Hennessy because every bottle of VSOP you open will taste exactly the same. Giboin is very proud that he sells a great deal of his brandy to one of the large houses.

When the conversation lags for a moment, Craig asks him if his brandies from the Fin Bois region are typical. Triumphantly, François replies, "Well, you must ask Courvoisier, which has been buying my eau de vies for many years!" We pause to talk about his relationship with Courvoisier. He sells fifty hectoliters a year to Courvoisier and keeps twenty for himself, with which he does projects like those he does with Charles and us.

Houses like Courvoisier blend and caramelize to ensure each bottle is like the last. We explain that we like the variation between selections, at which point Charles interrupts to remind François that we are using these young brandies in mixed drinks. "Only in mixed drinks?!" François seems a little aghast. "No, no," we insist, not just in drinks. Charles continues to explain that because the brandies are mixed with other ingredients, the subtle variations do not matter so much. "So, when you mix these for your clients," François asks, "you don't explain that this is by François Giboin from the Borderies, that I have made a mix with Charles . . . ?" François seems worried he may not be getting credit with our guests for these selections he generously bottles for us.

"We do. We do. Of course."

"And your clients are interested by this?"

"Yes! Yes!"

"I have to visit these bars, Charles." He smiles and pauses meditatively. "Okay, I bring the coffee!" Our producers never quite fathom what we are doing with their booze, as hard as Charles tries to explain.

For François, a "bar" is a place you go to have a coffee, or a beer, or a pastis, maybe a gin and tonic; it's the place he stops in to read the paper. The notion of a cocktail bar where mixing spirits is taken as seriously as cooking is totally foreign. We want to explain to him that we love to see the brandies change year to year. This is how it should be, like vintages of wine. That consumers expect something made from agriculture to taste identical year after year is a crime against nature. We always feel a little embarrassed that we mix with our friends' spirits. Our greatest fear is that they might think we don't take their craft seriously, that we are disrespecting their spirits. I think they see their brandies as finished products, meant to be consumed on their own. At times, we beg Charles not to mention it, but he—wisely, I think—always tells his producers the whole story.

Later that day, Craig will—at length—try to explain to François our philosophy of drinks as it relates to his spirits. François will look placidly at Craig, like a domesticated animal waiting to hear his name or the word "food," everything else being gibberish. When Craig has finished, François will nod in his beret, the small tendril at its peak moving in Craig's direction, and utter softly that word that offers resolution in any situation in France: *Bon.*

Later on, over coffee, François explains that his granddaughter, a baby, is having open-heart surgery. He notes that the father, his son-in-law, is in Morocco playing golf. Admirably, he says this in a kind, forgiving tone, elaborating, "This is very hard to maintain the work and the personal life today. She looks a very nice baby, but . . . *bon,*" he continues a little sadly, "I will bring the old Pineau." This insertion of personal detail is welcome and indicative of how these French producers like to do business, taking a meal, having an aperitif, sharing details of their family and asking after yours.

Just before leaving, François gives us tastes of his most recent eau de vies, fresh off the still. "Charles, he says, "I must warn your brigade that this is at 63 degrees." I ask Charles if he has the equipment in his pants to taste something at 63 degrees. The joking outside the grasp of the producer never stops, but it is not disrespectful. We love François very much.

Our time in Cognac is usually brief by comparison to Normandy and Gascony, and this stopover has been particularly efficient. From Dudognon and Giboin, we are able to buy young, single-barrel, grower-producer spirits. This means what is in the bottle was grown, fermented, distilled, and aged by one farmer. It is the fruit of one harvest in one year. When we taste their brandy, we are connected to one person as he or she occupied a very specific time and space in human history. No two barrels are the same, just as no two grapes are the same. I would be Luddite to insist these are the only spirits the world should enjoy, but it's worth pointing out that these kinds of bottlings are fast disappearing. I offer that they are worth exploring and that they are singular.

If these grower-producers are singular, what is their opposite? I contend that the large cognac houses aspire to uniformity. This quality is, of itself, not bad. The ability to maintain consistency in foodstuffs is emblematic of skill and progress. Fewer of us die as a result of what we eat now than when we drank small beer instead of dirty water.

To see how the other half lives, we sometimes visit large producers. On one trip, we stopped at Rémy Martin. Instead of being greeted familiarly by the proprietor in the driveway, we were received at the corporate headquarters by a slim, well-groomed, Hong Kong Chinese woman in her late twenties who spoke at least five languages. She took us on a well-choreographed tour for people in the industry, guiding us through beautifully designed interiors, strategically lit warehouses full of immaculate barrels posed picturesquely, building dramatically to the visual of a top-lit bottle of Louis XIII, which we would not be allowed to taste. A bottle of Louis XIII is about three thousand dollars, in no small part because it is bottled in Baccarat crystal. Most large producers of any spirit offer this kind of prestige bottling. Rémy Martin's version is probably the most famous. Throughout the tasting that followed, we would joke that now we are ready to have the Louis XIII. Our host, immune to sarcasm and irony, would efficiently rebuff each request.

"Now would be a good time to sample the Louis XIII . . ." Charles is the first to insist.

"No-no-no. This is not to be tasted." Our host would never smile. She remained severe in her skirt suit.

"This VSOP was very good. I think we're ready to enjoy the Louis XIII. Just a small pour . . ." Craig asks politely.

"No, my friends, this is not possible."

Something else funny happened on our visit to Rémy Martin. Our friend Sandoval was traveling with us. Sandoval owns a great, unpretentious bar that is now world-famous. I am very fond of him and he has done much to invite me further into a community he enjoys of bartenders, owners, and distillers. I am much less cynical as a result of our friendship, which grew quite strong as a result of our proximity when he was enduring a pretty ghastly separation and divorce. Anyone who's been through this shitty experience knows the pain and, more horribly, that this pain can last months if not years.

The "industry" tasting to which we were treated at the end of the Rémy Martin tour was interminable. From frozen shots of cognac in frozen glasses that underscored the neutrality of these brandies—when served cold, they taste like nothing—to strategic pairings of foie gras or chocolate with different "expressions" (a ponderous term used by the more insipid people in the industry) of Rémy Martin, we sat and listened to our guide's canned spiel about the brand.

Charles wondered aloud, beating a horse already long dead, "Would now be an appropriate time to try the Louis XIII?" He affects a puzzled facial expression like someone confused about the customs of another culture. Our guide looks silently at Charles, drawing contrast to her immaculate appearance and Charles's old greasy windbreaker and rock-and-roll hair.

We'd endured Rémy's version of all of the ways big liquor companies strive to make themselves seem modern, youthful, or relevant, and it was time for the culmination: Rémy as a choice for cocktails.

Our host paused, and then continued. "You are lucky because these Rémy cocktails were created for us by someone in your community. He is from San Francisco. I think you know him? His name is Jody Buckles." I felt some air leave the room and looked nervously over at Sandoval. He was white as a snowdrift, and understandably: Jody Buckles was the guy who'd been fucking his wife and, for salt in the wound, was a bit of a douche who took money from a lot of brands. Poor Sandoval. Without speaking, he excused himself to the bathroom, where he regrouped for some time.

I turned my attention back to our well-groomed host and experienced a moment's regret that we were using her time when we had no interest in the product. But she was dead-eyed and mercenary and completely immune to tone. She inhabited a world of prestige and excellence where some products were important and some were not. Companies like Rémy spend more money on marketing a spirit than they do producing it. They co-opt actors like John Leguizamo and talented bartenders like Jody Buckles.

As a child of the 1970s, I still believe in the possibility of selling out. I am guilty of judging a guy who develops recipes for a multinational corporation that is destroying diversity in a category of spirit. It reminds me of the indie band who sells a single to

Disney for a soundtrack; I forgive and understand it, but I can't love it.

Our time in Cognac is generally the shortest on these brandy trips to France. Cognac is the most popular brandy in the world, but not in France. The French prefer armagnac for a spirit of the grape, and more and more they are enjoying scotch or American whiskey during the aperitif and after dinner. Of course, the French drink wine with food.

While I'm cynical about the large producers of the region, the producers with whom we do business inspire me. I am tempted to characterize the state of cognac as a conflict between corporate interest and freedom-fighting grower-producers. This is reductive, but I do believe it's important to mark this moment in the history of cognac. The spirits of this region have been homogenized so that the world at large understands cognac to be a spirit distilled to a high ABV and colored and flavored with caramel, which gives it the subtle flavor of flat, warm cola. I am sure there was a time when greater diversity existed in cognac before the brandies of the area were seized as a financial opportunity. The world has kept spinning, and we are left to wonder what these great brandies might have been like before globalization and massive demand. Think Dudognon's few barrels a year versus Hennessy's annual fifty million bottles.

The Dudognons are proud this year *not* to have sold any brandies to the large houses. They have more security than producers in other regions, since their backup plan is always to just sell their brandies to the big four in a weak economy or off-harvest, but the great aspiration is to make brandies that are unique and their own. With Giboin and the Dudognons this year, we enjoy the restful pace of the French country producer. We slow down and sit a bit, make small talk, take deep breaths with each other, eat together; then we are ready to work, to taste together, to contemplate what we will take home to our guests. We find our rhythm here and are prepared for Gascony, for armagnac, the great agricultural grape brandy of France. I don't know if John Leguizamo drinks it, but we do—and it has, to use his words, "great character."

I study the back of Craig's head in the van as we roll out of Cognac toward the southeast, toward Spain, then Gascony. I see evidence of his scar and remember when he had the procedure removing a portion of his scalp. I feel a paternal attachment to his well-being; we've been together on this road for almost twenty years. I see Eric far forward in the passenger seat. He is smiling and speaking softly to Charles; I don't care what they're talking about. I study the bearded men from Marx Importers, and decide, after only a few days, that they are family. I am fond of everyone in the van. Leaving Cognac, I am resolved in my opinion of the historic region and satisfied that we have found, thanks to Charles, the right people to do business with here, and like traveling buyers since the dawn of history, we travel onto the next region in France, the country that curates its agriculture and produce thereof as though it were a museum.

Chapter Three

ARMAGNAC

ALL THOSE MOMENTS ARE LOST IN TIME, LIKE TEARS IN RAIN

On trips like these, we spend more time in the van than any other setting, and today the interior bears evidence of our hard use. However diligently we bang or wipe our boots before mounting up, we track mud into the vehicle, where a patina of drying clay coats the floor and walls around us. With grower-producer spirits, the dirt, so to speak, is in the bottle, informing the character of the fruit that the expert distiller preserves, and we love having our van and clothes caked with it. The van is a rolling barn on its way from Cognac to Spain, a four-hour drive that Charles will manage on his own. On our way out of Cognac, we drive through mani-cured, frozen vineyards that resist the ineffectual winter sun, whose optimistic light provides a soothing contrast to the stark winter vines. In the midst of the frozen landscape, we pass a cooperage: an unglamorous light-industrial facility that stores the aspects of unassembled barrels. No one is at work today, Sunday, or we might pay a visit. We are all quietly awake, watching the scenery pass.

The last two years we've dropped below the border into Spain for a night between our time in Cognac and our stay in the region of Gascony, where armagnac is made. Armagnac is the heart of this trip, and will be the most physically and emotionally taxing portion of the journey. Armagnac is where we will visit the most producers and taste the most brandy, and it is a region that is, at times, at a crossroads, torn between the traditions of agricultural spirits and a desire for greater commercial success. Armagnac will serve as an effective microcosm of what's going on around the world with spirits; we will have much to do and to contemplate, so this day in Spain has been a nice intermission the last two years.

I am watching Charles today carefully, like he's a sleeping lion. He has been in good cheer and particularly hardy this trip, which makes me wonder if we will later pay a tax. I am neurotic like this, vacillating between total ignorance of those around me and an excess of concern toward them. I am either vigilant or detached. I know now that this is, in part, symptomatic of having grown up in a chaotic home: a clenched attentiveness. I stare at Charles as he glares through the windscreen. He is such a thoughtful host that one can forget that he's organized this trip year after year for us, not as a friend but as a merchant. He does it to sell bottles. If we weren't performing as clients, he might not be so generous with his time and resources. Ours is a pragmatic friendship, based on a common agenda. This might seem sad, but I'd argue that if your work is important, you don't need to segregate it from the rest of your life. In fact, the more passionate you are about your living, the happier you are to be around people who share your convictions. The line between work and free time erodes and you are granted access to a curious bliss where one is always working and always free. If I have an extra Warriors basketball ticket, I'll call Charles or someone else with whom I can talk shop simply because I love it. We are lucky in that our work embodies our values, so the stakes are high on these trips. It is not enough to call them trips, and it is not enough to call them work. It's not enough to call Charles a colleague and it is not enough to call Charles a friend.

Our first stop is San Sebastián, where today the sky is a dramatic charcoal gray at dusk and the Bay of Biscay is violent and choppy, buffeting the coast with strong waves. We walk the town and stop in a bar where Charles has been before. The group drinks txacoli, a slightly sparkling dry and acidic Basque wine with low alcohol, and Spanish beer and eats *pintxos*. I can't help but think that this whole Spanish thing—the culinary obsession with Spain—has been blown out of proportion. Eating and drinking are always fun, and here it is no exception. The affordable wines are great and the bites are nice, too. But really, it's just an elevated version of what we enjoy in the United States. It is happy hour, and it is better than ours. *Basta.*

Hours later, we sit down for dinner at Etxebarri, a famous restaurant less than an hour from San Sebastián in Atxondo, where chef Victor Arguinzoniz is famous for working exclusively with wood fire. Smoked butter is on the table. The house water is Vichy Catalan, and I love its enormous bubbles and sulfurous minerality. Most of the dishes we try are simply and expertly grilled. But there is an incongruity between the rusticity of the food and the ponderous service. The waitstaff seem to serve us from a great distance. It is a family restaurant, so it's not the choreography of something like the French Laundry or Daniel, but it just doesn't feel friendly. I admit I'm guilty of a prejudice that there is a remarkable cruelty in the Spanish—after all, they delivered one of the great genocides of our history.

At dinner, we play a favorite game of Charles's. Throughout the duration of the meal, each of us chooses a bottle of wine for the table, which means six bottles of wine. I pretend to drink as much as possible, passing glasses off to Craig on my right and Leon on my left. This night's dinner in Spain is smoother than last year's, when we ate at a restaurant with a protracted wine list, which is always more of a determinant in Charles's selection than the food. Members of our party felt two of the five bottles we ordered were off, and an interminable conversation broke out about whether the wines were corked or oxidized or fine. Charles kept speaking French to the Spanish waiter, asking him his opinion in the wrong language. People tasted the wines over and over, and the conversation had that maddening quality conversations do when everyone present has lost their short-term memory from drunkenness and jet lag.

Finally I grab the check, which is about fifteen hundred dollars and does not seem quite worth it. I try to help Charles when we can because he has done so much to make this trip happen, including booking most of the lodging. Four credit cards in a row are rejected one after the other, but my Spanish is so much better than my French that I enjoy the ongoing communication about my cards.

We spend the night a couple of miles away, in Elorrio. In my limited experience, Spain has great affordable hotels. This hotel has that particular Spanish and South American charm where the finishes are a little cheap, but the designers' use of solid, bright colors throughout the interior leaves you invigorated. This is our third night in Europe, and we're home at close to 1:00 a.m., with eight hours until our call time—a luxury. Also, the jet lag is diminished and we may actually sleep for some hours in a row. Eight hours would have been wasted on us in the earlier nights—or at least this is the logic I ascribe to Charles as he propels us.

Breakfast in the hotel the next morning is very Spanish: bread, coffee, tortilla. Craig is in full strength. His rhythms oppose those of Charles, who had hit the ground running while Craig was debilitated the first couple of days by his customary Camut brothers' hangover. Craig has rejoined the group like the guy who took a nap at the party and wants to start celebrating just as the guests are leaving.

I think we have all been blocking out Marx's nephew. He continues to say things he is not sure are true. He's not a liar, but he would rather hear himself say something about what's in the glass he's holding, something that doesn't make sense, than say nothing at all. Charles, as I've mentioned, is very patient with him, which is touching but also seems to be no accident, as the boy's uncle is one of his biggest accounts. With the rest of us, Charles will not suffer gratuitous comments.

Eric loves breakfast. He breaks open his *pan de chocolate* in a pornographic slow motion, causing it to burst and cast flakes across the blood-red tabletop. You will not see him happier on these trips than with his first coffee of the day and the accompanying regionally appropriate bread, or upon the arrival of the cheese board, at which point he will rub his hands together histrionically, letting us know he is going to eat some fucking cheese. Really, Eric is a marvel. He is kind and patient at all times, to the point that I begin to take it for granted and want to crack it with my own irritability or passive aggression.

We drive a quick two hours back to France, to Gascony, home of armagnac, stopping just over the border at two of Charles's wine producers. Charles imports mostly wine, though spirits have long been a passion of his, resulting in his authorship of books about each of the three spirits we're in France to buy. People drink wine in greater volume, which means more bottles, which means more money for Charles Neal Selections.

The first winemaker is in the AOC Jurançon, which is just across the Spanish border and about a fifth of the way to Bordeaux. We're guided quickly through a tasting by the son of the proprietor. He is just a kid, maybe twenty or twenty-one. I sense his desire to get back to his friends and roll joints and talk to girls. Still he is warm and helpful, even though it is Sunday afternoon and we're late. They make nice, simple wines from the grapes of the region: Gros Manseng, Petit Manseng, and Courbu. Ranging from young, dry wines to late-harvest wines with botritus, the wines all have pleasing acidity and compelling qualities of tropical and stone fruit.

The second winemaker is recently separated and has dyed his curly mullet a youthful black. He is in the commune Madiran, still in the Pyrenees in the southwesternmost part of France, French Basque country. Despite the national border, the people and landscape appear much like those of San Sebastián and environs. The red wines of this region are the most tannic, astringent, inky wines you'll ever know. While you taste them, you feel like you are going insane. Your gums retreat from your teeth and you feel like a cackling skeleton. Everyone's mouth becomes black and medieval from the juice. As one might imagine, the tannic structure of these wines allows them to age well, and they are good accompaniment to the protein-rich cuisine of the area.

These quick stops have been largely for Charles's benefit; we are not here to buy wine, though I sell a lot of Charles's stuff, particularly from Gascony, at our restaurants. However, we benefit from this rest day, too; we can relax and play the part of tourists, enjoying our own sensual experience without having to be so accountable.

Before calling it a day, we make our first armagnac stop in Gascony at Domaine du Miquer. The barrel we bought from him is one of the best purchases of last year. We want another to back up the current one.

Jacques Miquer is a farmer. He wears tall rubber boots and a winter coat, and his brother is haggard and seems close to death from any number of causes. Presumably, they run the domaine together, though we've never really spoken with the brother, who appears once or twice a visit, passing zombielike across our field of vision in the background toward his next task. He nods congenially in our direction, a slowly burning cigarette gripped between his lips. Already we are enjoying the contrast of armagnac with its urbane cousin, cognac. Armagnac is a more agricultural spirit than cognac. The brandies of the region are vinous or winelike, maturing in the cask and also in the bottle, and more than in cognac, the variety of grape can be quite significant. Single-vintage, estate bot-tlings of brandies from specific varieties of grape value the fruit and mineral qualities of the grape as much as the traits of the oak barrels in which they rest. The mineral content of last year's selection from Miquer was what most moved us, reminiscent of mushrooms and the forest floor.

What follows is one of the most anticipated and idyllic stops of the trip. Brasserie Lebbe is a brewery (and its own ecosystem) somewhere way off the beaten path in Gascony. On second thought, "brewery" is probably too grand a term. It's more like a room with some brewing equipment and a bunch of old wrenches. Pierre Lebbe and his wife grow barley, raise goats, make goat cheese, and produce a wonderful Belgian-style farmhouse ale. The barley is used to make the beer. The spent wort from the beer feeds the goats, whose shit fertilizes the barley. The goat's milk engenders the ripe, acidic cheese, which we eat while standing around the brewery with Pierre, drinking his fresh beer that has a goat's head on the label.

We have a view of the calm valley, and on this visit, the fading light is pink and heartbreaking. We buy the beer in 750-ml bottles with the plan to sell it at Trou Normand and Bar Agricole, where we struggle to get people to order it because it's in such a large bottle. We plan to start serving it by the glass, like wine, pouring five-ounce portions of the fresh, grassy ale from the bottle. I hope people buy it. I want to be connected to this place where we spend time with hundreds of uniformly brown and uniformly sized goats. They are sportive and seem well cared for. On our first visit, Pierre was pro-tective of them, hurrying us out of the tent where they were fed and milked. Now they have built a grand barn with forty-foot rafters.

I love the place. I love the goats. I love the beer. Lebbe is what Eric would call a "mental screensaver." I close my eyes and I can clearly recall the goats' lustrous brown coats, the moist green mead-ows and hills that surround the eighteenth-century building where the family lives and brews. With great clarity, I recall the smell of barley and the smell of healthy goat and the smell of fresh beer.

For the three of us who work together, these trips allow us to fall in love again. We'll take deep breaths and file these moments away for when we are worried about money and sick of each other.

We arrive at around 9:00 p.m. in Montréal, a jewel of a small town that bears little external evidence of the twentieth, let alone the twenty-first century. Narrow stone roads wind toward a town square, centuries old. We are only an hour late. Those of us who've been here before are a little anxious. We're eating at Chez Simone tonight; Charles's brother-in-law, Bernard, is the proprietor, and he is a motherfucker. He thinks it is charming to insult people; for example, he calls Eric a faggot for being a vegetarian. We understand that this is Charles's family and what you do is pay your respects and support the man's restaurant. "Restaurant," however, is a misnomer here. It is Bernard's *court*. You pass a three-hour aperitif grinning as though you're listening to a story Stalin is telling, hoping desperately that Bernard won't turn his sadistic attention toward you. When finally you have surrendered to starvation and are about to leave, he brings out a little foie gras. Then you'll wait another half hour or so until a meal starts at midnight. It is uncanny. I will say to Craig or Eric, "If the food doesn't arrive by 11:30, I'm out of here." As I'm walking for my coat, some food emerges. Like all great torturers, his intuition for his victims' threshold is perfectly accurate.

Earlier this year, I spoke to Charles's wife, Nathalie, about her brother. She speaks English with a sexy Gascon accent. She and Charles have lived all over the world, and the two of them still see rock shows almost every week while raising their two worldly daughters. I joked about Bernard, implying he could be difficult. Nathalie corrected me by saying he is a monster, telling a blurry story of a cassoulet Bernard made a couple of years ago. Charles wanted him to do the cassoulet à la Toulouse and something went wrong. Nathalie elaborates, "Then Bernard is coming. Like an eagle." She put both her hands up, palms toward me in the universal signal for stop. "Like a bull. A bull on fire. Like someone grabs his balls! It is complicated. My mother. She is traumatized." After a few years of being held hostage by Bernard, I was reassured to learn about how his own sister perceives him. Nathalie, at the age of fifty, is a force of nature, often dancing alone until four in the morning. She is a flight attendant for American Airlines and a worthy partner for Charles.

Tonight there are some members of the local rugby team hanging out at the bar of Bernard's restaurant, blind tasting through a series of bottles wrapped in sleeves. The wines are pedigreed and we enjoy guessing what they are, but these guys are massive and they have that frat guy energy that leaves you with two choices: either you party with them, or you're homosexuals that they want to punch.

Craig makes some drinks with Bernard's wife and their fourteen-year-old son, who's interested in our trade; he has been working on some flair techniques and owns plastic cocktail shakers for the safe practice of flipping and tossing. Charles's mother-in-law is there as well: a quiet, mirthful woman in her early eighties, I'd guess. She eats and drinks very little, but loves to be around people. Craig flirts respectfully with both of the women present; I think we are all grateful for the relief from the sausagefest of the previous days.

I pretend to be fascinated by the kid's Larousse French bartenders' guide, avoiding any contact with Bernard, who roughhouses with the ruggers, casting insults at Charles. Tonight is unique in that we start eating at a reasonable hour. The food is an extension of Bernard's sadism; our first course is a whole soft-boiled egg immersed in about five ounces of truffle cream, at least 2,000 calories. The second course is an entire lobe of foie gras poached with peas, an entire lobe for each of us. Then strangely, mercifully, the food stops. After forty-five minutes or so, Charles investigates in the kitchen. In this the twenty-first century, Bernard is having a painful episode of gout. He is resting on his back on the kitchen floor. Gratefully, we are spared the ensuing three courses and obligatory dessert. We flee the bar.

We walk the block to our *chambre d'hote*, and I turn on my iPad to watch Bernardo Bertolucci's *The Conformist*. I am amazed at how much of Coppola's style in *The Godfather* comes from this. All those celebrated American directors of the 1970s just stole from the Europeans. Within ten minutes, I fall asleep. I am too exhausted to worry about how it might all go wrong, how my businesses might fail, how my wife might leave me, and how, as a result of all of this, I would be forced into a shared living situation with middle-aged men who play video games.

Before leaving the United States, Charles sent us an itinerary. Here are the objectives exactly as he wrote them for our penultimate day in Gascony:

Monday 26: Armagnac visits
9:30 Domaine d'Ognoas
11:00 Château de Ravignan
12:30 Domaine Boingneres
Lunch at Domaine Boingneres
17:00 Domaine de Baraillon
20:00 Dinner at Château de Briat

It is our most ambitious day of this or any trip: six producers; two meals with Armagnac nobility, which means two prolonged aperitifs—and all in less than twelve hours.

Charles joins us for breakfast at the *chambre d'hote*. He is wearing a winter coat over a T-shirt that says FASSBINDER in a font popularized by Metallica. Eric devours bread and cheese and drinks coffee from a white bowl; who knows what our lone vegetarian will be able to eat today?

When Marx's nephew is awake, we wait for him to eat something and then we mount up. The mood in the van is good. We are ready for a long day's work. The day begins auspiciously as we arrive on time at d'Ognoas, which is a bit of a museum with its château and grand facilities pronounced against a pale, pale-blue winter sky enwreathed by dormant vineyards. Craig cheers, "I'm gonna taste some brandy-wine today." Then Charles, "Let's burn this fucker to the ground!" This facility is run by the government. It serves as a vocational school for the trade of distilling in Armagnac. Also, it is an educational facility, teaching anyone who visits about armagnac. They are not our favorite producer, but we usually find something we can use. They are expecting us, and we have a long, somewhat canned tour led by Aline, an elegant, middle-aged woman in a pantsuit who speaks English very well. All the facilities are well maintained. D'Ognoas boasts an old still that has seen more than one hundred years of continuous operation. We had hoped to keep the tour brief somehow, but no chance. By the time we reach the tasting room, it's already been more than an hour. They are very organized and the tasting is a good one. Aline has laid a table with a well-organized series of bottles. We taste a number of brandies made from single varieties—Folle Blanche, Columbard, Ugni Blanc, Baco—which gets us grounded in the unique personalities of each grape. These varietal brandies are a great example of how armagnac is a more agricultural brandy, bottled often like wine with a single variety of grape and a designated vintage. This means of releasing brandy emphasizes the grown, base material of the brandies, the fruit of which is quite different from the ubiquity of a single variety in cognac, Ugni Blanc, and the general assault on the flavors of fruit with oak. We love tasting these bottlings that vary greatly from grape to grape and from vintage to vintage.

We move on to try a grand assortment of blends of different varieties and vintages spanning decades. Clearly, we were expected and we are gratified at the gracious treatment. As we are making to leave, a man in a heavy winter coat interrupts us. He gives a short speech in French, saying basically that he is grateful to Charles for his visit and all he has done for the domaine. It is solemn and stiff, as though he is wearing a broad sash and holding an enormous key in his hand. We take our gift bags with half-bottles of highly oaked Ugni Blanc, which is not something we'll sell. We've opted for a cask of Folle Blanche, which d'Ognoas will bottle at 44 percent. In addition, we've bought an affordable cask of Ugni Blanc, also bottled at a higher ABV, which we can use much as we would bourbon. It's relatively neutral, more about the barrel aging than the fruit, rendering the spirit a more compelling alternative to big American whiskey. With something to sell next year in hand, we are off to a good start.

In the van, we are lively and joking. "Remember, Craig, at Baraillon, you're on." Charles is trotting out a standard. The running joke is that we trade sexual favors by Craig with the daughter and heir of the Baraillon estate. The fantasy is that her old parents keep her locked up and she has a simple, incorrigible lust that Craig must satisfy with trembling knees under the porch while we have an aperitif in their cold tasting room. "I'm up for it!" says Craig.

"One barrel per episode of coitus. We expect three barrels at least."

Because we're already hours behind, Charles calls an audible and steers us to Boingneres directly. We will visit with Ravignan later in the day. At Boingneres, the plan is to have lunch before seeing the still and the *chai*, where the barrels age. Martine Lafitte, the proprietor, is an elegant woman in her sixties. She smokes for the duration of our time together, pausing briefly when food is on the table, distracting her from her primary purpose of inhaling cigarette smoke. She smokes extrathin cigarettes, like Virginia Slims, that she pulls from a sleek, square packet. Martine lives with her housekeeper, Marie-Claire, who is generally in the kitchen but is very much a part of the visit. She has a short, monastic bowl cut and wears dungarees and a men's shirt. She will often comment from the other room or make one of those many flatulent French noises with her mouth to express disdain or bemusement. In hopes of expediting the aperitif, I keep refilling the group's champagne glasses as quickly as possible. We open the second bottle. Craig and Eric help by drinking more and quickly. Our plan is thwarted, though, when Martine shouts to Marie-Claire in the kitchen, who emerges with a third bottle of champagne. We've now ensured one of the longest aperitifs of the trip because this third bottle is not consumed, and we all sit eating olives and salami while Martine smokes.

At lunch, Charles and Martine speak of other producers in Charles's portfolio. She is curious about Stéphane de Luze, with whom we're having dinner later. Charles is gently critical of Stéphane, but I do not join in. This trap is the equivalent to sharing your negative opinion when a friend talks shit about his wife or mother; it's fine for him, but hands-off for you.

Each year we've eaten there, Martine decorates the dining room table with a simple centerpiece featuring a French and a US flag. Lunch begins with a lot of foie gras, just the lobe served room temperature with a baguette. Gascony is known for a few things. It is the birthplace of d'Artagnan, arguably the sexiest of Dumas's musketeers; of course, it is the land of armagnac; and it is the cradle of duck in France, if not Europe. We eagerly anticipate the cassoulet, confit, and, of course, foie gras. While foie is legal again in California (there was a short ban), I still cannot resist it in these parts, particularly as the foie here is gamey and pungent. Our domestic foie seems anemic by comparison. Charles will yell at you if you spread the foie. He says it's Parisian bullshit. Just lay slices atop the bread. For our main course, we have a nice roast hen and then a memorable dessert: *fromage blanc* sprinkled with a little raw sugar and a splash of armagnac. You stir it all up and it is fabulous.

After lunch, we pass an hour at the *chai* and stillroom. It is the most beautiful still we see each year. Gleaming and copper, Martine's workers keep it in immaculate condition. Craig interrupts Martine in the stillroom: "Charles, could you explain to us how distillation works?" Charles pretends not to hear and we move on to the *chai*, which is as beautiful as the still. All the barrels are in tidy rows, stacked two high. Martine distills single varieties and ages them largely in Gascon wood. This is not unusual, but for her the unwavering use of the oak of this region is a dogmatic principle. She always bottles at cask strength, which means no water is added at any stage of the process; these brandies are made only from fruit juice and they are never diluted, leaving them at a higher percentage of alcohol by volume, which yields flavor and character. This preference may be confusing, as we generally like spirits that come off of the still at a *lower* ABV. Distilling to a lower alcohol percentage means the distillate has more of the character of the base material, the fruit or grain, and less pure alcohol. But in Martine's case, bottling at higher ABV means that she has not diluted the spirit with water, which leaves a richer more flavorful spirit.

Martine is an exemplary distiller, and her brandies are always among our favorites. Yet we do not buy them to mix in drinks. Martine would never sell us something at a discount or while it was young, which is sad for us; we are looking for newer brandies that will engender compelling cocktails, not so much these contemplative, consequential bottlings by this master. She knows the value of her inventory. So, we buy bottles of vintage armagnac from her for gifts for our favorite employees and have her sign them for us. On one of the bottles she writes, "*Vive l'armagnac!*" I kept that bottle, a thirty-year-old *cépage noble*, for myself and I love to study the expressions on my guests' faces when I pour them a splash after dinner or before bed. At thirty years, this brandy is just crossing into the third stage of *rancio*, a Spanish term, meaning "rancid," which describes the evolution of flavor in wines and brandies that spend a long time in cask. By the third stage, this brandy has spent a great deal of time in a barrel in the old *chai* with its own unique cultures of fungus, and it shows characteristics of nutmeg, tobacco, eucalyptus, and cedar. All of these qualities shine in conjunction with a bright spine of fruit and acidity that mark the vinous quality of the best armagnacs.

Sometimes as we travel from spot to spot, I imagine an aerial view of our white van moving along the country road, or even the expanding line that links one location to the next on the map, as in old films when the protagonist is traveling. The van has its own gravity, holding us together until we stop and the sliding door opens, allowing in the cold air, which pulls us out outward. We're like the characters in *Scooby-Doo*, I think, moving from adventure to adventure in a van of their own. In our van, a stoner and a talking dog don't eat huge sandwiches in one gulp. Rather we argue about music or ride in silence thinking of our obligations at home. As we move across the southwest of France, the landscape vacillates between small forests and expansive vistas. We mount and descend rolling hills surrounded by beautiful, agricultural land. Sunflowers grow all over here, but not at the height of winter. Even though the land is frozen, it appears swollen and fertile.

Ravignan is next. This is a grand Armagnac estate. It has a true château: a haunted, gabled, Gothic structure that also appears on the label of the brandy. This grandeur is definitely more common in Bordeaux, Burgundy, or Cognac. Armagnac is generally a bit less opulent. But the castle at Ravignan has been in this family for generations; the Ravignan family is literally nobility, with titles and lineages. Still, it is a humble operation. The distillation and *chai* are in the same barn, and here is where we encounter Jocelyn, the nephew of the property's owner, who is now serving as the manager of the domaine. We've been to Ravignan, but have never before had the pleasure of meeting Jocelyn.

When you first see him you think, *Jocelyn cannot be real.* He is proportioned like a snowman: a huge round head atop a round torso. He has enviably thick strawberry-blond hair that he parts decisively in the center. His face can only be called cherubic, with full rosy cheeks and lips that constitute a small, intelligent mouth. He is heavy but buoyant and conveys tremendous energy in his every movement. I love him. He dresses the part of the nobleman: he is in a perfectly worn waxed cotton jacket, immaculately knotted scarf that crests just below his chin, and high leather boots. He speaks almost perfect English with just enough French accent to enrich him as a character. Anything Charles says he considers earnestly, nodding and looking down before speaking. "Yes, Charles, we might have something like that." Or, "Charles, do your friends care for this vintage?" His appearance, his dress, his mannerisms are all so elegant and so stately, like a character in a P. G. Wodehouse story. He is the kind of fellow you imagine urging you to enjoy another glass of claret: "The decanter stands by you, sir!" I grow so impressed that I do something rude: secretly, I start taking as many photographs of him as I can.

Ravignan is a really strong producer, and with Jocelyn's guidance, we are able to secure a great cask of young armagnac.

Next is Baraillon. It's already completely dark, and we are as late as we've ever been. We're supposed to be at Briat by eight for a dinner, but it is past eight now and we are doubtful to finish this visit in less than an hour and a half. We are committed, though, to visiting each of these producers today. Charles is a little brittle on the drive. He's been trying to reach his brother-in-law, Bernard, who was supposed to join us at Briat with Charles's sister- and mother-in-law. Bernard's gout is still acting up and he sounds as though he may flake on the evening, which leaves his sweet mother dressed, ready to dine with the nobles, and stuck at home. This development fuses with a week's accumulation of tardiness, and I can see Charles is cooking a little, seared by tension and frustration.

Eric rides shotgun, wearing a pea coat and charcoal watch cap, lean and unshaven with his Hapsburg chin. He has always ridden in this seat, most likely because he is the number-two driver with masculine credentials second only to Charles.

The placement of this visit between Ravignan and Briat seems appropriate. Unlike the other two sophisticated distillers, Baraillon is a more country producer. They have shit on their boots and the tasting room is utilitarian, about a hundred square feet with dirty floors and some forty vintages displayed on a bland, linoleum table-top; the oldest bottle of which is from 1901. We did a cask from 2010 the previous year. The brandy was definitely indicative of the Baraillon style: deep notes, earthy and pungent with aromas of mushroom and dirt. The more time we spent with last year's cask, though, the more we grew concerned it had been adulterated with caramel. Charles prefers that we not ask producers directly if they've added caramel, as he feels the question puts them in an embarrassing position. Our selection from the previous year was just a little too rich for a barrel so young. Young brandies, three to five years old, will never be finished masterpieces. As the brandies haven't had time to take the full character of the charred oak barrels where they rest, we expect to smell and taste more subtle traces of the flavors of vanilla and, still fainter, wood tannin. I like to think of the brandies we buy for our restaurants as showing a "promising adolescence." We are lucky because the market values old spirits, whereas we prefer to mix with spirits that are younger and there-fore more fruit driven. We are most excited about the qualities of the organic material that engender the brandies rather than how they are aged after they've been distilled.

We find this only really succeeds with producers of a certain caliber, grower-producers who shepherd the product from the seed to the bottle. For grape brandies, armagnac is best for our needs. These are the finest agricultural brandies in the world, and when the vinous qualities of the grapes that comprise them are aged skillfully for decades, they are among the most beautiful spirits in the world. I remain extremely prejudiced in favor of the *vigneron* (grower-producer) who controls every facet of production. Usually, the person who makes a spirit is not the one who grew, fermented, and distilled the fruit or grain that constitutes the finished product. The benefits may be largely intangible, but I believe in them. Virtually all spirits in the world are created from a segregation of labor where the farmer is not in connection to the distiller.

I stare at all the vintages set out on Baraillon's table, a little overwhelmed. Even though we are so late, the lovely old couple who own Baraillon put out some cured meats with bread, a bit of a reception for us. I continue to stare at all the bottles. They all seem too dark and they are far too uniform in color. My palate is blown out already from the long day of tasting and the absurd lunch at Boingneres. Doubting myself, I share with Charles my suspicion that almost all these vintages have caramel or *boise* which is generally some combination of sugar, oak chips, or lower-proof brandy that can be left to macerate in a barrel or tank. Like caramel, it is added to the spirit to give the impression of maturity or, to be fair, to make the product more consistent. While we strive to avoid *boise*, we are willing to sell brandies that deploy it at times. In addition to *boise* and caramel, producers may legally add *petites eaux*, which is an eau de vie whose strength has fallen below the required minimum of 40 percent volume. *Petites eaux* can be used to dilute finished armagnacs and cognacs and, as they are often aged in casks, they can enhance the color and flavor of the brandy as well with the natural qualities of the oak barrel.

Charles is already fried and isn't interested in my opinion: "Do what you need to do, man. We all wondered why you bought the last barrel last year." By "we," he means himself and the K&L Wine Merchants guys: the Davids. K&L is a tremendous retailer that sells spirits on premise as well as by mail. One of the Davids, David Driscoll, writes a great column about spirits. He travels some of the same routes we do, and his archive of notes on spirits is excellent, conversational, and informative. The Davids are the biggest retail buyer of Charles's stuff. We are the biggest on-premise buyer, but we can't compete with the Davids' enormous buying power, and I am shamed at the thought of Charles and the Davids wondering why we'd selected a certain barrel. I leave the tasting room before trying the galette the owners are slicing.

Baraillon is in the middle of the woods, and it is peaceful and dark. I can smell the *chai* and its mildew and the trees, and I am pleased to be taking deep breaths of fresh air here in the country. As someone who is chronically late, I empathize with Charles. I have had many days when I've run late throughout, feeling more and more frustrated with myself, incapable of finding a place in the adult world. I think many of us have found ourselves in this peripheral industry because of such shortcomings. But as the Buddha said, "The late man is curious." He is fascinated with what currently engages him and it is hard to leave. Charles honors his producers. He never makes them feel secondary. I have noticed that the producers ask where else we have been. They inquire of Charles, as if they were asking about his other lovers. Charles makes them all feel special.

Before too long, everyone else emerges. Charles finds me on the way to the van and apologizes. I didn't expect it, but I am grateful in my seat in the van as we move toward the final stop, Château de Briat. With his apology and my few minutes of privacy and fresh air I'm restored, ready for the end of the day. We've been up since seven, and it is now ten and dinner is nowhere near. The day will be at least twenty hours long.

I wonder for a moment if I should warn the others that Charles is a little grumpy—especially Craig, whose strength and cheer keeps mounting in exact correspondence with Charles's depression. Craig jokes tunelessly, "I'm glad I didn't have to provide intercourse as barter for any barrels of spirit."

At last we arrive at the large oval gravel driveway of Château de Briat, in the Mauvezin-d'Armagnac, a commune in the Landes department in Nouvelle-Aquitaine. The white van comes to rest beside the stillroom, an eighteenth-century barn that sits beside the château, which once was a hunting lodge of Henry V. By "lodge," I mean a structure more opulent than all of our homes combined. Among other things, the property boasts paneled dining rooms, libraries with twenty-foot ceilings and eight-foot fireplaces, and, of course, its own staff. Stéphane meets the van as it pulls into the courtyard. It's 10:30 and a soft rain is beginning to fall.

Stéphane is the son of Gilles de Luze, who partnered with Charles some years ago. Gilles was passionate about the domaine and about Briat, working hard to champion the cause of the independent producer in Armagnac. In the late 1990s, de Luze formed an alliance with four other producers: Yves Grassa from Château du Tariquet, our friend Martine Lafitte from Domaine Boingneres, Jean de Boisséson from Château de Lacquy, and Pierre Laberdolive. Together they were the Cru Legendaires. The group advocated the production of traditional, cask-strength vintage armagnacs from their independent estates in the famous Bas-Armagnac region. At Briat, they distill to only 52 percent, resulting in assertive, compelling brandies. In 2003, Gilles and his wife, Adeline, died in an automobile crash as they were driving home from an independent producers' salon in Lyon. Gilles was fifty-three. The de Luzes left one son, Stéphane, who, in his early twenties, suddenly found himself as head of the château.

Knowing this story, it is hard not to project a sadness onto Stéphane. He seems reluctant in his leadership of Briat. Soon after his parents' death, Stéphane enlisted the help of his cousin Jean de Mareuil. The first time I visited Briat, some years ago, I met both Stéphane and Jean. They were continentally handsome and dressed as though for après-ski, with warm sweaters and boots. I felt as I had when I first arrived at Yale and found myself in the company of a Vanderbilt or a Rockefeller. Any insecurity is largely of my own creation, because these are human beings with all the idiosyncrasies that attend the species. Still, someone with a title or descendant from a title, in my experience, embodies a quiet detachment that must be the consequence of that singular life.

On that night, Jean took control. Sunburned, in his Breton sweater, he invited us enthusiastically, "Let's go chill out and eat some *jambon.*" He was comical in his cheer while Stéphane was laconic and diffident. Jean punctuated our every comment: "Oh! You like the Jack Daniel's! Oh! You were joking!"

We tasted through some vintages, encouraged at each turn by Jean while Stéphane remained quiet. I suspected that Jean had formed a parasitic relationship with his cousin. The two handsome Frenchmen were doing fashionable events together around the world to promote the brandy, the way Hennessy might cultivate awareness of their enormous brand. Jean's hip youthfulness didn't match the gravitas of the château or of the beautiful, structured armagnacs it has historically produced. On that first visit, we also tasted a couple of side projects: "Scherzo," a bright aperitif, and an orange cordial not unlike Grand Marnier. This kind of diversification generally doesn't bode well. I'm always sad to see a great distiller try to make his or her product more youthful, devaluing the cultural capital of generations of work.

We returned a year later and Jean was gone. Stéphane didn't say much, but I inferred that his cousin had been a mistake as a partner. Stéphane joined us for dinner at the home of Charles's mother-in-law. I sat by him and he still seemed wistful. During dinner, he commented that all he really wanted to do was hang out with his wife and kid and practice scuba. His wife worked for one of the great fashion ateliers, which is interesting when you consider that Louis Vuitton is becoming one of the more powerful distributors of spirits. Their portfolio includes Hennessy and Belvedere among many others. We've never met Stéphane's wife, but we know she has used the château for fashion shoots—which makes me sad, though it is understandable.

Tonight we are not invited into the château. Instead, we'll be spending the evening in a converted barn Stéphane has developed for professional entertaining. He likes the idea of renting the château sometimes, and he prefers to entertain clients in this space, which is not shoddy. A large open fire is at its center, over which they are cooking a joint of venison: a tribute to Stéphane, the noble, from a citizen who'd killed the deer on his estate.

Tonight we meet a new character. He is beautifully dressed in tailored trousers and blazer with a lovely, pressed shirt and a scarf knotted in one of those ways only the French can manage. He speaks effortless English and is congenial and enthusiastic in a way that reminds me a little of the departed Jean. As the evening progresses, we learn that he is helping Stéphane with marketing. The previous year, we discovered that Stéphane was going to do some *négociant* bottlings, meaning he will purchase spirits from other distillers and sell them on under a version of his label, "Fief de Briat." In Armagnac, most *négociants* just bottle the bought spirit under their own label, making no mention of the original distiller. This practice is not unheard of, but in other regions, like Scotland, the *négociant* or merchant bottler will feature the name of the original distiller.

With the Fief de Briat label, Stéphane can capitalize on his great name by selling other folks' brandies but, sadly, this could compromise his status as a grower-producer. It makes me nervous.

I am talking a bit to the marketing guy and, despite myself, come to like him more and more. He had worked as a French tobacco attaché to Cuba, where he'd participated in the development of a number of pretty cool cigars, including the Cohiba Siglo XX, which debuted while I lived in Havana. He loved Partagas, which are dark. I'm more of a Montecristo No. 2 guy, which features a looser draw and lighter tobacco. Our well-dressed friend, let's call him Jean Michel, smoked three or four cigars a day and had no problem taking down a double Corona. He was a more serious smoker than I, but I was grateful for a Partagas Robusto from the case he brought. I pass the time with Jean Michel, comparing notes about Cuba. He talks about it like a sex tourist, like most men I've met who spend time there. I feel absurd for nodding and listening when a man says something like, "The mulata women of Havana are very fine, yes?" He's the kind of fellow who's decent company if you leave politics at the door and you don't mind listening to stories: the story of having a cigar with Jeremy Irons, the story of having a cigar with Galliano, the story of having a cigar with Maradona.

Jean Michel mentions that he's helping Stéphane with packaging, another potential death knell. In the high-ceilinged barn, he had set up a little display of four new bottles—"new" bottles in that they are not shaped the same as the classic brandy bottle, the kind with sloped shoulders that is used commonly in armagnac and cognac. This new bottle is square-shouldered and had brightly colored labels. Each bottle is a different proprietary blend, a youthful approach, and the kind of thing I've seen too many times, not just in armagnac but in the greater spirits world as well.

I know I'm being unfair; Briat needs to survive, but this is cheesy. It is branding, and a great producer really can survive if he is simply attentive to the quality of his product. I cling to the cigar and contemplate the tension behind my eyes and the exquisite exhaustion. It was approaching midnight and we still hadn't eaten. Nicotine is not relaxing, but a forty-five minute cigar forces you to stop and contemplate. This pause is welcome, as I notice the others drinking more to wash the long day off of them. Charles insists that Craig, now looking a little absent in the eyes, make the group some mixed drinks with the new line of brandies Jean Michel is helping to market. Craig dutifully begins to perform the task, moving deliberately, like a harried marionette. The others take turns at a snooker table. The night is beginning to splinter.

I met Craig fifteen years ago when we worked together at a fine-dining restaurant where we had to wear beige shirts with band collars and aubergine vests. We made thousands and thousands of vodka sodas, vodka tonics, cosmopolitans, and lemon-drops, an empty infinity of meaningless drinks. At thirty, we were starting to suspect we might not become the famous artists or writers we'd anticipated being as undergraduates. This business spoke to us, though. We enjoyed practicing the physical skill of making drinks, which demands its own choreography as well as the Buddhist practice of *metta*, of loving kindness toward your guests. You couldn't just pretend to love them; you had to actually love them. We advocated for our guests, ensuring they felt cared for, supported. I'm sure psychic injury may have landed us in this trade, but none of us choose our careers. They are determined.

As time passed for me, the beauty of serving gave way to the importance of connecting with people who share our values. We've looked for years for people unwilling to compromise. On this trip, as with each year, we renew our optimism and our community. We know maybe ten or fewer people who truly produce in the most mindful way, and there are fewer and fewer each year.

I met Eric about ten years ago. We worked together briefly before recognizing we were kindred spirits. He is a quiet, sincere guy who loves the trade. He, like all of us, looks for meaning in his work. Eric, in particular, hungers for connection to beauty and kindness. This is why he put 250,000 dollars of his own money into our business. This money was largely the result of the life insurance benefit from his father, who died when Eric was a boy. Eric and Craig are sensitive guys. They want to feel good about a career that a lot of people shit on. I figure I'm the same as them; and this is why we've come to Briat for dinner at eleven in the evening. We're here to find meaning.

Jean Michel carves the joint of venison in a manly, hospitable way. "I will be the father," he jokes. He has put on a creased apron and holds the large carving fork and knife ceremoniously. The meat is served with some roast vegetables and a couple of wines that Jean Michel has an interest in selling. He would never ask Charles directly to import the wine, just as he never asks us to consider his new bottlings of armagnac. I have to admit this is a pretty civilized way to sell.

The cheese board hits the table with some lightly dressed endive. Peripherally, I am aware of Eric wielding the dull cheese knife as though it were a Masamune blade. Motherfucker loves cheese. Another great meal. It's approaching two, and I light a second small cigar and step outside to talk with Jean Michel. When a soft rain begins, he moves back inside and I enjoy another private moment of fresh air. This estate is also in the middle of the woods. The château stands out pale against the troubled Gascon sky.

By the time I make it back inside, the evening appears to be disintegrating a little. Marx's nephew has asked Stéphane if he has any weed. Stéphane coolly suggests we finally make our way to the *chai*.

Even Charles had agreed that the previous year was a little painful. Stéphane didn't seem to have a good handle of the inventory compared to someone like Miquer, who shot directly to the cask he was discussing. This year was only worse. Stéphane couldn't find anything. We stood around for awkward five-minute increments while he searched for a 2010 Baco or a 2009 Folle Blanche. When he finally found what he was looking for, or at least something close, he extracted samples awkwardly, like an actor playing the part. When we were home from the trip, Charles threw out his notes of the Briat tasting. He didn't trust himself because it had been at the end of such a long day and we'd all scorched ourselves. Also, I think he had no faith in Stéphane to bottle the cask we'd actually sampled. He is actually starting over with Stéphane. As I write this, Charles is in Gascony with the Davids.

Finally, we are in the van after saying our good-byes to Jean Michel and Stéphane. Some are quiet and some are talkative. Leon and Marx's nephew talk to each other about what they might want to pick up for their shop. Craig chats freely about the evening and is jokingly critical of Stéphane. "That motherfucker needs to get his *chai* in order! He doesn't know his Baco from his Folle Blanche!"

Charles interrupts from his throne at the steering wheel. God only knows how he is able to drive. "What the fuck are you talking about?" His interjection has the effect of a parent pulling the needle off a record. The ensuing silence is palpable—it fuses with the darkness outside the van while it moves through a symmetrical canopy of gaunt trees, reaching out to each other overhead, covering the road and giving us the sensation that we are traveling deeper and deeper into the night.

"Charles, don't you get at all discouraged?" Craig sounds unsure of himself.

Charles offers no quarter. "I have no idea what the fuck you're talking about," he says.

"The new bottles. That guy . . ." You could hear the hint of a smile in Craig's voice, his subtle prayer that this was not serious.

"He's showing you around his *chai* at three in the fucking morning," Charles says, "And you judge him."

In the van, all is still. No one moves or turns his head to look at anyone else. Charles grips the wheel and stares forward. Inside there is a feeling of being stuck, but the van is decidedly in motion, racing through the corridor of winter trees. I don't blame Charles. He's written a book about armagnac. He and these producers are married, and really no one else is brokering these kinds of friendships. We really should be, and generally are, unilaterally appreciative. We don't need to be critical of French men with beards and turtlenecks who feed us like we're family and sit up with us until three in the morning.

Craig won't let the embers die: "No, I just think . . ."

"We can't *all* be Bar Agricole!" Charles says. He is accusing us of being snobs here, which is maybe not unfounded as we are looking to buy grower-producer spirits to use in cocktails. This is as pissed as I've seen him. "When you get back to California, you can drive down Highway 17 to Soquel and buy brandy from a guy named Dan Farber if this isn't good enough for you." So confident is Charles in his lovemaking that he is pushing us toward another's bed. Dan Farber is a nice man. He distills brandy in the Santa Cruz Mountains south of San Francisco. He grows Columbard grapes and didn't sell any inventory until he'd been distilling for fifteen years, letting his inventory mature and his *chai* accumulate valuable microbial character. This accumulation of stock is normally the privilege of cash-rich producers, but Dan has supported the inception of his distillery with wine sales.

"Charles . . ." I can't see Craig's face, but his tone is heartbroken.

"I can't fucking believe you!" Charles has turned off the music and we are all roasting in the silence.

"Look, I didn't mean any offense," Craig continues. This, I think, would have been a great place to stop. "But it is sad to see Briat falling apart . . ." I can see Eric in the passenger seat shaking his head, so subtly; we will agree later that Craig really should have just stopped.

"What the fuck are you talking about?" Even Marx's nephew is silent. Looking straight ahead.

"He needs to get his *chai* in order. It's ridiculous . . . "

It went on. The rest of us sat upright. Occasionally, one of the others would interject to try to make peace between the two of them. But they were both drunk and exhausted and strangely lucid. The momentum of this long day could not be slowed. It propelled each of them in his unnamable emotion. They held in this pattern for about twenty minutes. Charles could not forgive and, maddeningly, Craig couldn't manage a simple, unconditional apology.

I am silent. I'd tasted a little of Charles's temper at Baraillon and I want no more. I am quietly embarrassed for having been so opinionated throughout this trip. I really should just be saying thank you to Charles at every juncture. We can be a little high-minded about this stuff and I'm sure it irritates Charles, who is violently averse to pretention despite his own love of Fassbinder and rock opera. At the same time, I have tender feelings for Craig, who weighed less than a hundred pounds until well into high school. When he did grow into himself, he became very handsome and eloquent, but he still carries about himself a sadness and vulnerability.

When Charles finally drops us outside the *chambre d'hote*, just down the street from Bernard's café at three in the morning, Eric and I ask Craig if he wants some company while he smokes his last cigarette. He is trembling and crying softly. The last twenty-five years have led to this moment and I don't begrudge Craig his tears. Middle age is painful sometimes.

He is at its precipice and, like me, thought he might have found the trick to make this work mean something. What we saw at Briat tonight is like the scene halfway through a period piece when our protagonist coughs without context. We've seen it before; we know the cough foreshadows a death by consumption. Briat may never become Rémy Martin, but Stéphane has started to move, tentatively, away from what his father fought so hard to protect.

To taste a spirit produced in the same way and from the same material it was made a hundred years ago is to connect through the experience of taste with our ancestors, to know how they lived. It is time travel and communion. Disconnected from this past, we are forced into a present and a looming future where scotch is all but dead, where tequila is sadly changed, where independent rums born from the African diaspora are being systematically expunged from the world. To judge a small misstep so sternly may seem unfair, but we are protecting our identities. We dread becoming just bartenders: shills for shitty brands, not champions of the beautiful.

A category of human experience is disappearing from the earth and I, like Craig, am paying close attention. We are in the luxury goods business, though; we are not freedom fighters. Nonetheless, we aspire to connection with people and products of substance, and to see someone who was doing the *right* thing start to do the *wrong* thing frightens us that a tradition might be ending. Surely, change is inevitable and lamenting it is part of living and of dying, but we can take note, like anthropologists, and mark this time, saying: "Once, human beings produced spirits in a certain way . . ." Let's pause to taste them before they are gone.

PART TWO

AMMUNITION?! THIS IS NO TIME FOR AMMUNITION!

Chapter Four

CUBA, PART I

THE REALITY OF CULTURAL CAPITAL

I have warned Eric and our employee Jay that they should bring as much cash as possible. In the airport, I notice Eric stopping at a cash machine and I grow a little nervous; he seems to be grabbing only a few hundred for the trip. Yesterday, I withdrew six thousand dollars in mixed bills and buried it like a brick in the bottom of my Filson backpack. Still, even in 2016, a year after diplomatic relations between the United States and Cuba were restored, you can't use an American ATM or credit card in Cuba.

I came here for a year in 2003 with considerably less money, stalled in another relationship, smoking too much grass, and convinced I couldn't stay at the Slanted Door selling Southeast Asian–inflected vodka drinks flavored with ginger and lemongrass any longer. I'd visited Cuba several times at this point, usually with my best friend from college, Ashley, who first experienced the country as a rower at the Pan-Am games. He had met Fidel and even spent time training with the Cuban boxing team. We were both intellectual communists and fascinated by the Cuban experience and all its successes and failures: 100 percent literacy and health care; world-class education free to all of Latin America; sports, arts, and music, all of a quality that transcends the country's size, population, and GDP. At the same time, Cuba embodied a profound sadness and impatience. Many people wanted to leave—not forever, just for a bit—and couldn't, and those who left weren't allowed to return.

The more time I spent in Cuba, the more I felt its contradictions. In 2003, I resolved to live there for a longer period of time in hopes of finding a truth about this country that is only eighty miles from the United States but is further away than anywhere I've ever been. I saved some money and found I could study Spanish at the University of Havana in a program, very affordable, oriented toward foreigners. I rented an illegal apartment in Havana Vieja, the oldest and most exquisitely decaying part of the town. Legally, any foreigner had to rent lodging through the state; I rented this place secretly. Havana Vieja was alive with horses and carts, bicycles, the famous old cars, ice shavers, sugarcane presses. This was when I cemented my relationship with Cuba's elemental staples: sugar, coffee, lime, bananas, rum, beans, rice, aspects of everyday Cuban life that would inform the way I think about bartending for the rest of my career. Unable to trade freely with its neighbors, Cuba has been limited for the last fifty years on the level of ingredient, which frustrates but also leads to a deeper relationship with these components, which I have enjoyed in great variety. From *congrí* to *moros y cristianos* to *frijoles negros* and *arroz blanco*—a few of the many ways in which people found to serve beans and rice—to the five or six coffees I'd have a day—their bitterness mitigated by the sugar that was the color of desert sand on every counter—to the numerous combinations of rum, this same sugar, and lime to the bananas of ever-changing sizes, turgor, and sweetness, I tunneled deeper and deeper into these flavors and textures and experienced how they changed with my mood, with the weather, with the time of day. Without imagination, this limited palette could feel myopic, but what resulted for me was a more evolved relationship with this place through those materials that thrived here. I left Cuba believing innovation and diversity really didn't matter so much. What excited me was the possibility of a more profound understanding of fewer ingredients.

Now I am back in Havana, two years after my last visit and thirteen years after I'd studied and lived there. I am in love with the country and I loathe it. To use a word that's wielded all too casually in this world, Cuba is an enigma. The more time one spends there, the less one understands it.

One of my favorite stories about the Cuban Revolution comes from a Che Guevara biography. When Fidel's revolutionary army, some sixty men, first landed on the shores of Cuba after training for months with Castro in Mexico, they were greeted by the CIA, most of the Cuban military, and members of the US Navy. Someone had tipped off the Cuban government, who then enlisted all the support they could to suppress what was expected to be a failed invasion. Che describes walking behind one of the designated ammunition carriers as they sneaked through the woods upon landing. As Che describes it, when gunfire broke out, the man who was carrying the ammunition dropped his precious cargo and took off running. Che called out, "Compañero, you are forgetting the ammunition!" His comrade, face white with terror, looked over his shoulder toward Che and shouted, "Ammunition! This is no time for ammunition!"

Cuba defies the world's imagination in all that it has accomplished while retaining such a human scale: built by humans, run by humans, fraught with human frailty and absurdity. Like Che mocking his own bravery, the nation of Cuba is at once painfully earnest and absurdly carefree. The integration of these opposites is the wonder of Cubanismo, and the reason why, at the end of this trip, I will not be surprised when this country, which lists rum among its proudest exports, will make it impossible for us to visit even one of their national distilleries.

On this most recent visit, in 2016, I'm traveling with three guys who've never been to Cuba. The first is our old friend Eric, elegantly

Euro as ever in his narrow jeans, windbreaker, and Adidas Sambas. New to our troupe is Jay, our latest protégé. He speaks Spanish well and seems wise beyond his twenty-nine years. That said, traveling with someone always reveals the truth of their character. We are hoping Jay will run Obispo, the rum bar that is a few months from opening at the time of this writing. He is very handsome and very earnest, with a perfectly casual thin beard, at times wearing atelier coats to bartend. He holds down the bar at Trou Normand these days, but he demands attention. He has other opportunities, and while he wants to work in this trade, he needs to be sure he is learning and gaining responsibility. This intensity keeps me honest, ensuring I'm present at Trou Normand doing tastings as often as possible and spending time seated at the bar watching the guys work. Jay and I will have a coffee once a month or so to check in while we wait for the rum bar to unfold, and he will often remind me that to work with me he turned down a position with Patagonia that would have allowed him to travel extensively throughout the Americas. Demanding employees can be difficult, but I prefer them; they tell you what they need, and if you honor their desires, they are generally faithful and content.

The third companion is none other than Charles Neal and, as usual, he has managed to arrive first. Upon clearing customs, we encounter him on his second beer, perfectly at home in his shorts and a T-shirt; this one has the words "VON TRIER" printed in the same font Van Halen used on their self-titled album cover. "We made it, boys," he says. He shakes each of our hands solemnly, as though we've found each other after the Battle of the Bulge. Customs had been a little arduous, entirely indicative of what is to come. The deceptively short lines at passport control shrink at a maddeningly slow pace, inspiring a couple of us to hop nervously from line to line like at the grocery store, betraying we are from San Francisco, where everyone pretends to be mellow but is really tight-assed, honking from cars, giving the finger from bikes, glaring self-righteously at cars that dare penetrate the plane of the cross-walk we occupy as pedestrians.

On the other side of immigration, I learn the backpack I checked (not my carry-on with the six grand, thankfully) is lost, and I spend a half hour wandering around the baggage claim talking to indif-ferent Cuban civil servants. Finally, one pointed behind a curtain as though I were stupid and, strangely, behind this curtain was my bag.

A first note about Cubans: most of them are civil servants, as the Cuban government is the chief employer of the entire island. From airport security to the taxi drivers to the hotel clerks to the waiters and the classically trained musicians who perform all over the island, everyone is working for the state. Private enterprise is allowed, if not encouraged, but business owners pay something like 80 percent in tax. So, in a way, they are working for the state as well. Marry this phenomenon with the fact that Cubans are educated and beautiful and it makes for a fascinating dynamic. Cubans are vastly unimpressed with you. They don't care if you want ice cream; they aren't concerned you've been waiting an hour; they're not worried that you can't find any toothpaste.

Charles, here for the first time, is keen to remark on the way the female airport security and clerks dress, comfortable in their stiletto heels and tight skirts. They wear uniforms, but they are far from the sexless costumes you'd see in US customs. "I'm quickly form-ing a positive impression of how women dress in this country," he remarks. "I mean, these women are really expressing themselves." Cuban sexuality is an indomitable force. My anthropological two cents is that, among other things, the island has been largely cleansed of the Catholicism that dominates the other Spanish-speaking islands in the Caribbean, which yields a kind of pride, as in the opposite of shame, that is always salient in interactions with men and women of any age.

Again, couple this quality with education. Cuba is famously the only nation with 100 percent literacy, which began during the revolution when Castro's forces taught everyone who enlisted to fight in the revolution—from farmers to destitute laborers to housebound mothers—to read. So, renting a car or ordering an omelet is generally an encounter with an empowered individual with a working knowledge of Marx who feels your relative wealth is the consequence of slavery and theft. It is an exquisite subtext that confuses people who have traveled elsewhere in Latin America, where you will get a lot more *para servirle* (at your service) for your money.

I leave Eric and Jay with Charles to have their first beer; I am off in search of the driver ostensibly hired by Amador, who will be the fifth member of this contingent. Amador is a friend and Cuban national living and working in San Francisco. I met him through Curtis Dubbs, who was Amador's professional and domestic partner. The two of them work with fabric. I collaborated with them on aprons and napkins for both of our bars. Amador and Curtis work with the finest fabrics from all around the world, and they are fabulous. They will appear at one of the bars with an eighty-year-old heirloom denim merchant from Japan, or the youngest, most avant garde importer from Mexico City or India. Both make their own essences and are draped in curiously flattering, though sexless, garments of their own creation. To hug Amador is to dive into an olfactory ocean composed of juniper, cedar, sandalwood—so ethereal and intoxicating that you never want to leave.

The newest bar I'm planning, Obispo Rumbar, aspires not to be too culturally specific, but it will take much of its inspiration from the time I've spent in Cuba and, obliquely, from the beautiful bars down here. I've hired Amador as an informal consultant on the bar; for this trip, I'm covering his flight and lodging in hopes that he can help us conquer the bureaucratic wall we'll need to scale to get inside a Cuban distillery. I am suspicious that Amador may be a bit of a flake; he and Curtis have recently separated and Curtis had expressed some concern about his drinking, which doesn't really alarm me, as most of us in this industry need to come to terms with our relationships with substances, be they alcohol, cocaine, or salty food.

During our layover in Panama, I received a text from Amador explaining his connection was fucked up and he'd be getting to Havana much later. I should instead look for Yan at the airport; he will drive us to the apartment Amador sorted out for us. I'm nervous, as I am the one who planned this trip. Charles's trips are usually wired very tight and, as he's written books on each of the regions he shares with us and maintains great relationships with his producers, we are able to get a great deal accomplished.

This trip will be something different. It is a crude, exploratory trip. Amador and I have been trying for months to arrange visits with distilleries and no one will bite. While tourism from the United States to Cuba is now legal for the first time in fifty years, the trade embargo between the two nations hasn't been lifted and the possibility that Cuban rums will be available for wholesale in the United States anytime soon is quite unlikely.

Generally speaking, Cuban rum is light and dry. In this case, "dry" refers to the amount of congeners and/or esters in the finished distillate. This is in contrast to high-ester, very aromatic rums like those found in Jamaica, in particular two independent distilleries I've visited: Hampden Estate and Worthy Park. Both are beautiful, plantation-style estates that produce Jamaican-style rums with long, open-vat fermentation. Hampden Estate is particularly fetid and microbial in its fermentation with stinky, moldy facilities that enrich the long, slow fermentation with so much character. Furthermore, these distilleries introduce *dunder* into the fermenting molasses. Dunder refers to the liquid remaining in the boiler after distilling a batch of rum. It is introduced to future washes to flavor them and help them ferment. Dunder acts like a sourdough starter with its own particularly aromatic legions of bacteria and other microbial colonies. Think good, stinky cheese; good things come from filthy circumstances at times.

Sadly, the United States is so clean-obsessed we miss out on a lot of these pungent pleasures. Similarly, Cuban rums are offered as a civilized alternative to the funkier Jamaican rums. While Hampden Estate would have an ester count of around 2,000 parts per million, a Cuban dry would be more like 200. Fermented in cleaner circumstances and distilled to a higher alcohol by volume, these more neutral rums have found their place in the cocktail canon. Bacardi popularized this style with rums that are distilled to almost complete neutrality, leaving them more like vodka than a challenging, high-ester rum.

In 2016, no Cuban rums, or any Cuban products, are available for wholesale in the United States. Similarly styled rums that are made elsewhere, by producers like El Dorado or Brugal, are available but don't hold the allure of the Cuban article, in no small part because they are forbidden, I imagine. Even so, we usually have a couple of bottles of one of my favorite truly Cuban rums, Havana Club, behind the bar: gifts from friends or procured ourselves at a duty-free shop.

Much has been made of the possible end to the embargo between Cuba and the United States. Novices speculate that opening trade between these neighbors will result in an erosion of Cuba's identity. In fact, the opposite is true. Cuba is resolved to maintain ownership of its land and businesses, just as it has for the last fifty years. Its identity will only be fortified by United States trade, which frightens those opposed to the lifting of the blockade, as that trade would render Cuba akin to Switzerland or a Scandinavian country: rich with cultural capital, strengthened by its social programs, and, now, with greater overall wealth to share among its citizens. I suppose we are hoping to contribute to this elevation of the Cuban economy: an advance landing party scouting the possibilities of the eventual rum trade between the United States and Cuba.

Rum is without question the most diverse category of spirit; really, the only definition or prerequisite is that it be a distillate of some by-product of sugar or the sugar production process. This includes but is not limited to fresh-pressed cane juice (cane being the grass from which sugar is made) or molasses; more eclectic rums are being made even from materials like sorghum and corn syrup.

I became obsessed with rum when I was introduced to *rhum agricole*, made from fresh-pressed sugarcane rather than molasses or another by-product. The man who introduced me to *rhum agricole* is Ed Hamilton, the self-appointed "Minister of Rum" and founder of the online community *Ministry of Rum*. If you ask him how to reach him, he will say, "Just Google 'rum.'" Fifteen years ago, when I first tasted with Ed, a giant man with a significant walrus moustache and hair to the middle of his back, he had been living for years on a boat and traveling all around the Caribbean, which allowed him to become expert in the category and befriend some really cool, unexposed distillers, who trusted him to bring their rums to the US market.

There is something wild or unfinished about Ed. The guy spent quite a while off the grid and he has been all over the world, so his company has a Melvillean quality that informed my first taste of *rhum agricole*. The best of these rums come from the island of Martinique, a state of France, where appellation rules dictate that they must be produced from the fresh-pressed juice of sugarcane grown on AOC-certified land. No other rum is curated to this degree, and this attentiveness yields spirits on par with the greatest French brandies, in my opinion. To smell them, as I first did with Ed, is to encounter the wildest, most vegetal qualities of the fresh sugarcane, and a startling array of smells and flavors: green olive, ocean floor, fresh-cut lawn, salty pineapple mixed with fresh banana. My first tasting was revelatory to say the least; the connection of what was in the bottle to what had grown in the ground was so compelling that I would never think about spirits the same way again. Once you taste great terroir-driven booze, you will never go back. It's why I called my first place "Bar Agricole."

Alas, most rums in the world are made from molasses, an agricultural inevitability linked to the history of the sugar trade and the colonization of the Caribbean. I love to imagine how marvelous the technology of sugar production must have seemed at its nascence. For the first time, humanity harnessed one of the four key flavors—sweet, sour, bitter, salt—for its own use. The quest to satisfy this global sweet tooth led to one of the greatest colonial land grabs in history. Every empire hurried to the Caribbean, one of the only places in the world where the cane plant flourishes, and appropriated agricultural land for the production of sugar. The by-product of sugar refinement is molasses, a boldly aromatic dark sludge that is redolent of sugar and the earthier aromatics of the oxidized cane plant. Molasses is used widely as a sweetening agent in the American South and in other regions and communities of the African diaspora. The combination of the sweetness of the molasses and the heat of the climate made for a synergy that all but guaranteed fermentation. *Tafia* is the first known distillate made from the refuse of the sugar production process; it was mostly consumed by local populations in sugar-producing regions. Tafia would evolve into rum, which, as we all know, became a valuable commodity in its own right. The agriculture of sugar was maximized now with the production of two great exports: refined sugar and rum.

The centuries of history that feature these commodities and the trade routes that facilitated their distribution are inextricably linked with slavery. Without slavery, we do not have rum. This connection informs the mystique of rum: slavery, rebellion, revolution, pirates, murder, royal navies all contribute to how compelling the liquid is even before you open the bottle. Worth repeating is that rum is slavery; to separate the two is irresponsible.

In every sugar-producing region of the Americas, slavers conveyed and imprisoned human beings, and in each of these places some kind of rum was usually made. Each of these areas was a cultural explosion, composed of the indigenous population, the colonizing forces, and the African communities that were forced to inhabit the area as well. The religions of these disparate cultures collided and inseminated each other—Santeria, Voodoo, Umbanda; the cuisines and languages of the cultures combined as well. From the Spanish-speaking islands of Puerto Rico, the Dominican Republic, and Cuba to the French-speaking Haiti, Martinique, and Guadaloupe to the English-speaking Jamaica and Barbados—each place where rum was produced is its own unique entity, but is united as a part of the African diaspora. The raw, fertile odors of the best rums are informed by, and linked to, the mayhem that is associated with a particularly painful chapter in human history that many would agree has not concluded.

Nowhere is the association between rum and slavery better understood than in Cuba. From the 1950s, leaders of the revolution would head up cane-cutting expeditions, making a point of doing the shitty work that had been relegated to slaves and the impoverished. The charismatic Che Guevara, after working a full week as president of the nation's banks, would head out into the country as part of these cutting parties. Even though he famously suffered from asthma, Che was not too good to do the work of slaves.

In Havana, the rum museum (Museo del Ron) begins with an exhibition of the horrors of slavery. Images of torture and subjugation are not the kind of saccharine prologue you would encounter in most distillery tours, but the Cuban state insists you face this part of the island's history. Not far from the museum, the main square where slaves were auctioned is commemorated with plaques and frequent reminders by the Cubans hanging out that this is where we sold human bodies. Restaurants feature "slave cuisine" and call it that, most notably at La Barraca in the famous Hotel Nacional. As mentioned, the population is well educated, and a sophisticated nationwide understanding of the institution of slavery is a cornerstone of that education.

Compare this to a country like Jamaica where the two primary, independent distilleries still run like plantations on properties that were plantations. The Worthy Park distillery is an achingly beautiful sprawl of more than ten thousand acres of sugarcane at 1,200 feet above sea level and is privately owned. As I mentioned, I love these rums and see them as emblematic of the earthy, even mephitic, Jamaican style. Even so, the legacy that informs these rums is complicated. The website makes no effort to hide the fact that "the Worthy Park Estate has remained this way since its inception in 1670." Only three families have ever owned the estate, the last of whom is the Clarkes, who have held the land since 1918. Its offices now occupy a remodeled version of the previous slave quarters. To walk its grounds or those of Hampden Estate, another beautiful independent property, is to walk among ghosts. The tall cane and Jurassic foliage, fertile with blossoms and small birds, almost feel sentient, keeping secrets of what has transpired here. Of course, this is a projection, but these properties, changed since the nineteenth century only in that the laborers are paid relatively little as opposed to being paid nothing at all, stand in stark contrast to the Cuban equivalent, where heads of state swung machetes for free.

The act of cultural remembrance is a recurrent one in Cuba and begins to account for the small nation's tremendous cultural capital. Cubans have guarded evidence of other aspects of colonization from the preservation, to the best of their means, of the colonial avenues and architecture, to the more recent conservation of cultural landmarks, in particular the historic hotels and bars of Havana. About eighty miles from Florida, the island was an ideal destination for alcoholic tourism, especially during Prohibition. Sloppy Joe's and El Floridita were among the world's most iconic cocktail bars. Yet they were emblems of the concentration of wealth in the cities that contradicted the abject poverty of rural Cuba. When the revolution reclaimed Havana in 1959, they must have been tempted to level these landmarks. Castro and his team immediately began reclaiming all the resources of the island from foreign interest, executing enemies of the revolution, creating a constitution that forbade Catholicism, and consolidating all the country's resources. Famously, Che Guevara set up camp in the lobby of the then–Havana Hilton and changed its name to the Havana Libre hotel, and the lobby is now decorated with photos of him and soldiers in combat wear.

But rather than destroy the hotel or turn it into public housing, the revolution preserved it as the destination it was, just as it guarded the identities of the Inglaterra, the Nacional, the Riviera, and the rest of Havana's legendary hotels. They maintained La Bodeguita del Medio, El Floridita, Sloppy Joe's, and other notable bars, rather than eradicating them for being evidence of previous colonial exploitation. For decades, Cuban nationals were not allowed into these establishments, despite being allowed to work in them. But the revolution has evolved in the last few years to allow Cuban citizens to frequent any and all businesses, in the same spirit that it decriminalized Catholicism.

As the birthplace of canonical drinks like the daiquiri, presidente, and mojito, Havana is a bit of a mecca for the cocktail enthusiast. Because the Cuban nation is empowered by the production of its rum and preserves even the darker corners of its colonial and pre-revolutionary history, we can order these drinks in their place of origin today.

I give up looking for our driver, Yan, get some change, and return to check on the guys, who are standing around a small round table speaking familiarly. The number of beer bottles has multiplied among them and Charles has bought me a coffee. No one is bothered by the delay, and I am feeling encouraged by my group's chemistry. Maybe we can transcend the profile of fake-mellow Californians with tight anuses and enjoy ourselves in the double onslaught of languorous inefficiency—that of the Caribbean coupled with that of Latin America. I am shaken from this meditation by a European-looking guy wearing enough product in his hair to leave it smooth and streamlined, pulled straight back, and a tastelessly large watch. It's Yan! Before we know it, we're bundled into a van, this time a Russian cargo-passenger Kombi driven by an acquaintance of Yan whose name we wouldn't learn, and headed into Havana, a half-hour drive.

What always strikes me about the drive into Havana is the realization that dawns on someone—first me years ago, and now my friends here for the first time—that there is no advertising. No billboards line the highway advertising . . . anything. A calm starts to possess you; unwittingly, you settle into a different dimension where the cacophony of commercialism isn't around to bother you. This quiet is compounded by the fact US mobile phones don't work, and compounded further by the absence of Wi-Fi on most of the island, excluding a couple of the nicer hotels, where so many have congregated to use the Wi-Fi that it functions about as effectively as the dial-up connections of the mid-1990s. So, we are stripped of our American armor, heading toward the apartments Amador arranged for us in the neighborhood of Vedado.

Our group is split between two apartments: a simple ground-floor affair for me and Amador; and a nicely decayed modernist penthouse apartment around the corner for Jay, Eric and Charles. We pay for our week of rooms up front to Yan through the driver's seat window. He collects the money without saying thank you, as though he were eating it, counts each of our stacks quickly, and leaves. Eric and Jay are a little pale because they've just paid for their week's lodging and the expense has devastated more than two-thirds of the cash they each brought. It's sinking in that they can't get anything more. We're only an hour into the trip, and suddenly they're on a very strict budget; I am feeling glad I brought too much money. (Though, really, there is never too much money. Or is there always too much money?) Charles watches calmly through his aviators. "I brought a French credit card; I can get cash if we need more," he says.

"Supercool," I say in a French accent.

We have a few hours to kill before we're scheduled to meet Amador at 11:00 p.m., so I suggest we walk to Havana Vieja, along the Malecón, the road that encompasses Havana and skirts the coastline. It is a dramatic route, with the water that separates us from Florida to our right and the decaying cityscape of Havana to our left. The nineteenth-century colonial buildings are grand in scale and proportion, and you might think you were in Paris until you look closely at their state of decay. Most of the buildings are painted soft, matte pastel colors to compensate for the deterioration. Waves collide with the sea wall to our left, occasionally splashing over and dampening the wide sidewalk.

One of Cuba's beauties is that all of the buildings are appropriated for the people. Normal citizens occupy these waterfront buildings. Kids play soccer with an old, half-inflated ball. Middle-aged men stand with their shirts off, arguing good-naturedly. An old woman sweeps a stoop.

We arrive at the Prado, the stunning, turn-of-the-century tiled pedestrian street that divides Havana Central from Havana Vieja. It is lined with proud, old trees full of singing birds. Kids roll by seated on old skateboards. Cuban lovers are everywhere, walking hand in hand, smoking, talking earnestly to each other.

The Prado leads directly to Parque Central, the center of the old town. It is shrouded by giant palm trees that stand watch over turn-of-the-century iron benches and is surrounded by some of the city's grander architecture: the recently restored Gran Teatro de La Habana; the Inglaterra, Telegraph, Plaza, and Central Park hotels as well as the Manzana de Gómez, the Asturian Center, the Payret Cinema, and the Capitolio building. Crossing the park we pass the famous Esquina Caliente, or "hot corner," where a single conversation with a constantly changing cast of participants has continued for twenty-four hours a day for years. Baseball is the chief topic on L'esquina Caliente though others are indulged. All day a group of almost entirely men of various demographics argue animatedly, pointing at each others' faces, stomping their feet, throwing back their heads and laughing at the ridiculousness of what someone's just said. It is perfect twilight and the air is heavy and still as we enjoy the seam between daytime and night. A block off the park in the direction of the bay is our first historic destination, El Floridita.

The famous bar is at the top of Calle Obispo, the road for which our new rum bar, Obispo, is named. Its now-iconic, pastel neon light is illuminated, the name written in an elegant midcentury cursive, and it casts an encouraging glow over the stucco exterior of the bar.

I have been to this bar many times, but my pulse still quickens a bit as I nod to the suited doorman, alert by the front entrance any time of day or night, and step into the room. As I cross the threshold, I savor the experience of being split down the middle, the fore half of my body plummeting in temperature as a consequence of the aggressive air conditioning, and the aft remaining, for a moment, appropriately warm. The motif of the room is Ferrari red with ancient fruitwood detail. A traditional quartet comprising two guitars, conga, and a vocalist who plays the claves performs in an alcove to the right of the doorway behind us. Famously, Cuba produces an infinity of trained musicians, many of whom play in tourist destinations like El Floridita. Initially, I was tempted to reject this ubiquitous music as cheesy, but over the years I've come to appreciate the truth that the state is educating and employing all these musicians, and they play a virtuosic and inarguably beautiful version of the island's traditional music. This group is about halfway through "Commandante Che," one of my favorite songs from the revolution. We opt for the bar and move toward four open seats at the right end of the wood counter. The two bartenders are stout middle-aged men—one with short-cropped, thick silver hair; the other shaved to stubble—who move confidently through the folk dance of making blended daiquiris. The red-lacquered coolers that constitute the back bar are emblazoned with the slogan *la cuna del Daiquiri*, "the cradle of the Daiquiri," which is no subtle clue as to what one orders at El Floridita.

Like the old cars and deteriorated architecture, the bars here in Havana are a time capsule. The menu features many of the same daiquiris and Cuban standards that were included in the first version of the menu, published in book form more than half a century ago. In that nearly perfect bar book, all the daiquiris are described as frappé, which would have meant shaken with crushed ice until the drink was the consistency of a Slurpee. Now the bartenders use blenders, though one may order a shaken daiquiri. And when one does, one will enjoy the spectacle of a Cuban career bartender expertly shaking a daiquiri in a small cobbler shaker, moving the shaker rhythmically and decisively at a 45-degree angle from the right ear toward the ceiling, each movement creating a two-beat pulse of ice against stainless steel . . . *shicka-shicka* . . . *shicka-shicka* . . . *shicka-shicka.*

Eric orders one of these shaken daiquiris and the other two order the standard blended version. I order an aged Santiago rum to kick off what will turn out to be a pretty unsuccessful excavation of the category of Cuban rum. Many, if not most, career bartenders will tell you that their favorite drink is the daiquiri, which is a drink you can make tens of thousands of times and not make perfectly. It is composed, epically, of four ingredients: rum, lime, sugar, and ice. All drinks are a balance of two or more of the four flavors: sweet, sour, bitter, and salty. None is more archetypal than the daiquiri, reportedly invented by Jennings Cox in the eponymously named Cuban mining town of Daiquiri. I and many others are doubtful that this was the first time these components were integrated and poured into a human mouth, but this is the history of the bar—borne of academic laziness and passed down by word of mouth. We always take the bartender's word for it, and this trust is a mistake because your bartender is categorically full of shit.

While the origin story of the daiquiri, like that of most mixed drinks, is likely apocryphal, it can still guide us to the historical significance of the drink. When it was ostensibly born in the nineteenth century, humans had only been refining sugar for decades. The flavor of crystalline sugar was something new and utterly remarkable. Ice, another key ingredient, was a delicacy, especially in the Caribbean where it was likely shipped from New England. Today we take the modulation of temperature for granted. But consider what it must have been like to have something cold to drink on a hot day hundreds of years ago. Add to that limes (who knows when we learned to suck on limes?) and rum, a distillate that was relatively new in the context of human history.

To truly enjoy a mixed drink, let alone make one successfully, you must valorize your ingredients in this way. You are wielding the building blocks of human history and civilization with every mixture. The daiquiri has been ruined by those who don't afford it this respect, which is why, even late in the midst of this so-called cocktail renaissance, most of the planet thinks of an adult slushie when the word *daiquiri* is mentioned. Consider also that the daiquiri could only have happened in a place like Cuba with its necessary collision of cultures: the Europeanization of folk-distilled tafia into a dry elegant spirit; the anguish of slavery that begat the sugar and the rum; the second generation of colonization from the United States, whose military and tourists occupied the island for decades and helped empower the bar culture of the twentieth-century Havana. This is just a cursory unpacking of the daiquiri. We all know the type of cocktail enthusiast who will take exception to a number of the details I've offered.

Jay is quiet, and Charles is predictably unimpressed. "Yeah, really, this is just too sweet." His head is tilted back slightly, allowing his thick, oily, collar-length hair to rest gently on his athletic shoulders. Aware that he has our attention, he exhales through his nose into his thin beard and shrugs. "Guys, it's not great." This is why we love him. Those three order another round: a presidente, a Papa Doble Daiquiri, and a mulata. The Papa Doble was the usual for Ernest Hemingway, who frequented El Floridita. In fact, this frequency is commemorated by a statue of the dead Nobel laureate—who did more to promote Cuba as a drinking destination than anyone else in the English language—perched at the far end of the bar. Hemingway is said to have once written, in Spanish as economical as his acclaimed English prose, "*Mi mojito en* La Bodeguita. *Mi daiquiri* en El Floridita*," describing his two favorite Cuban drinks and the bars where he enjoyed them. At least that is how the myth goes; like many myths, this one is likely untrue, disaffirmed by drinks researchers more rigorous than I.

The Papa Doble is a double daiquiri with no added sugar and the addition of some grapefruit juice, sweetened with only a tiny amount of maraschino liqueur. In many bars in the United States, different versions of this drink are called the "Hemingway Daiquiri." Reportedly, Hemingway would crush six to twelve in a sitting. I'm

sure the absence of added sugar did wonders for his hemochroma-
tosis and diabetes.

Eric, like me, is stoked about what he's seeing. We whisper to
each other.

"At first, the blenders bummed me out," he begins.

"Me, too, but now I get it. Time froze in the middle of the century
here and the blender was still a pretty cool thing. If I'm making a
thousand frappés, I'd be crazy not to use a blender."

"Exactly, it becomes the fifth ingredient to the drink. It's totally
forgivable . . ." His head is tilted close to mine, and I can hear the
nervous gulping sound he makes at the base of his throat when
he is nervous or excited.

Now the bartender is making the presidente. It's like seeing
Bob Dylan play "Percy's Song" in the year 2015. A cynic would dismiss it, saying it pales compared to what we would have seen at
the Gaslight Café in the late '50s, but the cynic is wrong. We are
witness to history, and actually the presidente served to us here in
2016 is delicious. The sturdy barman performed the drink deftly,
compiling the ingredients in the empty vessel before adding ice
and stirring silently, keeping the ice still while rotating it as one
solid mass, causing the drink to swirl with a whisper as the drink
is integrated and diluted.

The presidente is another classic, hardly as well known as
the daiquiri but revered by rum enthusiasts. When it first came
to prominence in the early twentieth century, it would have been
called an "improved" cocktail. In its most basic form, a *cocktail* is
a combination of spirit, bitters, and sweet. That formula became
known as "the old-fashioned," because as bartenders adjusted or
improved the cocktail, the customer needed to specify which type
of drink they wanted ("an OLD-FASHIONED whiskey cocktail,
please"). The improved cocktail takes that original balance of bitter
and sweet and adorns it with aromatic ingredients. In the case of

the presidente, curaçao, vermouth, and grenadine are added to the mix, but the core structure is the balance of the sweet (curaçao and grenadine) with the bitters. It must succeed on that bilateral level for all the aromatic drapery not to overwhelm the drinker.

Back in the real world, Charles is criticizing his second round. "Yeah, this one is too sour and just tastes like a Slurpee." He furrows his brow like Warren Oates in the film *Badlands*, as if he were forbidding his daughter (the daughter who will help murder him) from being with Martin Sheen. One side of his mouth is turned up scornfully, the other disengaged like that of a stroke victim. Jay, meanwhile, is drinking the mulata, a drink I was nervous about putting on a menu a few years ago because of the loaded name. Again, here in Cuba, the appropriation of the term is a gesture of empowerment. Of course, the drink—a daiquiri with a touch of dark crème de cacao, rendering it the color of a stirred latte—is a little sweet, but to see and taste this drink in the spot where it has been continuously made for more than a half a century is gratifying. The Santiago de Cuba twelve-year rum that I've been contemplating the last hour is, on the other hand, not compelling; it is riddled with caramel and bottled at an uninteresting 40 percent, a percentage frequently chosen by industrial producers to maximize yield and minimize tax obligation as the product moves between nations.

Withdrawing from El Floridita, we step back across the threshold into the embrace of the early evening heat. We turn right down Obispo, which is still covered with pedestrians, most of them Cuban, moving slowly in both directions on the ancient street, which is cast in shadow as a result of the ever-frugal Cubans using as little electricity as possible. This darkness contributes to the timeless quality of our walk through Havana Vieja. Terraced three-story colonial buildings line the avenues where people congregate in the night air.

Our dinner that night is at Doña Eutimia, a restaurant Amador has booked for us. I have my first plate of *ropas viejas* of the trip:

braised, shredded beef with cumin and garlic, served over rice. Eric and Jay order a dish of fried eggs with *moros y cristianos*, which is black beans and rice served separately, not to be confused with the legendary *congrí*, which is black beans and rice cooked together, generally with pork fat, though that is an extravagance for the islanders who have been on a ration for almost sixty years. We are all relieved as we watch Charles successfully pay for dinner with his French credit card.

We stroll a bit, back through the plaza of the cathedral and onto a side street, where we duck into a rum bar we'd passed on the way to the restaurant earlier. The two men are cleaning up after an early closing. The senior of the two, with a long head and a buzz cut, a little like *Sesame Street*'s Bert, faces us amicably and asks if he can help. I mention that it seems hard to visit distilleries in Cuba and ask if he has any suggestions about how to get access to one. He exhales boldly through his nostrils and concedes that it is difficult. He encourages us to start at the Museo del Ron and see if any guides there would be able to help. I'd received this suggestion from several Cubans already but thank him politely. He continues to explain a bit about the nature of rum in Cuba, in which he clarifies that a total of eight *maestro roneros* (literally "rum-men" or "rummers") maintain the quality of all the rum made on the island. In 1860, there were one thousand distilleries on the Island; as of 1982, there were four, which produced all the different marks (brands) of rum coming out of the nation of Cuba. One of these is Havana Club, which is in partnership, as we know, with Pernod Ricard. The other three make up the company Cuba Ron; they are Ron Santiago de Cuba, Cubay, and Aguardiente de Caña. Each of these sell retail bottlings, but also sell *aguardientes*, or unaged rums, to merchant bottlers and blenders around the world.

This methodology reminds us greatly of American whiskey, particularly bourbon, where large industrial distilleries will sell many different retail labels and sell spirit to be bottled by other producers as well, understandably, as these spirits are commodities foremost. A company like Jim Beam will release scores of bottlings under different names, for example, Booker's, Basil Hayden, and Knob Creek. Interestingly, the Soviet Union underwent a similar monopolization and standardization of its vodka until 1992, when the market was opened up and small, independent distilleries proliferated.

The barman who helped us introduces himself as Abel. We shake hands and tip him for the advice and information, then continue on our way.

We are due at eleven at the Nacional to meet Amador, so we walk back toward Parque Central, where the conversation is still raging at La Esquina Caliente. At the row of cars for hire near the Plaza Hotel, we choose a barrel-chested guy who's leaning against a 1953 Chevy, and the five of us mount comfortably and head toward the Nacional along the Malecón, which is teaming with life now. People of all ages sit on the sea wall, blurring together to comprise a second, human wall. They play musical instruments and drink beer or, even better, rum if they are lucky, or just pass time together in that Cuban way beneath a waxing gibbous moon; a popular superstition dictates that you must kiss someone on the Malecón to be sure you will return to Havana. This I have done, and I keep coming back.

Our beautiful 1953 Chevy chugs and gasps to mount the moderately steep hill toward the hotel. Like most of these vintage cars, the original engine was long ago replaced with a soviet one, most likely that of a Lada. The entire island was mechanized with US machinery at the inception of the blockade. When the US parts and goods dried up, the Cubans were left in an industrial crisis, watching their infrastructure collapse as the American machinery began to degenerate. This dilemma fostered the *amistad,* or friendship, between Cuba and the Soviet Union, which helped the revolution mechanize anew; nonetheless, Cubans have kept a number of these huge, old American engines running, at times going so far as to manually fine their own replacement parts.

After paying our driver and mounting the steps to the hotel, we cross the lobby and exit again to the terrace bar where we settle into the comfortable wicker chairs of the Nacionale's terrace to wait for Amador, who is Cuban, which means he will likely not arrive at 11:00 p.m. as promised.

Time for the first cigar. The *mesero*, or waiter, presents a modest portable humidor, a simple box built from cedar, which is best for storing tobacco, with a thick lacquer on its exterior that was dissipating in patches from frequent handling. The case is well stocked with various sizes and hues of cigar, each one with its own beautiful band and insignia. The names—Romeo y Julieta, Hoya de Monterrey, Montecristo—conjure ghosts and legends. I decide on a Cohiba Robusto, which Jay selects as well. We enjoy the spectacle of proper cigar service as the *mesero* lights the cigar with a thin strip of cedar, never touching the *puro*, as the Cubans call their cigars, to his lips but rather pulling the lit cigar rapidly lengthwise and parallel to the floor to create a suction that draws the air through the cigar. We accept our lit cigars from our caretaker and settle into the stuffed cushions.

I order a fifteen-year-old Havana Club and the others ask for their first mojitos of the trip. Before drawing on the thick Cohiba, I fill my lungs with air to be sure the rich concentrated smoke isn't pulled into my lungs. Sucking gently on the cigar, like a thumb, I fill my mouth with the creamy, dense smoke that is pleasantly cool as a consequence of the expert wrapping of the cigar; this temperature is one of the clear indications of a well-made and well-stored cigar. Cigars left out in the open can become dry, which leads them to burn hot, yielding a scalding smoke that leaves the sensation of astringency in the mouth. These cigars are in perfect condition, and Cohibas are the BMW of cigars, immediately recognized and celebrated by even the least-experienced cigar smokers; it's a prestige smoke, but with its redolence of cedar, cracked pepper, leather, and moist earth, deserving of the reputation. Cuba is the perfect climate for smoking. The ambient humidity preserves the moisture of the tobacco, ensuring the cigar burns slowly and coolly, and the languor of a still Caribbean night helps me to slacken. The ennui of a day's travel and walking seeps into the cushion and wicker beneath me.

The mojitos arrive. I consider my second old Cuban rum of the day, and then pass it around. Before tasting it, Charles looks at me pointedly, as though I may be trying to poison him. It seems to have a little less caramel added than the Santiago from earlier in the night, but none of us are thrilled by it. The drinks are more compelling, largely because of their historical significance.

The mojito, like the daiquiri, is one of the world's great mixed drinks, and is still consumed in its country of origin. Consider the daiquiri and its simple equilibrium of sweet and sour and its refreshing chill. Add to this little machine the technology of carbonation and you have the precursor to the mojito, the rum Collins. The category of Collins fails to impress much these days because people take ice and carbonation for granted, but at its inception, the Collins must have amazed: a long, cold drink that tickled the nose and palate with exploding carbon dioxide. Add two more components to the rum Collins—fresh mint and aromatic bitters—and you have the mojito, a more complicated drink that balances three of the four principal flavors: sweet, sour, and bitter. The drink must be concentrated so the addition of the ice and seltzer do not overly dilute it. If one had to criticize this first round of mojitos, it would be to describe them as too sweet. Cuban sugar is elemental and flavorful, though, so you can almost forgive its overenthusiastic use.

We are big fans of uncomplicated drinks. A sour, a gimlet, a Collins, or a straight-forward five-ingredient punch are all drinks that are so simple that they must be made very carefully. We favor these rudimentary recipes, traveling the world looking for the best spirits with which to make them, and we're wondering how to handle the question of a dry cocktail rum for Obispo. The Havana Club three-year is the gold standard for this category. Aged for three years in American oak, which is generally bought thirdhand from non-American producers who have already used the repurposed American casks, it is then thoroughly filtered, removing all color and evidence of barrel aging. The resulting spirit is round and softly aromatic but hardly something you would spend a lot of time pondering when served neat. This spirit is for cocktails, like affordable dry gin or young American whiskey. The base materials from which these spirits are made don't figure as it does with armagnac, scotch, mezcal, or an agricole rum.

Contrast the expedience of these rums, though, with the cigars of Cuba, which are just as we would have our favorite spirits: handmade simply from elemental agricultural materials that are allowed to cure naturally in their own element, with nothing added. And compare the rums to the musical culture of Cuba, and the dance. The country knows what is fine and insists upon it. Their rums are not their purest luxury good. Instead, they are like spirits have always been: a way to make the most of the nation's sugarcane crop. Rum is what they do with the molasses when they are done making their lovely sugar, which should have its own abbreviation on the periodic table of the elements.

It's 1:30 a.m. and we are finished with our cigars, so the time is right to give up on Amador. We share a taxi back to Avenida de los Presidentes and separate, planning to meet at Hotel Presidente tomorrow.

For years, my best Cuban friend was Leticia, whom I knew from when she dated Ashley, my best friend from the United States. She would make *congrí* and chicken, or black beans and white rice (or spaghetti, a strange favorite in Cuba), and we'd sit after dinner in her dining room. I would smoke a large cigar and she would smoke cigarette after cigarette, unfiltered Populares. She could inhale a quarter of a cigarette in one deep drag, exhaling menacingly through her cavernous nostrils. Often we would play dominos with her family; her father served with Che, and tells an amazing story of when the comandante granted him forty-eight hours to get married.

It was Leticia who explained to me, "Tadeo, to be Cuban is to be waiting. The embargo strangles us and we are waiting. Waiting for there to be more money. Waiting for our family members to come back from Miami. Waiting to leave." When I asked Leticia if she didn't like Cuba, she was emphatic: "But we love Cuba! We love the revolution!" This paradox is one I've encountered frequently in Cubans. Yes, to be Cuban is to wait. I loved Cuba then, with a more detached perspective than my friend, of course, and I also found it depressing. I will still love Cuba after this bizarre, most recent trip when my colleagues and I also will be made to wait by its byzantine bureaucracy.

Chapter Five

CUBA, PART II

UNBUTTON YOUR TROUSERS . . .
THIS IS HOW WE DO IT, MAN

I lost twenty pounds in six months when I lived in Havana Vieja. I would start the day with a piece of bread and a coffee in the morning; for lunch a small sandwich or pillowy street pizza, which is basically what Native Americans call fry bread, with a fleeting quantity of pungent, shelf-stable Cuban cheese melted over it; then two coffees with golden Cuban sugar between lunch and dinner to keep the mood aloft and brain firing; for dinner, usually, a *cajita*, or "little case," a meal served in the street by a home cook who had a pot of chicken on the stove and would serve it with some black beans and rice. You'd return your plate to the host when you were finished. When the pot was empty, the kitchen was closed. To get there in the first place, you would ask in the street if anyone was cooking nearby and be directed to an alley or up some stairs where you'd see people standing and waiting or eating. It's harder to find this kind of service in Havana today; this might be due to the stronger economy or Cuban nationals having access to all the restaurants from which they were once excluded, but I am only supposing.

I was thirty-three then, the christological year, a difficult age for someone who is directionless. Christ died at the same age, and he'd already refigured all of civilization. Since college, I'd always been sure I couldn't stay in the restaurant business. I still operated under that misconception as I studied Spanish in Cuba, to what end I didn't know. While living the life of a student, I was interested by the same things as before: food and drink. I loved being free of the shame that surrounds food in California. Here in Cuba, the idea of pretending not to be hungry never figured.

I made friends with a guy named Willie, who was a taxi driver and a *guapo*, which is basically a small-time criminal who is willing to use his fists. He was my height and started asking if I had any extra clothes or shoes. We'd run into each other at the park regularly, and before long he was taking me to his favorite places to eat. We were most regular in the kitchen of one woman who served braised chicken with black beans and white rice. Willie would get us two huge portions that we'd devour together, then two more bowls of the chicken, rice, and beans. After we'd finished, he'd invite me to lay back and unbutton my trousers, following his lead. We'd recover from our meal that way, reclining against the wall in that woman's kitchen. "This is how we do it, man," said Willie.

During the day, I jumped from coffee to coffee. Cubans cut theirs with chicory, leaving it supple and less bitter. One thing that was always in abundance was, as I've mentioned before, the beautiful sugar. Unlike the refined sugar I'd always used behind the bar, these amber crystals retained more of the earthy qualities that are usually stripped from the refined sugar. I'd take my coffee with two spoons of it, enjoying the burst of energy from the synergy of sugar and caffeine. I'd been blind, using white sugar all those years. So I was there in Cuba to get away from the hospitality business, but I was forced to admit it was what interested me. I loved having a cigar and watching the bartenders work in the big bars, and with Leticia I loved going to the national ration stores where Cuban nationals redeemed their state-issued coupons for food and other staples. I enjoyed the hotels and I loved the greasy street pizzas that cost a quarter.

Here now, in 2016, I wake without an alarm at seven and feel surprisingly jet-lagged for only a three-hour time difference, but the Caribbean is strangely far away, almost impossible to reach in a single flight, particularly if you are bound for Cuba. I had heard Amador come in early that morning, so I choose not to wake him yet. I head to the Presidente for my first *café con leche* of the day and use the painfully slow Wi-Fi on my phone to reply to the most pressing emails from the previous day. The others arrive with wet hair and fresh T-shirts and do the same.

I see an email from my overwhelmed bookkeeper, Chris, saying there might be a problem with the State Board of Equalization. When Amador still hasn't arrived an hour later, I run back to the apartment to see if he's awake. I am already keeping score a bit, as I've paid for him to join us, and I resist the early urge to be irritated. I'm not three blocks into my walk when I notice him walking toward me in the distance. He has his long hair in two pigtails and is wearing a kind of short-sleeved coverall with cropped legs—a great look. "Hey, dude . . ." His voice is languid and peaceful, like he'd been screwing all night. My initial irritation fades at the pleasure of Amador's company. He may prove to be useless, but he's cool to be around.

After we've all gathered at the Presidente, we embark on our first mission of the day. The plan is to get started at the Museo del Ron and try to gain a little momentum toward visiting a distillery. Amador argues with the driver of an enormous green Pontiac convertible; he refuses the deal of twenty pesos for the convertible and puts us in two Ladas at ten convertible pesos each. I'm wedged in the back with Eric, who leans familiarly into me in the cramped, soviet backseat and raises his voice to speak over the suffering engine, "What did we accomplish by taking two cars for ten each when we could have the wind in our hair for twenty total?" He and I are both bald.

We bend over in the small car and watch the Malecón pass again, much less populated than late last night, when the cool air made congregating on the sea wall preferable to crowded, stifling apartments. I think of when I was younger and less cynical, and how I would spend nights on the Malecón, sharing bottles of rum with musicians and hustlers.

We get out of our Ladas at the base of Obrapia, the street on which I lived in 2003. We walk to the Museo del Ron where I've already been, but our plan is to try to find a guide who can get us into a distillery. I sit in the stultifying heat of the open-air lobby, watching other tourists mill around waiting for their tour, until I hear a bell ring. "OKAY. ENGLISH TOUR!" someone shouts. The others and I turn our heads listlessly to find the source. "COME. OVER . HERE! WHERE. AREYOUFROM?"

"Mexico," one couple says. "MEXICO!" he echoes.

"I . . . AMADOLFO. MY. NAME. MEANS. NOBLEWOLF. IN. ENGLISH!" he says in the same flat, discordant English I first noticed in well-traveled Dutch people when I was a teenager staying in hostels. "I. WANT. YOU. TO PREPAREYOURSELF. TO. LEARN. ABOUTTHERUM. OF. CUBA." Our little group is already pretty arrogant and accustomed to private tours and access to real distilleries. The thought of being dragged at a snail's pace through this museum, which isn't even a functioning distillery, is dispiriting. We endure Adolfo's tour: the scale model of a refinery and distillery, complete with a model train delivering the sugarcane; the hall of slavery, which is actually compelling with its daguerreotypes representing the insane brutality of Western European colonialism; the seven-minute film expediently describing the distillation process and the history of the Havana Club distillery, ending with a depiction of the Cuban custom of pouring the first drops of any newly opened bottle of rum onto the floor or earth for the benefit of our ancestors; the scale model of an aging room and a hammering, atonal description of the aging process. "THE. RUM. THAT. EVAPORATES. ISCALLED. THE. ANGELSSHARE. BECAUSE. THE. RUM. IS. FOR. THEM. THE. ANGELS. THESE. ARE. VERYHAPPY. ANGELS. IN. HERE." Then the tasting room, where we are all given a half-ounce portion of the Havana Club seven-year rum.

I am so disheartened by the tour and the waste of time and money it has been that I sit a moment in the tasting room, which is part frontier apothecary and part tropical cantina. Less discouraged than I, Eric and Jay corner Adolfo to get what we came for: someone who might help us gain access to a still. I give Charles my seven-year. I know already that he doesn't care for it because at the conclusion of one of our French tasting trips, I'd bought him a glass of it in a cigar bar in Saint-Germain. He tasted it and looked at me through my cigar smoke, paused a moment, and said, "That's it?"

Jay and Eric return in good spirits. "Okay," Jay begins. "Adolfo says the best thing to do is to go to the Havana Club offices and try to arrange for a tour. He was cool. Not as big a pain in the ass as he seemed during that tour." Jay has an address in his hand and it is in Vedado, not so far from our apartments on Avenida de los Presidentes. We head off toward the Malecón to find a car back across town.

This time we treat ourselves to a fine, burgundy-colored Pontiac. As we approach the address of the Havana Club headquarters, Amador speaks quietly to me: "The thing is, I think it will be better if you speak to the people here. You will appear to be important businesspeople, which is better than just talking to me, to some Cuban black guy." I am a little irritated at the truth becoming evident, which is Amador isn't going to be much help on this trip.

Later that night, he will offer an opinion: "I think this trip you need to just get the lay of the land," he says. "Don't try to get too much accomplished. Maybe we will meet some of the right people this time. We can come back . . ." I am certain that I won't be bringing Amador back. I've enjoyed following his Instagram since this trip together and seeing that his life is a continuing series of sponsored trips around the world; in each of the locations, he looks hip and engaged, and he is always gracious. I do not mind. The world cares for people like Amador, and despite my mild frustration in the Pontiac, I am glad to be with him today, pressed up against him, smelling the strong bergamot of his eau de cologne.

We enter the Havana Club compound, which offers its own Cuban type of opulence. Brightly colored plastic deck chairs surround a small sunken swimming pool, the surface of which is adorned with leaves from the sheltering canopy of tropical trees.

We are greeted professionally by a tall, handsome young woman who introduces herself as Agathe, another good Cuban name. The foyer where we introduce ourselves is cool and appears quite Spanish with its Moorish tile and vaulted ceiling. I set forth in my halting Spanish, now decidedly more campesino after a recent year in Central America, to explain the purpose of our visit. Amador watches quietly and Charles fidgets; he hates my Central American Spanish and begins interjecting shortly with his *c*'s pronounced as *th*. Furthermore, he is sure I wasn't playing the industry card sufficiently. He joins in: "I am an importer of brandies and other spirits to the United States. I actually worked for your sister company, Pernod Ricard, and was the leading salesperson for one year." All of this he offers with a Castilian accent that would befit a newscaster. Agathe seems more confused.

Every citizen on the island has been at war for sixty years, waiting obstinately for the deliverance of the revolution, a time when the blockade is lifted and there is no threat to their insular way of life. The attitude is not a conscious one, but manifests in different ways: defiance, irritability, but often also grace, as in this instance in which we babble at a young woman, born after the fall of the Soviet Union, who has all the time in the world.

And I suppose this revolution is one I want to join—the country got it right; their rum sales compensate for all the damage that industry did to the region. We walk away from Havana Club with a plan. Agathe has explained that we need to write a formal email to send to the heads of the distillery who will then extend us an invitation. Where will we send this email? Excellent question. We must call a phone number, entrusted to us by Agathe, after 9:00 a.m. the next day to ask for the appropriate email address, because Agathe cannot give this email address to anyone, nor would she feel comfortable calling on our behalf.

We strategize aloud about what to say in this ineffectual email that we will probably never have the opportunity to write, as we walk toward Hotel Presidente. There we will get a second installment of Wi-Fi and a late afternoon coffee with a spoon or two of that amazing Cuban sugar that keeps you afloat.

The time is after five and I am ready for a cigar; the others discuss making daiquiris at one of the apartments. I head back to my apartment resolved to have a shower, move my bowels, and then meet Eric, Charles, and Jay at their place, which has a balcony with a view down Avenida de los Presidentes to the Malecón. At my place, I am only able to lie on my back on the small soft bed for about fifteen minutes, as I take deep breaths and let pass through me the physiological symptoms of financial worry that have plagued me since opening my own business.

I feel guilty whenever I leave the bars for trips like this one, but I know we need to do this to understand where we fit in the global market of all we sell. The cultural capital is part of what we sell: the stories that surround these spirits. We are always looking for the true story, which is particularly evasive in Cuba this week. Or, more accurately, the true story in Cuba is particularly crazy making.

The world of spirit sales is a minefield, and people tend to proceed naively and destructively into it as, simultaneously, the world of a certain kind of spirit production is ending and another is beginning.

One cannot speak of Cuban rum without mentioning Bacardi. At the time of the revolution, Bacardi was successful, but nothing like what it would become. Afraid of being stripped of their wealth, the owners fled the island and established what would become one of the largest drinks companies in the world, doing billions of dollars of revenue a year. The Bacardi brand has been linked to any number of overt and covert military and commercial operations designed to overthrow the Cuban government as well as the state-owned Havana Club brand of rum. The Cubans developed this brand in Bacardi's absence and championed it as their own premium brand, ultimately partnering with the Pernod Ricard company to ensure global distribution and influence, though it's important to note that Cuba will never sell more than half of its interest in a company or Cuban real estate, ensuring that the socialist country will never again be owned by foreign interest. A war has also raged between Bacardi and Havana Club for the right to use the name "Havana Club" for distribution in the United States. Bacardi purchased naming rights for Havana Club from the Arechabala family, who made the rum until its distillery was seized by the revolution, and it has been trying to distribute a rum in the United States under that label for years.

At the time of this writing, Bacardi has achieved licensing of the Havana Club name in the United States market. The United States is the number-two consumer of rum of all nations in the world; conceivably Bacardi would do anything to prevent Havana Club from securing that market, not only because they want the business for themselves, but also because this revenue would strengthen the Cuban nation and vindicate the nationalization of all commerce and resources on the island. Historically frustrated, displaced Cuban nationals, like the Bacardi clan and many others, would be even more removed from any claim to what the Cuban revolution appropriated.

So, what does this mean for someone looking to open a small rum bar in the Mission District of San Francisco? As a small business owner, I am always trying to mitigate the terror of failure and bankruptcy with the aspirational. And what is more aspirational than the Cuban revolution? We don't know if Cuban rum will be for sale anytime soon in the United States. Charles, as an importer, has an abstract curiosity. The rest of us are opening a bar that features recipes calling for the dry, Cuban style of rum, and we should know of what we speak even if we can't sell the real article for the time being. We are here to learn about the category. If, on the unlikely chance, we develop a relationship with a distiller that anticipated the liberation of the American market and gives us a jump on selling some Cuban bottled to our specifications, so much the better.

I breathe deeply and feel my weight press against the coiled springs of this tiny mattress. I drift toward sleep, but I catch myself before the precipice of unconsciousness and feel a moment's joy of being free of anxiety, which fires me awake. I splash room-temperature water on my face, swallow a glass of water from the pitcher in the refrigerator, and head back out into the Havana dusk. The streets are crowded with traffic: buses, motorcycles with sidecars, Lada taxis, and the occasional American taxi packed with Cubans heading to different locations, a kind of improvised carpool that predated UberPOOL by decades. A miscellany of Cubans stand outside my apartment, sharing the day's events with each other, laughing, some with their shirts off, others dressed in clerical uniforms for the concluded day's work in an office or hotel. Many smoke, but few drink or eat. Tobacco is cheap and abundant here in Cuba, but food and drink are not. Conversation is its own entertainment here, as we've seen on La Esquina Caliente, and we witness it every day in the streets of Havana.

The other apartment is just around the corner; I let myself in with the keys I took from Eric before we separated. I find Jay is the only one at home, but he is a welcome sight with his two big Partagas cigars, robustos we light joyously with a piece of cedar. Charles and Eric show up an hour later. They are quiet and low energy as they shuffle around putting things away from their cheap plastic bags. When pressed, they share they've had a typically Cuban shopping experience, accumulating their list of staples from three or four different shops, but they have arrived with the three essentials in hand: a bottle of the Havana Club three-year-old, limes, and beautiful Cuban sugar. Eric and I begin slicing the limes in half and juicing them with our bare hands into a large glass pitcher. Charles and Eric admit that they paid twelve convertible pesos for a street pizza that should have cost only twelve Cuban pesos. (Another maddening aspect of Cuban civilization is their two forms of pesos: one is convertible and traded internationally, intended for tourists to use. The second is intended only for commerce within Cuba and has a value $\frac{1}{20}$ of a convertible peso, and is used by Cubans in ration stores, secondhand shops, and street stalls. They are generally not accepted in the state-owned stores intended for tourists.) "This fucking country," Charles complains. "Two kinds of money. What the fuck. I don't believe it." I'd explained it when we landed, but I don't think it registered. Amador arrives in the midst of the discussion and confirms that our friends should have paid a fraction of what they did for the two deep-fried pieces of dough with ketchup on them. Eric and I add sugar very slowly to the mixture of rum and lime juice until we feel the acidity of the drink is perfect: a decisive tartness that leaves one salivating and the palate clean and refreshed, rather than coated with sugar.

"This is good, but I think it's a little tart," Charles decides just as we finish pouring some of the pitcher for everyone present, and the aperitif devolves into a good-natured argument about Charles's manners and what constitutes a really good daiquiri.

After the aperitif, some of us apply deodorant and others shower, and we meet on the corner from which Amador takes us to one of his favorite *paladares*, or privately owned restaurants, which is not far from my companions' penthouse apartment. The setting is a beautiful nineteenth-century home that has been converted into a dining room lit by an abundance of candles that cast a satisfying, primitive light over original paintings that cover the formidable walls of the main room. Our hosts know Amador and treat us graciously, offering us a tour of the place, which is well equipped, with a gleaming tiled kitchen and a full bar that occupies a separate room.

After the dinner, we order as many rums from their spirits list as we can; by the end of the trip, we'd get a sense of the category even if we couldn't set foot in an actual distillery. The confused waiter takes several trips, carrying a glass in each hand rather than using a tray. Eventually, a score of rums are spread across our white tablecloth, interspersed with a couple of coffees and desserts. We labor over the glasses for some minutes, smelling, squinting, holding them up to the light, pouring a few drops into an open hand and rubbing palms together before smelling them and seeing if they are sticky as a consequence of added caramel. Each of us makes quiet sounds, hinting at a general sentiment of disapproval: a groan here, a sudden exhalation of breath that is also a short laugh. Forced to say something about this mediocre array, I offer that I dislike this one the least. Charles immediately responds. He's in a combative mood, which is usually entertaining.

"Thad," he begins. "You have taste. I can't believe you would tell me this rum is good."

"I'm not saying it's good. I'm saying it's the least shitty . . ."

"It's riddled with caramel. I'm ashamed of you . . ."

"They all have caramel!"

"I don't even know why we're here if you're going to be so lazy! I'm ashamed of you!" His brow is furrowed and he squints, turning up the left corner of his mouth. He is disgusted, or he is pretending to be disgusted, which doesn't really make a difference, shaking his head very slowly to the left and right.

It is a selection of aged and unaged rums from each of the three main distilleries: Cubay, Havana Club, and Santiago. The painful truth is that these are all distilled in large column stills that create a relatively neutral but unremarkable spirit. First patented in 1822 and also known as continuous stills, column stills are constructed in such a way that no one needs to mind them. Gradually, the spirit rises through a long shaft—or column—that holds a series of metal plates. As the alcoholic vapor reaches each plate, it will condense again from the slightly lower temperature of the metal, then turn again to vapor before graduating to the plate above. The alcohol moves up this ladder until it becomes light enough to escape out the top—this light weight corresponds to an extremely pure alcohol. The heavier wines or *tails* will not make it to the top, which some feel robs the spirit of character, and this technique generally allows some amount of *heads* or lighter wines to escape out the top, which can give the inferior liquors a faint odor of nail polish remover or formaldehyde.

Big column stills are the tools that are used to produce millions of gallons of flavorless vodka as well as industrial solvents. These stills generally aren't behind the most compelling distillates. Those that we taste tonight, the ones that are said to be aged, were augmented with caramel; we will recall from our time in Cognac, these additives are the most expedient affordable way to give young, mediocre spirits the impression of age and prestige. As we taste more and more, it seems clear that the only mark we might consider using at our bars is the classic and young three-year, clear Cuban dry rum, which offers a much less chemical and much more pleasing, round flavor than a clear spirit right from the column.

Barrel aging allows some of the less appealing esters to blow off, and the charred oak imparts a mellow sweetness that remains even after the color associated with the barrel aging is stripped from the spirit by thorough charcoal filtering, an unusual practice that leaves a rum that is barrel aged and clear at the same time. What remains is a sweet, clear spirit with a cleaner late finish than an unadulterated spirit from a large column still.

I think we, as a group, have three naive hopes for this trip. First, that we might find some small-batch artisanal distiller in Cuba. Second, that some of these large-production, column-distilled spirits might rise above the others. (After all, armagnac and agricole rum are made with column stills.) Third, that we might gain access to a production facility in Cuba and achieve some kind of expertise in the category. At this point, we are disabused of all but the third fantasy, and even that one seems less and less likely. With that goal in mind, we resolve that Amador will call Havana Club in the morning in hopes of finding this email address, and then we will get on some Wi-Fi and send the email in question, earning us backstage passes to the Havana Club distillery. While we wait for Amador to work his magic, I will show the guys a couple of my favorite museums: el Museo de la Revolución and el Museo Nacional de Bellas Artes.

As we leave the *paladar*, Amador shouts after us that he will stay and chat for a bit, presumably with the handsome chef in the beret we'd met on our tour of the kitchen. We retire again to the balcony of the penthouse, where Jay, Eric, and Charles finish the bottle of Havana Club while I enjoy an Hoya de Monterrey. As the hours wane, Charles's Spanish grows less Castilian and more and more *del campo*, as he adds further diminution to his nouns. At eleven, he asks for *un trago mas* ("one drink more"); at midnight, he requests *un tragito mas* ("one little drink more"); and by one in the morning, he is demanding *un tragitito mas* ("one very little drink more").

I wake the next morning without an alarm at 7:30 and continue my experiment of simply applying more deodorant and bug spray rather than showering, the morbid trial of a married man abroad. Amador is still unconscious, so I leave him undisturbed and step into another hot and humid Havana morning. I arrive at the Hotel Presidente first, and have time to read the latest email from my liberal arts degree–holding bookkeeper, who explains that our liquor license had been suspended "technically," but we should be fine to sell liquor while we sort out the issue. I feel a cold tension settle between my shoulder blades that isn't diminished by a second *café con leche*.

We don't bother waiting for Amador and after the others have communicated with their wives or girlfriends, posted on Instagram, and made sure their world isn't burning down, we head in a big Ford back to Havana Vieja, where we walk through El Museo de la Revolución. There, Charles stops for a time before a photograph of Vilma Espín; el Museo de la Revolución is particularly inclusive of women who were involved in the revolution, bearing arms or helping in the home, schools, or elsewhere. Vilma is frozen in the height of her youth in this picture; wearing a beret tilted expressively to one side, she smiles confidently in loose-fitting camouflage clothing, long before she would be married to Raúl Castro. Again, Cuba feels like a big family and Vilma seems like a relative. I feel at once the optimism shining on her face, sadness at her death in 2007 when she was only fifty-eight, and optimism again that the revolution survived her. It all happened so fast. I watch Charles take a photograph of this photograph and am touched later when he and I discuss how moved we are by the same exhibit.

We walk without talking toward a hotel to eat, tacitly agreeing not to mention the letter to the Havana Club leadership that none of us has the energy to write. We have a quick lunch, omelets, at the Hotel Sevilla, and then I want to go to the Casa del Ron, which, contrary to what its name would suggest, is one of the few places where I can buy legal cigars with a proper *factura*, or receipt, which allows me to take them out of the country. After a flirtatious conversation with the woman in her sixties who handles the humidors, we turn our conversation to rum. She confirms what we know: that all of the brands come from only a few distilleries. She offers, though, that the Cubay distillery is quite close and we might be able to simply get a ride there and have a look. We hire a car and ask the driver if he knows where this distillery is, based on the directions the woman has given us. He does and we are away, finally, with a sense of purpose. Immediately we are of good cheer, like whalers who have heard "thar she blows!"

I watch mile after mile of Havana Vieja pass by. Endless pastel colors, colonial facades, beautiful people of all ages in tight, revealing clothing walking, laughing, arguing, flirting, kissing without shame on the broken streets. Finally, we arrive at what we are assured is the distillery: a strangely squat, two-story building with ornamental columns. Charles interjects quite audibly, "I think this is some bullshit." We hurry up the staircase and inside, where we are greeted by a muscular, bald man who immediately begins to bargain with us, offering a tour followed by the opportunity to buy cigars. They are clearly forgeries, sitting out in the open air with bands that look as if they were produced on a color copy machine. That said, Cuban forgeries are often better than legitimate cigars from other countries. They are probably made by someone who worked at one of the factories from leaves that did indeed grow in the finest terroir in the world for cigar tobacco.

I manage to duck this guy and take a turn through the small building. It is another distiller's museum—more of a tasting room with some models of distilling equipment than an actual distillery. We are the only people there and we wonder, as we would discuss later, what is this guy's game plan? What are the odds that someone is going to happen by this place and pay for a tasting before buying some forged cigars? Our man's name is Leonardo, and he turns out to be very affable and inclined to help us. He listens intently as we explain we are just hoping to see the interior of a distillery, and Leonardo says, "*Te puedo ayudar.*" I can help you.

Our driver hasn't left—he is smoking a cigarette and talking on his telephone in the capacious Ford. Leonardo engages him in an animated discussion of directions; Cubans always seem to be arguing, but I never see evidence of residual bad blood. He takes a cigarette from the driver's pack of Populares, the state-rationed brand, puts it behind his ear, and calls us over by tilting his head quickly backward. There were six of us, sitting three abreast in the front and back bench seats, our strong scents mixing with the ubiquitous Cuban smells of tobacco and diesel. Leonardo is chatty, talking to us first of the NBA, which is one of Charles's and my favorite topics, then fielding questions from Charles in his elevated Spanish. A typical Charles question: "So, I'm done working for the day, and I'm Cuban . . . where do I go? I mean do I have a beer at a bar, or do I go home and have dinner with my family? Or do I stand around in a park?" The conversation flows freely, and Leonardo has an easy way about him that quickly earns our confidence.

We arrive at an address in a light industrial neighborhood, as far as I could tell, in the very furthest southeastern corner of Havana. We park before a warehouse with a large open sliding door. Leonardo invites us out of the car and leads us toward the open door that from our perspective, looking into the sun, frames only darkness.

A stocky man steps from the darkness and stops us from entering with his bulk. As my eyes adjust to the light, I can see the interior of what seems like an empty warehouse. A moment of quiet, clipped Spanish passes between Leonardo and the sentinel before Leonardo looks over his left shoulder and beckons us in with a reverse nod of the head. We step between the two Cuban men into the warehouse, which smells distinctly of alcohol. As my eyes further adjust, I see farther into what appears to be an ancient bottling line, with its conveyor belt and spigot for filling. We grab our phones to photograph our first evidence of any aspect of the distilling process when two other men appear and start to shout at us. "Get out of there!" "*Para! Para! Para!*" ("Stop!") They move between us and the bottling line and walk us out of the facility. One of them wears a sleeveless white shirt that has stains on the front that look as if he's been eating spaghetti sauce. Another wears a nondescript gray uniform and the third is in cutoff shorts and no shirt. We move away from this motley, improvised security detail and begin laughing.

Absurd though it seems, the citizenry's protection of these facilities is not without cause. Cuba has literally been in a state of martial law for sixty years. While it may seem to us that the Cubans are protecting state secrets, the reality is on hundreds of occasions people from other countries have tried to murder officials—even going so far as to try to get Fidel an exploding cigar—and blow up public buildings. We should not mock them; they are conditioned to guard the security of their state. They likely think we are just tourists, but a real history exists in Cuba of terrorist attack.

I've never felt physically threatened in Cuba, though I have heard Cubans speak often of machete violence, which has unnerved me at times walking through Havana Central in the pitch-black night, but has never seemed a practical threat. The country is safer than any other I've visited in what we call Latin America, which is why we'd followed Leonardo so casually this afternoon. These men weren't going to hurt anyone, but they were not going to let us casually tour the plant either. Back in the car, Leonardo consoles us by saying he has learned the location of a distillery; it is closed now, but we can visit in the morning. I borrow Leonardo's phone to call Amador, who has had no luck reaching anyone at Havana Club. I hang up, decide that Leonardo is a bit of an upgrade from Amador, and negotiate meeting him at the Presidente at nine the next morning; if he isn't there by 9:30, we will assume he isn't coming. Leonardo feigns indignation at the possibility he might not show. "*Si digo voy, voy . . .*" We ride quietly through Havana Vieja, enjoying the old spring-loaded seats that rise and fall gently with the concussive effect of the ancient suspension. Pressed against my colleagues, sweating, I experience a moment's peace. We are dropped at Parque Central across the main path from La Esquina Caliente, near an array of iron tables and affixed chairs where I'd taken chess lessons when I lived in Havana Vieja.

I had taken my lessons from Orelbe, who hustled me masterfully the day we met. We played one game and I dumped a piece and lost; we played another that lasted more than an hour, during which I stretched my cognitive abilities to their very limit, contemplating every move until I was positive before moving my piece. Orelbe would close his eyes and exhale slowly and loudly through his nose, suggesting I'd made a great move. We played until I had a king and a pawn to his king and I was in a position to promote. I had won and, looking up, saw that we were surrounded by enthusiasts of the game, some of whom slapped me on the back and said, "*Bien hecho.*" ("Well done.") We played the next game for a beer and I lost. I made a stupid mistake and I'd already learned I could beat him. Orelbe won the next eight games, and it was he who finally insisted we stop, looking humbly down as he put his old, plastic Staunton set in a cardboard box and folded up the tattered paper board on which the pieces had rested. He looked up, catching my eye, and the corners of his mouth rose while his eyes grew moist, then he began to laugh quietly as I gave him the price of nine beers. One of the onlookers asked me if I knew who he was before sharing that Orelbe was, at the age of eighteen, a national master, one of the ten best players in the country. I couldn't be angry; I was so fascinated to learn what it is to be a victim of this kind of con. We talked amiably for half an hour as it grew dark until Orelbe offered me lessons, which I accepted and enjoyed twice a week for the duration of that winter.

And what does this story have to do with rum? For me, everything. In other parks, on other rum-producing islands, there aren't young descendants of slaves who have been educated by the state and sponsored for international travel to play chess, funded by the revenue of that island's rum sales. I do not consider art in a vacuum, and I do not consider spirits that way either. It's about more than just the quality of the spirit; I allow myself to be biased by story and by community.

Yet the rums that we've been tasting on this trip are not amazing; they're fine for daiquiris, but that's about all you can say for them. And then, the irony is, it will probably be years before I, or more likely my younger employees, can pour these spirits behind a bar in San Francisco. So, again, why are we even here? We are considering a platonic ideal: what we would sell if we could. We are here to learn what we would most like to have available to us. And to learn why we are precluded from learning about these spirits, or seeing them, let alone buying them. This clarity is hard to come by in an industry that invests billions of dollars in marketing, often lying, about their products—to consumers, to bartenders, to people like me. I could fly free once a month, visiting large distilleries as their guest, toeing their party line and blindly pouring their shit at my bars, without asking any hard questions. Sadly, many people who write about this industry accept this special treatment.

We walk from the park to La Bodeguita del Medio, another of Hemingway's supposed favorite bars, where the mojito was popularized (although not invented, as popular legend claims). We find a table in the back to escape the din of the house band, which is excellent, but we are tired. Four mojitos arrive as I light a Montecristo No. 2. *Mojito* means literally "little wet one," which reveals the drink's purpose: a quick cooling draught from a time when air conditioning didn't exist. To drink a mojito is to stop, put your foot on the rail, and cool down with the effervescing synthesis of fresh mint, lime, Havana Club three-year, and the beautiful, ever-present, crystalline Cuban sugar held in opposition to dashes of angostura bitters. Sadly, this round is not made with the gravitas the drink demands: it's too sweet and not cold. I taste mine and let Eric finish it, giving my full attention to the Montecristo. We watch the international crowd spill in and out of the century-old interior, every inch of which is covered with encouraged graffiti. Charles is pleasantly cynical. "This place is about as compelling as Jim Morrison's grave." We sit quietly and comfortably for forty-five minutes or so, long enough for those of us smoking to finish their Montecristos. After a long day of walking, we're fine taking two yellow Lada taxis back to the apartments where we regroup for dinner.

After showering we walk to this evening's *paladar*, which is one of the restaurants visited by Barack and Michelle Obama; apparently Michelle enjoyed it so thoroughly that she returned the next night with her girls and without a reservation. Tonight Vedado is consumed by a blackout and we walk through the stillest of nights: pitch black with people congregating on street corners, chatting languidly, not eating, not drinking, maybe smoking. Cats move across the road; one black-and-white fellow follows us cautiously for many blocks. The *paladar* is similarly peaceful, luminous with an abundance of candlelight compensating for the blackout. A gas-powered generator on the patio makes a noise like a quiet lawn-mower engine, giving enough electricity to keep the kitchen working. We eat slowly in the dark and enjoy a visit from the chef, another friend of Amador. Eric is enjoying Cuba and is always at his most lovely after a couple of drinks, though he never crosses over, a true gentleman. Seated beside me, he whispers enthusiastically, "Thank you for sharing this place. A lot comes clear here. I mean, a lot is confusing as well, but it opens up so many great conversations."

I smile and nod, grabbing him on the shoulder and adding, "I'm so happy to be here with you."

"These old bars . . . to see where people have continuously drunk the same drinks for more than half a century. Well, it's exceptional. Thank you. I'm not discouraged about the distilleries. We understand this place more. We understand these rums more. I am better educated. Thank you." Eric puts his hand on my shoulder and makes sure I make eye contact. He does this whenever we toast, ensuring that he locks eyes with everyone raising a glass. This adherence to custom will drive him to crane his neck, peering around someone's head, while reaching dramatically, around a torso or through other outstretched arms, to be sure the glass in his hand meets his target's while locking eyes, resolutely.

After dinner that night, we try another ten rums and none of them are memorable; Charles berates me again for rating them from worst to least bad. At this point, we've tried tens of rums produced on the island. It's become clear that small-batch, independent craft distilling isn't happening in Cuba.

The next morning, Leonardo meets us at exactly 9:30 a.m., interrupting my attempts to get online. Eric has succeeded and finally has word from our friend Julio, who owns a famous tequila bar in San Francisco and relates that in dozens of visits he hadn't been able to gain access to a single distillery. We feel vindicated a bit, and this news augurs the adventures of the next forty-eight hours with Leonardo.

Leonardo ushers us into a new American taxi with a different driver from the day before, who drives us directly to a distillery; unfortunately, it is a distillery that produces industrial alcohol, most notably hand sanitizer, a depiction of which, over an outstretched hand, is featured on a plaque on the exterior of the factory. Charles shakes his head. "We can't get a fucking break," he says. "Blocked from even seeing them make hand cleaner." We realize that we had not clarified to Leonardo that we were hoping to see a distillery of rum.

Accustomed to seeing seven distilleries in a day with good preparation, we are beginning to accept that we may not see even one true distillery in seven days. But now Leonardo understands that we want to see rum exclusively, and he has a new idea. He leads us to an administrative building on La Rampa, back in Vedado. From the lobby, he phones the Minister of Sugar, whose dominion includes sugar by-products, that is, rum. The minister is in a meeting; he will call back in an hour. To kill an hour, we go to el Museo Nacional de Bellas Artes, where Leonardo pays his own admission in Cuban pesos. We pay the much higher tariff in convertible currency. We split up and wander the museum separately. I go directly to Jorge Arche, whose bright palette and stolid, thick-trunked subjects play cards and drink rum at a small table or in various postures of repose. For years, I had a print of one of Arche's paintings, *Primavera o descanso*, on my wall. A sturdy young man lies on his back in a verdant field. His hands are folded and cradling his handsome head as he stares placidly at the sky. One of his legs is stretched out straight and the other is bent at the knee, against which his buxom lover reclines. Her dress reveals cleavage and the young man's shirt is open to the waist. The woman distractedly toys with a plant that grows beside them. Given they are not interested in each other and are loosely clothed, one imagines they have recently finished making love. They are the picture of rest and comfort, lying there in the sun. For me, this captures the ideal of Cuba, and the ideal of rum. The possibility of real rest. Of real passion.

When the hour is up, I return to meet Leonardo at the pay phone. Now the minister is having coffee. He will call again in forty-five minutes, which I pass in the modern wing, which is not my favorite. Cuban painting is quite European in style, adhering to the canonical traditions of each period, until about 1960 when the paintings became more propagandistic. One of my favorites is a large piece depicting many heroes of the revolution in a comic fashion, very much like the animated film *Yellow Submarine*, saturated with primary colors and simple line representations.

By the time I make it back to the pay phone, Leonardo is engaged. I have no energy and find a bench, on which I sit and watch him on the phone, making bold gestures with his hands that his partner in conversation cannot see. Twenty minutes pass before Leonardo replaces the handset in the cradle and walks across the outdoor lobby of the museum toward me. The minister can't help us; he suggests we visit the US embassy and ask that they make a formal request of Havana Club, which will, of course, honor such a request and make us welcome. If he can help us with anything else related to sugar, we should surely call.

Charles, Eric, Jay, and I squeeze into a Lada taxi and ride to the US embassy, where we wait in line to speak with the *ayudante* ("assistant") out front. "Oh, man," he says in capable English, "You should go to the Havana Club offices. They are near here."

Us: "We tried that."

Him: "Well then, man, you should go to the Museum of Rum. They can help you there, those *guías* know what's going on . . ."

Us: "We went there and our guide sent us to the Havana Club offices."

Him: "Okay, look then. Just drive out there. When I was working in tourism, I would just take groups out there to see the distillery."

Us: "Well, is there someone we could call just in case?" He uses a ballpoint pen from his breast pocket to write a number on a small piece of paper, and then directs us to a phone cabin two blocks away, which does not work until an irritated Cuban teenager gives me some Cuban pesos to try instead of the convertible ones.

After several calls without an answer, we return to La Bodeguita; this time, despite Charles's protestations, we sit at the bar and watch the bartenders work. The house quartet is playing my favorite, "Comandante Che Guevara." When they finish, Eric detains the guitarist, entrusting him with a collection of steel strings he brought as gifts. An amateur picker himself, he'd read that Cubans appreciate being brought items scarce due to the embargo. The guitarist restrings his instrument immediately, slaps Eric on the back, then in true *habanero* fashion asks him if he'd like to buy a CD. My kind, quiet friend buys the CD, which appears only to compound his pleasure of having brought a gift that was meaningful. I order a fifteen-year Havana Club to smell and cautiously ignite a Hoya de Monterrey robusto. I'm excited about the next ninety minutes of my life, the duration of this cigar.

Our barman has worked at La Bodeguita for eighteen years and is probably sixty-five years old, with short-cropped hair and a white guayabera. He works before a backdrop of shelves, replete with every mark of Havana Club and a number of sealed cases of cigars in addition to a stocked humidor. He scowls gently, as Cuban bartenders do, while he lines up a series of zombie-style highball glasses stenciled with the Havana Club logo. From a squirt bottle, he ejaculates about an ounce of lime juice in each glass, adds mint using tongs so as not to taint the yerba buena with his hands, then spoonfuls of desert-colored Cuban sugar and dashes of angostura bitters before free-pouring the Havana Club three-year, the foundation of his next fifteen drinks. As his clients call for mojitos, generally in foreign Spanish, he adds ice and tops them with seltzer. Unlike many of our career bartenders in the United States, our man's movements are unpretentious and meditative. My perch is off to the side by the front door, and I watch Jay watching our guy. He is relishing the same cigar I am, and I enjoy his youth and intensity as he studies the barman, helps those behind him pay and receive their drinks, and chats with his neighbors in perfunctory Spanish. With his beatnik beard and unlabeled military green cap, he does not look unlike many of the young men we'd seen on the walls of el Museo de la Revolución men who died long ago, but are remembered by this strange country that has formed a partnership with Pernod Ricard while ensuring its population has a working understanding of Marx and Engels.

I choose to remember the trip this way. An hour later, we'll be at the Hotel Meliá Cohiba watching the NBA finals, where I connect to the modern hotel's network and learn from a number of text messages and emails that Trou Normand has been shut down for the night for serving liquor while its license was suspended. All the blood in my body seems to run to my head, and I perceive the world through a myopic haze. My partners are enraged, as this failure is clearly my responsibility, and I have to return immediately. I pack quietly at the apartment, and leaving behind anything that I can easily replace back at home like toothpaste, deodorant, a pair of shoes, a pair of shorts. Someone can use all of this stuff. As I approach Amador's room to explain my departure, I hear a sonorous voice, which either means Amador is talking to himself, has company, or is speaking in his sleep. None of these options makes me keen to knock on his door.

The following morning, my colleagues will ride to the Havana Club distillery with Leonardo, where they will be allowed nowhere near the facility, and will be chastised for photographing the factory from tens of meters away. Eric later sends me a photo of the angry matriarch who shouted obscenities, flanked by male guards, as my friends drove away. He captured her in the photo, enormous hips jammed into a bureaucrat's skirt. Her government-issue uniform shirt is half untucked and she is wearing stiletto heels with her legs spread wide and triumphantly, one arm outstretched with a raised index finger as if to say, "I know what the fuck you're doing!"

So I am leaving. And the others are close behind. In our frustration, we are grateful to get out, but as soon as we are clear of Cuba we will want to return, as one always does when escaping the island—what exactly was that? I need another look. We didn't get the information we'd hoped for, but were educated in a more important way, one that only being in Cuba can offer. It is all instructive: the heat of the late afternoon, wrestling with the heady challenge of Cuban socialism and all its sophistication and absurdity, while you smoke the finest cigar in the world with a drink made from the simplest ingredients, and smell the sex and frustration in the air all around you. I will return to these memories, on some level, every time I pour dry, molasses-based rum into a glass, cocktail shaker, or beaker. *Primavera o descanso*? Spring or rest?

PART THREE

GIN A BODY MEET A BODY/COMIN THRO' THE GRAIN

Chapter Six

SCOTLAND, PART I

HALOO, GRIGALACH!

Our signal for fight, that from monarchs we drew,
Must be heard but by night in our vengeful haloo!
Then haloo, Grigalach! haloo, Grigalach!
Haloo, haloo, haloo, Grigalach.
—"Macgregor's Gathering," Sir Walter Scott

The last two trips I've taken to Scotland, about a year apart, have been with my stepfather, Lester, and midway between them his father died. We were both there, with hands on Les Senior, when he breathed his last breath. They, his breaths, had been coming more and more slowly and, while holding Les's feet, I wondered, *How many of these breaths does one get?* How valuable they become as we near the end.

We had known Les was very sick before our first of the two trips in August. A resilient and vital ninety-three-year-old, he'd begun to experience some chronic back pain, which he assumed was sciatica and soldiered on, only to learn later that what ached was actually metasticized cancer. This trip was important to Lester and to me, so we decided to go despite Les's critical condition—a loaded decision for Lester who had chosen to go through on a trip to Europe when he was eighteen, while his mother was enduring cancer; she died while he was away.

Les Senior died in November, months after we returned from our first trip. We held a memorial for him at Bar Agricole, in which he was an investor, six months later. Lester and I left for our second trip to Scotland four days after the memorial. Coincidentally, on the road in Scotland, I learned that my wife and I had finally been approved for adoption, which Lester and I celebrated in our own way together. He and I are close, and my love for him was further inspiration to adopt, as I am certain that our true families are elected rather than borne of blood. So a lot has happened for Lester and me around these trips to Scotland.

My work was not trivialized by these events but rather augmented. I wish for everyone that their career might feel meaningful in the face of death, in the face of parenthood, in the most concentrated moments of life. Apparently mine does, no more so than when I seek the most fabled spirit, scotch, named for the land of Sir Walter, Irvine Welsh, Sir Wilfred of Ivanhoe, Francis Begbie.

The first of our two trips was not long after the historic referendum vote of 2014, in which 86 percent of voters turned out, and ultimately Scotland decided to remain a part of the United Kingdom. Our second trip fell immediately after Brexit, the UK's unlikely decision to leave the European Union, painful irony for many Scottish who had chosen inclusion and collectivism with a country that would prefer isolation.

The bookends of these historic votes are notable to me because one cannot consider Scotland without its storied battles for independence and identity. This grappling informs the category of scotch whisky (the Scottish leave out the "e") as well, whose brands all draw on the rugged nation's epic history and topography, naming themselves after clans, lakes, rivers, hills, and historic events that celebrate the regionalism and sense of place within Scotland. We see scotch at a similar juncture as the country at large, trading on a reputation of fierce nationalism but, in reality, having undergone a kind of miscegenation that, at times, jeopardizes the identity of the spirit while contributing to the greatest popularity and commercial success of its history.

Having driven all around and across Scotland multiple times, I have my own visceral sense of the place. First, Scotland is more a part of Scandinavia than of England. At its northeastern tip, one is closer to Norway than to London. Scottish Gaelic is informed by the phonetics of the Norse language of the eighth-century Viking invaders who colonized Scotland and influenced the population's genetics, as they also did in Northern France. I am guilty of projecting a kind of barbaric pride onto the Scottish who inhabit an endless, savage landscape that is impossibly verdant while jagged and mountainous. Water is everywhere in the form of countless lakes, inlets, springs, and rivers, illustrated by the many Gaelic words to describe different bodies of water: *loch, logh, loch-uisge, abhain, awin, aven, sruth, allt, muir, fairge, cuan.* As you move through it, the landscape is constantly changing and beautiful.

To be in Scotland with its grass and rain and clouds and perseverant sun is to take one huge, restorative, fresh breath of air that lasts the number of days you are there. I am superstitious, breathing deeply through my mouth and nose as much as I can, keeping the window to the car open when possible, taking walks in the evening, pausing. I imagine what is surely a very anachronistic tableau of tribes roaming the terrain, living close to the land, carrying all they own in garments comprised of one large cloth, each clan tied to a territory, to a place.

The myth of the whisky grew out of this hyperregionalism. Scotch is made simply from three elemental ingredients: grain, yeast, and water. Actually, strangely, one other ingredient is allowed: the caramel coloring agent E150a. The grain most commonly used is barley, though scotch whisky can be made from any grain. Envision a more primitive time when a farmer might make whisky from his store of barley and the water of that area, likely with its own unique mineral personality. The producer would first add water to cause the barley to germinate, thereby increasing the sugar content of the grain, which will be converted to alcohol through fermentation. Before the grain fully sprouts into a plant, while it is still sweet, it must be drained and dried quickly. This is done in a kiln, which in earlier times would likely have been fueled by peat, the fertile ground cover of earth and decomposed vegetal matter that is particularly rich in the Scottish ecosystem. In some small towns, you can still walk down the street and smell the pleasantly acrid aroma of burning peat. When used, this aromatic fuel instills the barley with its own unique character, adding another stamp of the provenance of this particular whisky. This specificity is compounded when the distiller incorporates the water from that particular area into the fermenting sweet grain. Before the advent of industrial yeasts, the distiller would have relied on wild ambient yeasts particular to his or her plot, or inoculated the mixture of water and grain (mash) with a yeast culture that was maintained on the property, akin to a sourdough starter. Furthering the singularity of the eventual spirit would be the particularities of whatever simple, primitive still was made by the distiller or other member of the community. The resulting spirit would have been unexampled and inimitable, and to conceive of this time in the evolution of scotch is both inspiring and sad. Consider a school of small, sui generis spirits, hatched from a very specific set of circumstances, all of these combinations of unique grain, yeast, water, peat, and still, never tasted before and never to be replicated.

A more simple spirit (read: most other spirits) does not have as many variables contributing to its final identity as scotch does: there's the grain, the water in which it is germinated and fermented, the fuel that dries it, the yeast that causes fermentation, the construction and operation of the still, the barrels that guard and inform the spirit, and, of course, the human element that influences every stage of the process. At its best, scotch is a titan, dwarfing virtually all other spirits with its complexity.

Lester is only seventeen years my senior but has been one of my guardians since I was two years old. In his prime, he was the doppelganger of a virile Mandy Patinkin circa *Yentl*, with thick, tightly curled, dark brown hair and an imposing beard; now he appears much the same, but his thick curls and beard are dusted with silver, and he suffers cheerfully from a growing assortment of maladies, despite his appearance of great health and vigor. Lester and I are both Anglophiles, and our affection stretches to every island and corner of the empire. His favorite vacation is to hike in the Lake District of northern England where, in his vocation as a high school English teacher, he guided many groups of students, as well as family and members of his secular spiritual congregation in Olympia, Washington, where he has lived since taking up with my mother in 1971. On these tours, he was able to indulge his avocation: map reader and planner. Lester loves to navigate by compass over the fells of the green and craggy region; only recently, after years of shouted argument, did he concede to using a GPS on our driving excursions.

Lester is the perfect companion for these trips. Thanks to his skilled and painstaking planning, we are able to visit the right thirty distilleries in only a week; Lester arranges for the car, ferries, lodging, and dinner reservations at each inn along the way. On the plane, he is prepared with snacks: sealed plastic bags of sliced carrots, dried almonds, salami, and cheese. When we claim our rental car on the ground in Edinburgh, Lester realizes that it cannot accommodate my six-foot-eight frame, so he kindly insists on a different car, a large Volvo wagon, even though he will be sacrificing a manual transmission, which he much prefers.

At the time of this writing, Scotland boasts almost one hundred fifty licensed distilleries. Notably only six of these are technically independent—an astonishing minority. I have made it a priority to visit each of the independents over the last few years. The others are owned by companies, a majority by multinational companies. Diageo, which is the largest holding company with twenty-nine scotch distilleries, could combine their holdings with Bacardi and Pernod Ricard and the three companies would own a third of the distilleries in Scotland. This plurality is particularly interesting when we consider the Scotch Whisky Association (SWA), which is the nonprofit organization whose role, according to its website, "is to advance the global interests and profile of Scotch Whisky, our members and of the industry as a whole." Essentially, it is a governing body that decides how scotch can be made, packaged, marketed, distributed, and sold—and it is funded by the subscriptions of its members. One can clearly see how these large companies that are responsible for much of the organization's revenue might have a disproportionate influence on the identity of scotch internationally. For example, in 2008, the nomenclature of scotch was adjusted, a discussion of which can help us better understand the current world of scotch. Scotch is divided into three rough categories. Single grain scotches are composed of any mixture of grains and made in a single distillery; most notable of these are the single malts that are made from only malt in a single distillery. Blended malt whiskies are a mixture of single malts that can come from multiple distilleries. Last are the blended scotch whiskies, which constitute more than 90 percent of the scotch sold in the world. Blended scotch whiskies contain both malt whisky and grain whisky. Producers combine the malts and grain whiskies to construct a consistent house style. Some of the more popular blended scotch whiskies include Dewar's, Johnnie Walker, Cutty Sark, J&B, and Chivas Regal.

Much like those of cognac, the merchant bottlers who buy and blend whiskies have contributed greatly to the international success of the category and have also created a security in Scotland for producers, which would be a mistake to dismiss. Blended malt whiskies were called "vatted malts" until 2008 when the SWA decided that they would be called "blends." A subtle difference, but the result is that the unsophisticated consumer could easily miss the difference between a blended malt, comprised of only single malts, and the less rare blended scotch, which is the most affordable and least pedigreed option in scotch. One could argue that this new nomenclature favors the sellers of blends by eliding the category with the more exclusive vatted malts. A trivial example, perhaps, but we begin to understand how the SWA merits some scrutiny.

From Edinburgh we head toward Fife, where we are excited about visiting two very different types of distilleries. The first is Daftmill, one of the six independent distilleries, and one of the most charming distillers and distilleries in Scotland. Founded in 2005, the property is an old mill dating from the late seventeenth century. You arrive at the old, stone structure by way of an unmarked, tree-lined road, across which ducks scurry and along which lies evidence of children: footballs, brightly colored small bicycles. The mill was converted handsomely by its brother-owners, Ian and Francis Cuthbert, who detailed the weathered stone walls with kelly-green trim. All of the men who worked on the mill and all of the materials used, save the stills and *mash tun* (fermenting tank) made by Forsyths of Rothes in northeastern Scotland, come from within a five-mile radius of Daftmill. The Cuthberts farm their own barley and also operate a nearby quarry whose revenue funded the distillery project.

The previous year, Francis had met us for a tour after his day of work on the farm. We were waiting for him outside the distillery when he pulled up at a frantic speed, jumped from the cab of his old American-make pickup, then disappeared into what we assumed was the house for about ten minutes. He emerged with wet hair in clean work boots, a crisp pair of Lee Jeans, and a clean, loose-fitting plaid shirt. Francis has dark, straight hair, which he parts severely on one side. He is gaunt, with sunken olive cheeks, and his charcoal-colored eyes have pale dark circles beneath them. I kept looking at his right hand, held habitually palm up, for a cigarette, perhaps because he struck me more as a morose poet than a distiller. His posture was erect and athletic, though, as he guided us around the facility. The tour was a lovely, human one, largely due to Francis's constant self-effacement. He would sweep his floppy hair off his brow and smile nervously. "If you haven't guessed by now," he'd say, "I have little idea what I'm doing." We ended by tasting some of his finished whisky aged in a sherry oak cask and some aged in bourbon oak in his tiny cask room. To be called *scotch*, the spirit must be aged in a bonded (monitored by the government to secure payment of tax) warehouse in Scotland for at least three years in some kind of oak. Francis had whiskies that were old enough to sell legally, but he conserved the liquid, explaining that he will sell some when "it was ready," which is a quote I've heard several others joke about having heard him utter, including famous whisky writer Charles Maclean.

The Daftmill is unique in that it is literally the only distillery in all of Scotland that is growing all the grain it uses to distill. A couple of other distilleries claim to be phasing in their own growth, but for now Daftmill is an anomaly. The Cuthberts do, however, send it out to be malted—but then they mill, ferment, and distill the grain themselves. Francis explained to us that, as farmers, they'd been selling their barley for decades. "At one time," he tells us, "you just grew barley and depending, it would go to animal feed, distilleries, brewing." Now, Francis sells most of the family's grain to the prestigious producer Macallan. True agrarian distillers, they decided to withhold some of the grain and distill it themselves; Macallan buys about eight hundred thousand kilos and Daftmill keeps the other two hundred thousand. What's old is new again at Daftmill.

When you taste the Daftmill, and other grower-producer spirits or wines, you can relax and stop worrying about words like "prestige." I enjoy a spirit like the Daftmill not because it tries to be the best but rather because it hopes to be part of a category, connecting field and glass. Daftmill does not aspire to impress you; it simply aspires to make scotch. From the barrel, I notice fresh cereal qualities in the young spirit, as well as deeper, malty notes of chocolate and leather that integrate with both the sherry and the bourbon oak, with the characteristic qualities of dried fruit standing out in the sherry finish in particular. I experience a sense of connection to the crop in the field and to the beer it became briefly before being distilled. The bourbon cask, not surprisingly, instills a nougat quality in the spirit. Francis speaks softly as we taste. "Ten years later I'm nosing the spirit, thinking I could do better," he says.

As has been mentioned, tasting can be time travel connecting us to our ancestors, which inspires us, of late, to make things in an old-fashioned way, not simply because it may be more healthy, but also because experiencing the same flavors as our predecessors makes us feel less alone out here on the knife's edge of history. When spirits regress in this way, they will taste more like they used to, which is also to say, there will be less standardization of flavors. Each spirit will taste unique.

The other distillery we visit in the area of Fife is the Cameron-bridge, a grain distillery owned by Diageo that occupies the opposite end of the spectrum from Daftmill. Where one could drive up to Francis's property unannounced, Cameronbridge doesn't allow entry. I have had to arrange the visit to the closed facility weeks in advance. Diageo signs guide us to a large parking lot, across from which looms the distillery, covering what must be twenty acres, and appearing as antithetical to the twee Daftmill as one could imagine. It is not so much a building as an industrial complex, militarily secure and penetrated only by grim train tracks that bring in raw materials and take them back out, transformed. The architecture of the compound is ashen concrete, glass, and rows of stainless steel tanks with capacities of as much as a million liters. Industrial smokestacks cast steam and smoke skyward, unlike the charming, squat pagoda-style stacks we see in the vast majority of scotch distilleries built in the nineteenth century. The uninformed witness likely would never guess that this is a complex producing foodstuffs. It reminds me of the Monsanto plant outside of New Orleans: ominous and enormous.

To their credit, Diageo is very cordial in its accommodation of us and pairs us with the appropriately named Scott, who greets us professionally and warmly, especially considering we are three hours later than we'd intended. He wears glasses with German-looking, thick black frames and seems about my age, fit and well put together. His card describes him as the "Business Leader" dealing with process. After leaving our shoes and phones in a locker at the gatehouse and receiving a warning that we could take no photographs, we are given institutional shoes, hardhats, and fluorescent vests. Eternally merry, Lester looks comfortable in his vest and hardhat. He smiles expectantly as Scott explains that Cameronbridge has basically been a construction site for the last nine or ten years, constantly evolving and trying to increase production.

To begin to understand the scope of this place, Francis will produce about sixty-five thousand liters of spirit in a year at his Daftmill, compared to Cameronbridge which distills close to two hundred million liters of spirit a year. Daftmill wants to go back in time; Cameronbridge is a juggernaut, churning toward an inevitable future. From the guardhouse, we follow Scott across a pedestrian bridge and descend a flight of metal stairs, arriving on an expanse of tarmac. Hurrying to keep up with Scott, likely quite fit because he is traversing this corporate city all day, we are dwarfed by enormous tanks and nondescript gray-clad edifices.

We arrive at an office building and are guided to what appears to be a small boardroom, where Scott prepares to give us a PowerPoint presentation. He begins playfully with an apocryphal but humorous assertion that distillation began in the town of Alloa, where he was born and raised. Jameson, of Irish whiskey fame, is also from Alloa, so, Scott offers with a sheepish grin, it seems that the Scottish also created Irish whiskey. He embarks on a brief history of the factory, describing the various corporate mergers that shaped the identity of the place until Diageo took over in 1990 and really began to optimize production. Scott speaks without shame about Diageo's success in taking production from sixty million liters in 1990 to the quantities it accomplishes now. He was educated as an engineer and speaks eloquently about distillation. In the car afterward, Lester and I will agree that we learned as much from Scott as any other person we'd met. Cameronbridge is producing grain whiskies and neutral grain spirit, distilled to such a high alcohol by volume that it is basically a vodka, which is used in all of Diageo's blended whiskies, which include the behemoth, Johnnie Walker, Buchanan's, J&B, and Bell's. In addition to whiskies, Cameronbridge also makes all of the Diageo gins, including Gordon's and the complete line of Tanqueray products, as well as Smirnoff vodka. These clear spirits are produced from neutral spirits purchased on the open market, much of which is from the Sedalcol distillery in Yorkshire, which makes Cameronbridge look like a tiny grower-producer in Armagnac. This spirit is redistilled with the appropriate botanicals for each of their gins. The Smirnoff is not even redistilled—it is simply forced through ten charcoal filters, absolving it of any offensive character, or arguably any character at all.

I must admit I was shocked to learn, only a few years ago, that all of Diageo's clear spirits come from facilities like this one, which produce scores of supposedly different spirits—gins, vodkas, and blended whiskies—from the same base materials and neutral spirits.

This homogeneity is bizarre but understandable. For most of the twentieth century, humans worked to standardize and maximize the production of what's edible. What Diageo has accomplished is laudatory from certain perspectives. Scott explains the automated processes by which technology can eliminate certain *congeners*, or chemical compounds, that would negatively impact these spirits. He speaks often about *innovation*, a word that is also featured in Diageo's marketing material. He is proud to explain the ways in which, through a largely automated process the distillery, Diageo has achieved the highest "specifications of purity," a phrase that, to my mind, has a eugenic feel and does actually denote a real neutrality of flavor. As a scientist, he is excited by the developments his company has made, including the cultivation of one of the most environmentally responsible physical plants I've encountered, but he makes a point of differentiating Cameronbridge from the larger Irish whiskey distilleries that actually go so far as to deploy scientifically engineered enzymes rather than natural yeast. Funny, I think—even at this space station, people find occasion to brag about doing things the old-fashioned way.

Advances in technology are why inhabitants of the developed world enjoy an almost unlimited quantity of sterile, safe calories. We've come to take this abundance for granted, but early in the twentieth century these new technologies were a godsend. Scott is proud that the company is maximizing its output; now more of the world has the opportunity to enjoy scotch in the form of consistent blends. To Scott, it's "the same as it's always been" at Cameronbridge; after all, scotch was popularized as a blend. Single malts weren't widely drunk until the 1960s, when Glenfiddich began selling its malts in the now ubiquitous triangular green bottle.

Strangely, though, we are learning that the malts that inform these blended whiskies are also largely standardized. I am reminded that we live on a planet where consumers believe we should be able to enjoy the same exact flavor, at any time, in any city, in any country. Although we are outgrowing this entitlement with food (even institutions like McDonald's are forced to recast themselves as slow-food meccas), with alcohol we are slow to remember that the contents of this bottle are grown in the ground, are *food,* and may actually be more interesting if these contents don't taste the same all the time.

We leave Cameronbridge enervated. We've learned a great deal about what most of the world drinks most of the time, and in so doing have come to better understand the things we do like. Sitting in the Volvo while Lester methodically slices some Thuringer on a travel chopping board in his lap, I remind him that Diageo is an English company. "Do you find it allegorical that this English company is homogenizing and diluting these Scottish whiskies, all while trading on Scotland's rugged cultural capital?" Lester pauses in his work, holding the unsheathed Japanese travel knife in his right hand. I'm grateful he's taking the time to consider my long, bombastic sentence. "Hm. Well. I guess I do find it allegorical," he says.

We drive directly to the hotel, in the town of Fettercairn, and have a satisfying pub dinner of venison and fish and chips. My favorite thing about Lester is he enjoys his food, be it high or low, like me. Our bond is strong here as we both reward ourselves with food and insist upon enjoying it. We order the house charcuterie plate to be sure we have enough and leave the table feeling sated as we make our way to walk the small village, enjoying one of the longest days of the year. At 10:30 p.m. a pastel sun disappears into the horizon line, beyond the foothills of the highlands. The farmland surrounding us is washed in generous, pale golden light. I breathe this fresh, clean air as deeply and often as I can.

We arrive at the Fettercairn Distillery, luminescent in the impossibly late sunlight, and admire its classic appearance. Low, hand-built buildings are covered with thick, white matte paint and crowned by slate roofs to create a courtyard. The malting building is recognizable because of its pagoda-style chimney, capped to retard the exit of the smoke that was once used to interrupt the malting of the barley and instill the grain with its own unique humor. Fettercairn is in the Whyte and Mackay family of products, bought from Diageo and others by Philippines-based Emperador Inc. in 2014, and distills largely unpeated whiskies, though much of the whisky is used in blends, to which end Fettercairn produces a small amount of peated scotch each year.

We turn our back on the sunset and on Fettercairn Distillery and walk slowly back to the hotel, which lies just opposite the Fettercairn Arch. Romanesque and extravagant, particularly in this rural context, it was built in 1864 for $250 to commemorate an overnight visit by Queen Victoria. We pause beneath the arch and look at the quiet river that flows beside it. I reckon the stream is Caulecotts Burn, which I know from the Charles Maclean guide is the water used for cooling in the distillery. The water used in the scotch itself comes from the springs in the Grampian Mountains, behind which we'd watched the peach-colored sun disappear.

Tomorrow I would be much more inclined to visit Fettercairn if it used grain from the area, but I am guilty of a prejudice. Standing between the distillery's two water sources, within eyeshot of the defunct malting room, I am nostalgic for something I have not experienced—a mourning, perhaps, from the shared unconscious. What scotch must have been when each one was built from its own biosphere! Now, Fettercairn gets its premalted grain from outsourced maltsters who, while independent, kiln-dry the malt to their clients' specifications, dialing in an exact parts per million of peat. Fettercairn whisky is hardly terrible. Lester had one earlier in the bar before dinner, which I tasted. A twelve-year-old bottled unremarkably at 40 percent, it seemed chill filtered, meaning the temperature of the whisky has been reduced until fats and oils become less soluble and can be easily removed from the liquid, a practice that is practically universal and curtails the quality of most spirits in the world. The Fettercairn's character was largely a consequence of its mixture of sherry and bourbon oak finishes rather than its cereal origins. The tasting notes I've read accurately report its qualities of butterscotch, walnut, and spice. Of all the spirits in the world, I would place this firmly in the top 10 percent if only because there is a lot of garbage being made, but also because it's made from decent base materials and is governed by a domain that ensures it will be simply grain, yeast, and water with perhaps a little caramel color, much like cognac. These distillers use copper pot stills rather than the enormous columns you might see at a Bacardi facility, which means they are made in small batches, and by law they must be aged in real barrels for three years, which is actually more than you can guarantee for cognac or armagnac. But the compromises are so apparent. These decisions are expedient and in the service of greater revenue. That virtually all these distillers must operate like this likely means it's pretty hard to make a living otherwise, but still we are in search of those who compromise the least, or even not at all.

Miraculously, I sleep through the night on the first evening and wake with only moderate anxiety, which is quickly allayed by my anticipation of the "full Scottish," the reason breakfast is my favorite part of the day in Scotland. Lester is already at table, smiling to himself with his reading glasses on, which are secured around his neck by sporty, protective strings. His place setting is besieged by a collection of maps and his smartphone, a newly utilized travel tool. He has chosen tea this morning, always a difficult selection, as the quality of coffee varies so wildly in the United Kingdom. Once it was always instant and you just took tea, which is wonderful over there, particularly when it's turned tan with an ounce of milk (British dairy products are without question of a higher quality than ours). I see an espresso machine poised in the bar and pull the trigger on a latte. What arrives is an *afrocino*—scalded espresso crowned by an improbably turgid mountain of dry, compactly foamed, scorched milk, a disappointment. But now it's time to order, and I opt for the whole complement: tomato, potato scone, beans, link sausage, black pudding, haggis, a rasher of bacon, and an extra egg for two total, fried. Every lodging place in Scotland from the Inn at Gleneagles to the basest hostel offers the full Scottish. This style of breakfast is common throughout the British Isles, but the Scottish is remarkable in its inclusion of blood pudding and haggis, the former being the amalgam of pigs' blood, fat, oats, barley, and spices, all stuffed in a length of intestine. *Haggis*, for those who don't know, is a savory pudding built from a sheep's *pluck*, or heart, liver, and lungs, minced with oats, onion, suet, and spices, traditionally encased in the same animal's stomach though, sadly, more often now it is served in an artificial casing. Before a North American judges haggis without trying it, I ask, "Have you ever enjoyed a ballpark hotdog, whose contents are even less wholesome and advertised with less transparency?"

I savor my breakfast as I give Lester my attention and consider his morning's preparations. "Okay," he begins, chuckling to himself—something he does often, betraying an almost constant sense of amusement. "I've prepared three possible routes . . ."

I feel myself getting annoyed. "Why do you always laugh like that?" I ask. The only difference between me now and me at fourteen is that now I am able to apologize, which I do after we've decided on the route to Auchindoun Castle.

As opposed to my relationship with Lester, my relationship with my biological father was always a little Victorian, full of awe and deference. The son of a motorcycle cop, my "real" father did something we are told is common in the United States but really is not: he jumped social class. He matriculated at the University of

Chicago at the age of sixteen, then attended Yale Law School until he changed his mind and transferred into the English department, where he became a professor who has published books on Blake and Joyce, and is now retired in Sonoma County in a home he designed himself, a hay-bale and adobe temple of books, artifacts, and art he's collected over the years. He has always been a passionate home cook; I remember trying sun-dried tomatoes for the first time with him in the 1970s, and enjoying the fruits of his pasta machine only a few years later. I am sure without my father's influence I would not be in the food and beverage business, and I am even more certain that, without his influence, I would not be writing this book. He and my fourth parent, my stepmother Mary-Kay, who is a professor of classics and theater, insisted that I read, and I can remember watching many of the most influential films of my youth on LaserDisc in their Northern California living room. My favorite memories and most anticipated visits are when my father, Mary-Kay, and I sit around their kitchen table talking about novels, talking about films, eating my father's cooking.

My mother, with whom I lived most of the year, was very busy finishing school and embarking on a career in middle age. So while my relationship with my father and Mary-Kay was more cordial, my mother and Lester bore the brunt of most of my childishness, for which I am grateful. In fact, he still does.

Back in Scotland, Lester listens to my apology solemnly, his wintry afro bathed in waxing morning sunshine. "I know. Thank you for your apology. I'm used to it. Nothing will spoil this trip." I let my embarrassment wash over me quickly as we load up the Volvo and move toward our first distillery, Glenfiddich, in the notable Scottish town of Dufftown.

Visiting Glenfiddich is a formality. The whiskies are not my favorites, but I want to honor the historical significance of the distillery. As I mentioned earlier, Glenfiddich was the first, in 1963, to actively promote a single malt internationally. While everyone produced malts, they were, until then, generally sold internationally as aspects of blends, integrated with neutral grain whiskies.

Of course, Glenfiddich didn't invent the single malt style; most malt whisky in Scotland produced historically could be characterized as single malt before being blended with malts from other distilleries or neutral grain spirit. This practice proliferated at the end of the nineteenth century and the first half of the twentieth, when industrialization led to the standardization and increased production of blends. One imagines the wild variety of all the different small malts was difficult to sell, and merchant bottlers set out to standardize them, just as Richard Hennessy had the previous century in France. As consumers came to trust these blends, the producers manufactured more and more—and these blends became synonymous with scotch. To sell a single malt was a regressive move. Just as I've sentimentalized the way scotch may have once been, Glenfiddich invites the globe to sample what they first labeled as pure malt, in the strategically designed bottle, each side of which represents one of the elemental ingredients of scotch: water, air, and malted barley. (At that point, Scotland had not yet discovered E150a.) The idea of the pure malt would catch on, and these whiskies, comprising a single distillery run from a single malting, would be more widely known as single malts, and more and more of them would penetrate foreign markets. Brands like Glenlivet, Laphroiag, and Macallan would gain footing and begin to grow a significant market share over the next forty years.

I liken this to a trend in another liquid industry: coffee. Enthusiasts and merchants of coffee have come to describe this market change as "third wave coffee," which is, simply put, a campaign to understand coffee not as a commodity but an artisanal good. This has led to more attention and resources being committed to the sourcing of coffee and a valorization of the provenance and farmer of the beans.

So, think of 1960s-era single malts as the single-origin pour-over coffee from Ethiopia you paid too much for this morning. The coffee industry stands to learn something from single malt scotch distillers, who have a decades-long head start and have grown more and more expedient in their production, subcontracting more of the production process, relying on base materials from the open market instead of grain with a greater sense of provenance, and augmenting with colorants. It's hard to anticipate how boutique coffee importers might compromise as their small producers dry up, but I'm guessing the half measure would require a certain amount of exaggeration, if not dishonesty, in how the beans are characterized or advertised—which is exactly what has happened in the whiskey trade.

Lester and I take a quick look at a few more spots in Dufftown. First is Mortlach, a distillery that is historically significant because it boasts the most complicated distilling regime in Scotland: six stills of different shapes and sizes, one of which is called the "wee witchy" and is filled three times in every single run. At the end of the eighteenth century, Mortlach was one of the first producers to get real international attention, claiming the most private customers in Scotland, and reported to send allotments directly to all the United Kingdom in addition to the United States, Australia, China, and India. Today the distillery is closed for renovations; Diageo has purchased the property and is building a second facility that will enable them to double production, which means another distillery will be pulling grain from Diageo's enormous central maltings.

I am peeved leaving Mortlach; I've tried a number of great, old-cask bottlings from this property and now it's subsumed by the beast. I turn my irritation toward Lester, who is enjoying a metal cup of tea from the Thermos he filled at the hotel that morning.

"You don't seem to care what's happening here?" I hear myself complain. I talk to him like an eighth grader who has come to understand racism and can't believe his parents continue to work and pay the mortgage in this doomed civilization.

"No, I do care," he says. "I'm just taking some time to figure out what I think."

When all this is said and done, Lester will be among the most dogmatic of scotch enthusiasts I know, disinterested in anything but a couple of the most honorable producers we've met.

The second half of this day illustrates how distillery travel can be work. We visit Craigellachie, which was bought by Bacardi in 1998 and now contributes a great deal of its whisky to Dewar's, the flagship blend in Bacardi's portfolio. Less than ten minutes down the road is Aberlour, a quite handsome distillery, where the malts are fine, unpeated in style, with bright flavors of fresh fruit. But I know that all their grain is bought from the open market, commercial yeasts are used, and the whisky is aged in barrels bought as a commodity on the open market—more and more often from the United States, where bourbon producers are forbidden by law from using a cask more than once, a stipulation that accounts for most of the world now aging their spirits in American whiskey barrels. Some of the scotch may be aged in sherry casks, but then, they may very well be sherry casks made for the sole purpose of aging scotch, that is, washed with sherry, but never actually used to age the wine. These contrivances, like using science to engineer peat levels that have never existed in nature, feel like plastic surgery.

I think about the explosion of microbrews in the 1990s that continues today, which at first was very exciting, but the more I tasted, the more they seemed the same. Grain, yeast, and hops were all bought as a commodity, often from the same purveyors. All of these beers seem like Miller or Budweiser when compared to the farmhouse ale Eric, Craig, and I enjoyed with Charles at Brasserie

Lebbe, standing in a field within a stone's throw of the barley that spawns the beer and the goats that eat the same barley in the form of spent wort, which they will shit out, thus providing fertilizer for the same grain.

In our Volvo, on the shoulder of a single-lane road not far from Dufftown, I think aloud to Lester on this topic. "I used to think it was political," I say. I'm slicing a piece of sharp Cheddar cheese using only my right hand. With my four fingers, I pry the blade of the wood-handled French pocketknife through the body of the cheese toward my anchoring thumb, slowly and carefully. Still, in my forties, I'm worried an adult will see me using a knife this way and scold me for cutting toward my hand. "What's that?" he says. Lester's glasses are on, the off-duty strings that usually anchor them slack on his shoulders.

"Well," I say, "as I got into sourcing and agriculture more, I thought the work had more meaning because it was more righteous. I think a lot of people want owning restaurants to be political work." I wait for Lester's reply as he studies his topographical road map. "But it's not. This is the luxury goods business. Really it's about quality. What's the best. Not about being morally right. Just about being really good . . ." I hand Lester a piece of white cheese and he takes it wordlessly, as I continue, "I'm tempted to think then that my work is meaningless, because it isn't political. But that's the beauty of this stuff. It shouldn't be political; it's uniquely human, the inessential experience, the pleasure of tasting something for its own sake . . ." I grow self-conscious. I can remember talking like this in the passenger seat of our old Volkswagen bus as a sophomore in high school, on the way home from basketball practice, explaining to Lester why I should be the one starting at power forward instead of the senior who currently is number one at that position. I do not even mind when Lester replies with only one syllable. "Hmm," he says. He leans toward me, holding the book of maps open with his left hand so I can see it and anchoring our current location on the page with the tip of his right index finger. "We can probably see a castle *and* do three more distilleries today if we travel like this . . ."

Chapter Seven

NORTHERN IRELAND

BUT I WAS YOUNG AND FOOLISH

As a younger man, I lived near a castle in Northern Ireland for about six months, at an age when six months is a long time. I landed there after a first attempt to escape the restaurant business; I'd been working behind the bar at a restaurant I'd helped open called One Market, near the Ferry Building in San Francisco. Strapping, in my mid-twenties, I never dreamed food and beverage was my career. I rented a cottage in the tiny seaside town of Portrush with Julia, my then-girlfriend with whom I'd bartended, and my English friend Harry who was a student at Ulster University in the town of Coleraine. Julie and I had arrived at Portrush under dramatic circumstances. To digress further, we'd been living in Paris in a hotel that paid us room and board to hand out fliers at Gare du Nord to backpackers and other budget travelers. We'd meet the morning and afternoon trains from Amsterdam and choose our targets. Because of experiencing the frustration of the stack in my left hand not diminishing because no one will grab the single flier in my right, as though they were falling victim to a con by taking a fucking piece of paper, I'll always take a flier when handed one now. Anyone who arrived at the Hotel de Belfort with one of our fliers in hand that entitled them to a discounted "traveler's rate" would also earn us a few francs on top of the room and board we were guaranteed. We would learn at the end of the day from Mohammad or Bathshir, the North African guys who ran the hotel, how many backpackers we'd caught and they'd give us our francs.

Between the two trains, we had several hours to ourselves. I would generally pass them in Chez Jeannette, a proletariat lunch counter and café with a majestically deteriorated belle époque interior including a twenty-five-foot pounded tin ceiling and nicotine-drenched canary-yellow walls. I rolled tobacco then and would pass the few hours until the next train working on horrible, thinly veiled autobiographical short stories. If I had the francs, I'd eat a baguette with ham and cornichon served on a plate only half the size of the sandwich. I'd look discreetly up from my notebook and felt-tip pens to consider the workmen having their bread with a draft Kronenbourg at the counter. They wore work caps with brims and thick, dirty atelier coats, booted feet on the brass rail, hanging on tightly to the bar top with both hands as though they might fall over backward when throwing their heads back to laugh at the saucy woman who made the sandwiches. This was only twenty years ago, but Paris felt more provincial then, supporting its workers and small café owners who gave the town its timeless cadence. What Parisians did they'd been doing for hundreds of years in roughly the same way, eating the same foods, drinking the same beverages. At that age, when my own identity was so unresolved, I envied the culture that sustained and carried along French daily life.

I was falling in love and delusional about adulthood and the plot was thickening. Julia's ex-boyfriend, Jean-Franco, was a Sicilian kickboxer who was starting to come by the train station to look for her, and the hotel to look for her, and he'd show up places we'd planned to be: "*Quelle coïncidence!*" I had never experienced true sexual jealousy until that time and was naive about where it could drive the imbalanced. I remember a lecture from Harold Bloom at Yale about the sexual obsession of Othello. Vastly overweight, Bloom wore amorphous garments and wandered slowly around the neo-Gothic classroom, reciting, completely from memory, passages that spanned many pages. That day he indulged us. "My darlings," he said. "You are young. And many of you will say to me, Dr. Bloom, I am not susceptible to sexual jealousy. I understand that one human being cannot possess another. Yes, you are enlightened, as only the very young can be, but my darlings, the day will come when you feel you are being devoured by your insides and you cannot sleep and you would do anything for relief. You will experience this pain of sexual jealousy, and you will say to yourself . . . you will say to yourself . . . Professor Bloom was correct."

Jean-Franco appeared more and more frequently, uninvited in our daily lives, clearly following Julia. Then he began asking for just one more conversation with Julia, who'd disappear with him for a few hours and try to clarify that they could not see each other, even as friends, never telling Jean-Franco we were a couple.

Late one evening, he faxed a drawing of flowers to Julia, with the inscription that he was always thinking of her and he was glad they could still be friends. The drawing was creepy, childish in its execution, the work of a nitwit, his faculties diminished by his myopic pain. On the other side of Harold Bloom's predictions for me, I now have sympathy for Jean-Franco, though his actions were reproachable. One night, Julia and I were lying naked in the single bedroom in my little room in the Hotel de Belfort. We had just finished sex and were returning to our regular rhythm of breathing when we heard a knock. Instinctively, we both stayed silent. The knocking continued for an improbable length of time, steady and consistent like a metronome, but it very gradually grew more and more intense until after what felt like ten minutes he was banging so hard that the door was giving way, trembling at its perimeter everywhere but at the hinges and lock where the door was secured. Then, thankfully, the percussion stopped. We lay silent on the bed, looking at each other in the eyes, not allowing ourselves to relax completely or speak. After some minutes, I was beginning to decide he had gone when we heard a chilling sound; the person outside knocked one more time, not at all emphatically, one soft tap then a musical knock: *knock, knock-knock-knock-knock, knock, knock,* shave and a haircut, two bits. A moment's quiet, then the door buckled at a tremendous blow from the other side. Julia mouthed the words, "Get in the bathroom," and pointed confidently. I jumped up and made it to the bathroom and pulled the door to the bathroom shut, just as the door to the room was coming off the hinges.

A low point in my masculinity, I stood naked in the bathroom, just large enough to contain a bidet, a toilet, and me, and listened as Julia shouted at him, "Calm the fuck down!" I tried to comfort myself that she wasn't afraid of him and may have experienced something along these lines before, but I was bathed in shame. I felt relief as I heard Bashir arrive at the shattered door, bellowing. The shouting gave way to emphatic speaking, which dissipated to silence, after a few moments of which, I heard another knock—that of Julia on the bathroom door. I opened the door and we locked eyes before breaking into nervous laughter.

Despite the hotel being largely empty, Bashir and Mohammed wouldn't give us a new room with an unbroken door. From their perspective, Julia had taken up with another man and deserved whatever she got.

So, Julia and I packed all we had, slept for a few hours, and then, early in the morning, before J-F could come back, took the train to London to find my friend Harry, who was home on his winter break from college. We spent a restorative few days at his family's home in the village of Witney with his five siblings, eating cheese-and-pickle sandwiches during the day and smoking joints and listening to records during the night. I don't remember if Harry convinced us to come to Portrush, what some call a resort town on the northern tip of the coast of Northern Ireland, or if we invited ourselves, but we went. I found work as a bouncer in a very large nightclub a mile outside of Portrush, where young adults would travel from any number of rural communities, often on party buses, sometimes driving themselves, which was unfortunate given the levels of intoxication most of the punters achieved, using mostly alcohol, cannabis, and MDMA. This club, Kelly's, was a destination and would draw the occasional famous DJ (many of whom may seem meaningless now): Boy George, who played records at this point, John Digweed, Sasha. On those nights, I would often be put in charge of the stage because of my size, which was vastly preferable to the catalog of shitty assignments I'd received in my tenure at Kelly's, which on my first night began with literally guarding a locked, empty room.

In Northern Ireland in the late 1990s, I encountered fewer North Americans than I'd seen in any country, except Cuba. It was a tumultuous time in Northern Ireland. The advice Harry gave Julia and me came in two installments: first, don't speak of the Troubles, which is how locals here in the North referred to the bloody stalemate between Protestants and Catholics, and second, don't call it Ireland—call it Northern Ireland. Easy enough, I thought, until my first night in the Anchor Pub, which was built of thick, white plaster and warmed by a peat fire that smelled softly of iodine, salt, and earth. The patrons sat at long tables on a Sunday in the late afternoon, drinking Guinness and Smithwick's cream ale with the occasional whiskey or brandy. Julia and I were just meeting my friend Brian Ross, who was Catholic, a minority in that part of the world. As I came to know him, he would take me further into his community: buying some hash from an IRA man, parties that were a little unnerving. Brian called out to a middle-aged man at the next table, "C'moan Fergul, you big piece of shite. Give us a song. Och, you've got to hear your man, Fergul, he's good for a song. That's for certain." Fergul stood at his table and sang a folk song based on the Yeats poem, "Down by the Salley Gardens."

> *Down by the salley gardens my love and I did meet;*
> *She passed the salley gardens with little snow-white feet.*
> *She bid me take love easy, as the leaves grow on the tree;*
> *But I, being young and foolish, with her would not agree.*
> *In a field by the river my love and I did stand,*
> *And on my leaning shoulder she laid her snow-white hand.*
> *She bid me take life easy, as the grass grows on the weirs;*
> *But I was young and foolish, and now am full of tears.*

When Fergul finished, feeling a dangerous accumulation of moisture in my eyes, I said to Julia, "I like Ireland even more than I thought."

"What's that you say?" A fellow with a short neck and a crew cut with a very clean and low hairline, his face a little red with creases in his forehead, interrupted.

"Sorry?" I said, smiling unknowingly.

"Don't be sorry, big lad," he said, affecting that phony friendliness of the bully, a tone I would apprehend too often in Northern Ireland. "I was wondering what you meant by 'Ireland'?" He wasn't smiling now.

"Oh," I said, remembering Harry's advice too late, "Well, I suppose I meant the island of Ireland . . ."

He was leaning toward me now across the space between his bench and mine. "Are we in Ireland now, big lad? Is this Ireland?" He squinted. While he was physically very small, I was frightened of him. His insides seemed combustible. I was at a loss when Brian

Ross interjected, "Aw t'fuck Sean, don't be a stupid shite. He's just landed here. Don't you git a big head with us now. I'll tell you what. Big lad here will get us three short ones, and he'll be sure mine's a brandy." As I walked to the bar to order two Bushmills and a brandy, I heard Sean soften: "Just having a bit of craic, Brian; sorry 'bout your big lad. Now we'll see you on the brandy again!"

What happened when Brian was on the brandy is for another book. This was the spring and summer of 1996, a violent time in Northern Ireland. This was especially true for me personally: in my brief tenure as a bouncer, I learned a lot about the recreation of fighting. My second night working at Kelly's, I broke up my first fight, which was between two teenagers. I had them separated and said, "Now, look! This shit has to stop. Shake hands." They looked at me, then looked at each, other and smiled a bit before shaking hands. I walked away pleased with the peace I'd made and, after I'd made it about three strides, heard the two of them topple over in a graceless grapple.

It was exhausting work, as I didn't have the benefit of rage or alcohol to fuel me. But a strange honor existed among the bouncers. You had to take out your own garbage. The other thick-necked, short, bulldog bouncers would watch with crossed arms as one of us strained to remove an offender.

One memorable fight saw two combatants and two bouncers falling down a flight of stairs. One of the brawlers hit the back of his head on a stair, and once we'd stopped them fighting, walked half-conscious out the back door. I was holding the other fellow in a full nelson and driving forward with my legs to get him clear of the building. I heaved this young man out the door of the club as if he were a large game fish I'd played for a half hour then released back into the water. But then I noticed, ten yards ahead of us, the back of the head of the man who'd walked himself out half-conscious after the tumble down the stairs. A large opening was visible at the base of his skull, probably six inches across and an inch wide and deep. A curtain of blood streamed down his neck, coloring most of his white shirt. The fellow I'd let go of started to jog toward the injured man. I shouted, "No!" and started after him but was grabbed by two of my colleagues who held me as I watched the second man bury his fist in the opening in the other's skull, producing a meaty thud and a spray of blood. They pulled me back in and closed the double doors. "Big lad, once they're in the parking lot, they're not our problem."

The next night a dazed young man approached me at my station by one of the side doors, his pupils dramatically dilated. I could not help noticing a perfectly circular, fast-bleeding wound in his right cheek. This laceration was the consequence of another clubgoer breaking a pint glass while holding tight to its base then jabbing it in his adversary's face: "jarring," they called it. I was strangely impressed, as I'd read about such barbarism recently in the novel *Trainspotting*, which had a profound effect on me.

One of the worst fights I infiltrated was between two completely unhinged women on the dance floor, which was covered with spilled beer. As I was getting between them, I lost my footing on the wet floor and the three of us tumbled over and rolled around a bit until I was on my knees holding them apart at arm's length. They were losing interest in each other and started to walk away, in opposite directions, when one of the women's crazed boyfriends—who'd been sprinting across the enormous nightclub to dive from an improbable distance—tackled me in a flying posture, bringing me back down onto the wet floor. We rolled around for what seemed five minutes. Finally, I fastened him into a full nelson and started the marathon expulsion with my comrades looking solemnly on, thick forearms crossed over their barrel chests. After shifts like these, I would drink tall cans of Harp lager, brewed in Dundalk just south of the border between the North and the Republic of Ireland,

and neat servings of Bushmills that were called "short ones." I needed hours to relax, and many hash joints smoked with my friend Harry, who also worked at Kelly's bussing glasses. I was envious of Harry: British Islanders were more accustomed to recreational violence than I. It was doing my head in.

Eventually, I would learn that all these bouncers were UVF, the Ulster Volunteer Force. The UVF, for those who don't know, is the Protestant paramilitary organization that opposes the Irish Republican Army (IRA). I was in way over my head, which was evinced by an errand in which one of the senior bouncers, Jason, insisted I participate. "Big lad, come with us. Don't say shite, just stand there, right? Just stand behind us, big lad. It'll make sense." It didn't make sense. Jason had a crowbar in his hand and the other fireplug of a man had what looked like a rolling pin. The three of us walked a couple hundred yards to the caravan park—what in the United States would be called a trailer park—that abuts the immense property on which Kelly's sits, and walked some yards farther to a caravan, or trailer, with three metal stairs leading to a small metal door with a glass square window, about a foot across. Jason reminded me of my role, "All right ye, big lad. How's your form? Remember just stand there, big as fuck . . ." He was up the stairs in one bound and through the door that gave little resistance to his low powerful shoulder. The other UVF man was through the door like Special Forces, then I bent over and entered the caravan, where I could not stand fully upright. I stood in a very wide stance and bent my head slightly. The middle-aged man, who was already enjoying his new visitors, looked at me but had no perceptible reaction to my presence. "All right then, you're the fuck out of here by tomorrow," Jason said. I think he was reiterating this arrangement. "No worries, there," said the resident of the caravan, seated on a bench-style cot that could be fastened upright to the wall of the caravan when no longer in use. All I could do was stand silently and notice my breath. The caravan smelled ripely of Regal cigarette smoke and empty Harp tins, of which there were dozens strewn about the small caravan lined with artificial wooden paneling.

As we returned to the nightclub, the other two walked fast and ahead of me, speaking with each other lightheartedly in that impenetrable Ulster accent, laughing and lighting cigarettes. They waited for me at the entrance to the Royal Bar, which was an appendage to the club where older clients could sit and drink in relative brightness and calm. "Back to the main dance floor, big lad. Don't say fuckall to Sean." Sean Murphy was the head of security, Catholic (strangely), and was away on a surfing holiday that weekend. I would try to limit myself to a cigarette an hour working at Kelly's, but that night I smoked four times my quota until the lights went up and I ordered my carryout from the bartender.

That was the summer I learned about the Drumcree riots, basically an annual occurrence. Since the nineteenth century, the Protestants had been having a celebratory parade to commemorate the great victory of William of Orange, and in the 1970s, the route of that parade became more and more significant as the Unionists, those who wanted Northern Ireland to remain part of the United Kingdom, made a point of going through Catholic neighborhoods. This was perceived as gloating by members of the Catholic community, and they would retaliate, resulting in several deaths over several years.

The year I was in Northern Ireland, in 1996, after the parade, burning vehicles, presumably set afire by UVF, blocked all roads connecting Portrush to the rest of the world. When I arrived at work one of these nights and realized that only Sean Murphy, Harry, one other college student from Cornwall, and I were all that was left of the floor and security staff of about forty, I finally understood that all the guys I worked with were paramilitaries.

Bushmills will always be Northern Ireland for me and remind me of the violence and confusion I endured there as a young man.

The distillery itself is in the town of Bushmills, only six miles from Portrush. I first visited the distillery with my father and stepmother, who had come up for a visit from Dublin where my father, a Joycean, went for Bloomsday, a local celebration of the novel *Ulysses* and all things Joyce. To them, Portrush and the North seemed hard and joyless, unlike their beloved South. Like my friend Charles, who affects distaste for Parisians in allegiance with his family-in-law, I was disdainful of the South and its absence of strife—a strange frame of mind, looking back on it. One afternoon my parents insisted on taking us south of the border to Donegal, and I swear, as soon as we were across the national border between Northern Ireland and the Republic of Ireland, color returned to the landscape and architecture. People were smiling. Live music could be heard in the pubs. We ate fish and chips, drank Guinness, and I fought back tears as I felt a tautness that had been gripping me for weeks begin to dissipate, sitting there with my father, strong-shouldered and bearded. I didn't want him or Mary-Kay to leave. I wanted to get out of Northern Ireland and return to the comfort of a restaurant job in San Francisco, where I always had a hundred dollars in my jeans.

On their last full day, we all agreed we should visit the distillery, located in this tiny Protestant town where they painted the curbs red, white, and blue in honor of the queen. I was twenty-six and Bushmills was the first distillery I had ever visited. I don't remember much of it, except that the tour felt rehearsed. In the tasting portion, the host asked for a volunteer, and I obliged him. He asked me to taste a series of whiskies: a bourbon, a scotch, and Bushmills, and then say which I preferred. I had been drinking too much whiskey for a few years at that point and could easily differentiate the styles, choosing Bushmills intentionally each time while being sure to indicate I knew which was which, until the last when they gave me a taste of the relatively new Bush Malt and a Scottish malt. To our guide's disappointment, I pointed at the scotch. I left with a signed document indicating I was a certified whiskey taster, a qualification I've actually listed on resumes.

I now know that Pernod Ricard had already bought Bushmills when I visited in 1996, and that there was a diversification going on of their offerings: Black Bush, the green label Bushmills, Bushmills Malt. I didn't know then what I do now, but even so the visit felt a little rotten, there in the center of Ulster (the Protestant name for Northern Ireland), one of the most culturally specific places I've ever been. Twelve years later, Diageo would buy the distillery, and as of this writing is close to trading it to Jose Cuervo for the remaining half of the brand Don Julio. So the oldest distillery in the world, founded in 1601, in the birthplace of the column or column still, will likely be owned by a Mexican company and use engineered enzymes in their production. I remember learning to bartend in the 1980s and early '90s and being told that Unionists drink Bushmills and Republicans drink Jameson, and for a period of time these both have been owned by Diageo, which holds the Guinness portfolio, which includes Jameson whiskey and their eponymous, famous stout. The moral of this story is unclear or nonexistent.

Then I was twenty-six, and in the summer I would turn twenty-seven. There in Portrush, I was thinking of Jim Morrison, Janice Joplin, and Kurt Cobain, wondering if I, too, would die that year. I can only hope, twenty years from now, that my worries of today are as unfounded as those fears, but in fairness to my younger self, I was looking for meaning in travel, in place, in the spirits I drank—and now it is all a little wobbly. A kind of schizophrenia emerges when you love a whiskey and connect it, with deep emotion, to a particular place it claims to be from, only to learn it's not of that place in the way you thought. I find myself furious at companies that affect integrity and lie to consumers about their history and values.

One would need to take this stuff a little too seriously to write a book about it. And I do.

Chapter Eight

SCOTLAND, PART II

GIN A BODY KISS A BODY /
NEED A BODY CRY?

It is worth noting that in 1923, only a few years after an apex of production during the late nineteenth century, merely six distilleries were legally in operation in Scotland. Our industry is volatile and perilous. For this reason, we are all prone to compromise. For example, I use gin and American whisky in cocktails because it is more affordable and allows me to buy more of the bespoke spirits I love. These companies have to survive, and when they do survive and another, larger company is willing to buy them, it must be hard to say no. If someone offered me ten million for my two bars, I'd sell them in an instant and write more purple prose about the importance of not compromising. This is the direction of the species, but I hope to help you understand the truth of where we are in this project, to encourage you in the direction of the spirits that connect you to the place they were made, especially when the place they were made is somewhere you want to be. And the truth is, today, Scotland is somewhere I want to be.

Back in Scotland in 2016, Lester and I are nearing our castle, Auchindoun, the ruins of which rise slowly above the horizon ahead and to our right. We find an area to park near the unlabeled trailhead whose entire path is evident from the roadside, winding a mile or so through thick moist grass, to the ruins of the castle perched atop a strategic mound of earth. We set forth, both in our lightweight REI hiking boots, along the narrow earthen walkway, long stalks of grass whipping our legs and dampening our jeans as we make progress. I am invigorated in this moment, experiencing the same phenomenon another might have six hundred years ago. Informed by the same apparatus of sense humans have always trusted, I watch a castle built in the fifteenth century grow larger with each step I take. If I dig in with my senses, smelling the grass and earth, feeling and hearing the ageless wind, I am freed from any context of history and I am another human animal, having the same experience as my distant ancestor, free of self-consciousness, engaged. So I suppose I want my scotch to be like the experience of walking up to a castle. Ideally, technology has not extenuated my sense of the liquid; I like to close my eyes and travel through the flavor to the grain that engendered the whisky, just as someone experienced a similar flavor a hundred years ago. I am interested in spirits that are made in a noninterventionist way because how they taste is more timeless. In tasting spirits like this, I am united with all those who enjoyed a primitive concoction of barley, yeast, water, peat, and fire in the past.

I have pulled ahead of Lester a bit on the walk toward Auchindoun, enjoying the spring of the damp earth beneath the thin soles of my boots, cushioning each stride and enervating my ankles, knees, and hips that are beginning to ache chronically—the beginning of middle age, or maybe the middle of middle age. I pause to study a dead sheep at the side of the walkway—its mouth open wide, showing rows of brown teeth, a smear of red paint, indicating who owns the animal, marks the white fur coating its rib cage that I notice is not rising and falling gently as it once did.

The last hundred yards of the walk carry us up a steep incline to a plateau, where we are greeted by a tall, deteriorating stone wall, close to three feet deep and, at its most intact, about eight feet in height. I stoop and move through a doorway, and as I stand upright, I am separated from the castle, in beautiful disarray, by only a lawn, about ten yards across, bathed in cold Scottish sunlight and carpeted with violet heather. The bones of the castle are still intact and you get a sense that, really, this was a large family home with three stories. We can see the cellars on the ground level and the hall was on the first floor, with the living quarters on the second. A number of these rooms are relatively intact, with the occasional window breaching the sturdy stone fortress. Standing back from one window, through the aperture in the lichen-studded, slate-colored stone, I make out a continuum of rolling hills, the crest of each wearing sunlight that illuminates an endless variety of greens punctuated by groves of trees, farmhouses, and planted land with no end in sight, the furthest visible pale gray-green slope abutting a colorless blue sky.

Scotland does a mindful job of taking care of its national parks and monuments, and Auchindoun is no exception. We are able to wander up and explore the construction as though it were our discovery, until finding evidence of other visitors in the form of a large plaque, mounted at waist level, that describes some of the castle's violent history. Its earliest recorded mention is in 1509, when it was owned by Sir James Ogilvy who entrusted "the mains Auchindoun with its castle, fortalice and castle hill" to his nephew Alexander, who in 1567 would then sell Auchindoun to Sir Adam Gordon, a relative of the Earl of Huntley and an active participant in clan warfare. In 1571, Gordon ordered an attack on nearby Corgarff Castle, the possession of his rival, John Forbes, connected to the famous Mackintosh clan. Forbes would survive the attack and burning of the castle, but his wife, Margaret, and twenty-four other people, including his children, died. This violence was the consequence of religious and tribal rivalry between the Gordon and Forbes families, Catholics and Protestants respectively. William Mackintosh, seeking vengeance, attacked and burned Auchindoun, for which he was beheaded. The massacre at Corgarff is commemorated in the *Ballad of Edom o'Gordon*.

> *Come doun to me, ye lady gay,*
> *Come doun, come doun to me;*
> *This night sall ye lig within mine arms,*
> *To-morrow my bride sall be.*
> *I winna come down, ye fals Gordon,*
> *I winna come down to thee;*
> *I winna forsake my ain dear lord,*
> *That is sae far frae me.*
> *Gie owre your house, ye lady fair,*
> *Gie owre your house to me;*
> *Or I sall brenn yoursel therein,*
> *But and your babies three.*

We listened to a recording of the song by Scottish folk singers Malinky several times over as we drove toward Benromach Distillery.

> *O bonnie, bonnie was her mouth,*
> *And cherry were her cheiks,*
> *And clear, clear was her yellow hair,*
> *Whereon the red blood dreips.*
> *Then wi' his spear he turn'd her owre;*
> *O gin her face was wane!*
> *He said, "Ye are the first that e'er*
> *I wish'd alive again."*
> *He turn'd her owre and owre again;*
> *O gin her skin was white!*
> *"I might hae spared that bonnie face*
> *To hae been some man's delight."*

Any property would have seemed muted in the wake of the visceral experience of Auchindoun Castle and the subsequent history and poetry. Once, but no longer, owned by Diageo, Benromach uses water from the nearby Chapelton Spring, but, of course, the grain has no known provenance and the maltings are outsourced with a precisely calculated level of peat, 10 ppm phenols, with some experimental distilling happening throughout the year at higher and lower levels of peat. Where is the violence of this place, the tribal history, the uncompromising, long-haired beardness of this place? Not in this bottle.

The next day we drive to Wolfburn, the northernmost distillery on the Scottish mainland, and one of the six independent distilleries. It was begun by independent investors and is run by Shane Fraser, formerly of Glenfarclas, an old, independent distillery. The facility is remote and functional, a small complex of low-roofed buildings with aluminum siding. We arrange a tour, not with any of the principals but rather with a friend of the outfit, a retired police officer with no great knowledge of distilling but smart enough to have absorbed some relevant information. At this point, they have been distilling for three years and are about to release their first young bottling. Our kind host lets us try some of the young spirit out of the cask, never a chore for me, like appraising the potential of a fledgling athlete. Only just beginning to show its age in a mixture of different-size bourbon barrels and sherry casks, the young spirit is made with the water from the nearby Wolfburn (*burn* is one of the many words for "river" or "stream") and maltings from Bairds, a large corporate malting company. It has a light, fragrant style. One of the cooler things about the project is the label, with its primitive wood-block print of Scotland's mythological sea wolf that inhabits both sea and land. While this distillery required a whole day of travel for only one producer and our guide was warm though hardly expert, Wolfburn is a good one to check off our list and we look forward to tasting the older spirit. But clearly this is a financial venture as much as anything. With four years of operating revenue set aside so they can guard inventory and not cannibalize new stock, Wolfburn's two seasoned investors hand-picked industry insiders and seem to have a pretty clear plan; one wonders if they are flipping it (that is, developing a brand to sell on to a larger group for a nice payday). Who could blame them?

Next we are off to the islands, which is our favorite, really. From Ullapool, an early morning ferry takes us to Stornoway on the Isle of Lewis, where we are excited to revisit Abhainn Dearg Distillery, one of the most compelling places I've ever been. We have allowed ourselves time to visit the Callanish stone circles, dating from 1800 BCE, where we wander the forty-three by thirty-seven-foot round built of tall stones made from Lewisian gneiss, the coarse-grained rock commonly used for building on the island. Pathways lead from the circle in each direction, with single rows of stones to the east, south, and west, and a double row just east of north. From the sky, the collection of monoliths would appear something like a pagan cross. On this cold morning, we walk through the stones, feeling the full assault of human history, as we often have on these trips. My stepfather and I are wandering apart. I watch him from my place, a hundred yards away, assured he is relishing this moment as I do, affected by this physical evidence of the mystical history of Scotland, which continues to deliver this morning with its simultaneous rain and sunshine.

"Desolate" is a word someone might use to describe the route from the stone circle to Abhainn Dearg Distillery; one does not see much life; the landscape lining the jagged road is hard and low, comprised of shaggy Hebridean grasses and stone beneath the ever-changing Scottish sky that at this moment is a dark, stone-gray as it canopies the ancient stones disappearing in our rear-view mirror. The road *is* desolate and harsh, but it is also peaceful, even comforting, somehow indicative in this contradiction of Scotland as a people and a place. The countryside is stony and, at times, uninviting, but beneath throbs a boundless life force built of ample water tables and aromatic earth. As you study Scotland and travel its surface, you grow aware of a profound depth of resources, informed by its less-visible oil industry and brimming salmon farms that are often only apparent by the acre or so of thrashing fish at the water's surface in a pen in the midst of a loch. Studying a topographical map of Lewis, the island's countless small bodies of water give it the impression of having been shot by a shotgun, whose shot sprayed across the surface of the map. The road from Callanish is long and has only one lane, with the occasional shoulder that allows one car to pull aside to create space for the oncoming one—a custom that delights Lester, who chuckles to himself as he races to grab the shoulder and secure the pleasure of chivalry before the other car pulls to the left, then the courteous waves between drivers coupled with affable head nods.

We hug the northern coast of the island as we navigate westward along a small bay on a road that rises and falls, betraying the occasional dramatic view of coastline, which, with its white sand and cobalt surface, seems Mediterranean or Caribbean, though I know from experience it is not. At last, we descend to the base of a small valley between two steep hills, creating a little cove of the bay to the right. We pull into a gravel lot and see the unremarkable architecture of the distillery. Abhainn Dearg (pronounced *Aveen JERrak*) is the westernmost distillery in Scotland and, at the time of this writing, the smallest, producing thirty thousand liters per year. Its proprietor, Mark Tayburn, or Marko, is as elusive as Nessie, the Loch Ness monster. Both Lester and I have met him before, and, while he is not as expressive as a Northern Californian, he is diffident and warm in that Scottish way of not saying a single word of exaggeration. We've never received a tour from Marko. He's usually not there; maybe he's away procuring a cow or in Spain with his son getting a sherry cask. Lester is particularly driven to help me get a proper hour with Marko and a tape recorder, but it seems unlikely. On one occasion, when someone did answer the phone whom Lester felt *sure* was Marko, the speaker insisted Marko was away. The ones who do it for love have less time for you.

Marko was a slater, basically a roofer, when he decided to make a Lewis scotch, which is built with the water from the river that gives the place its name. *Abhainn Dearg* means "red river," and is named such for the massacre, centuries ago, of invading, then defeated, Vikings whose blood colored the river water. Charles Maclean describes the distillery as the most artisanal in Scotland and I, with my more limited experience, do not disagree. All of the grain comes from Lewis, and Marko will soon be using only crops he himself has farmed: 'Golden Promise,' an heirloom variety of barley, the *draff*, or husks, of which feeds his Highland cattle. The stills are handmade and derivative of those used on Lewis for illicit distilling, which look like witches hats, crudely cobbled together from rough copper. His grain is left to germinate on the concrete floor, and then dried in a small trough that is heated by a tiny hearth beneath it. Everything is rough and pleasantly unclean.

In Marko's stead, we are shown around by Joanie MacDonald, the matriarch of the place, who is one of Abhainn Dearg's three employees, including Marko. Today we walk around the small utilitarian buildings, which feel more like an eccentric's work sheds than a licensed distillery, and chat freely. Joanie has a wary, suspicious quality, letting your words sit on the table in front of you, so maybe you understand they are a little trivial, before picking them up and replying. She has thick strawberry-blond hair that is beginning to gray. Before helping out Marko, she worked for decades as a psychiatric nurse on the mainland. I mention that my brother is a psychiatric nurse and has his complaints about the state of the trade. "Och, it's nonsense," she says. "None of these people are crazy, they just want someone to take care of them." When asked if she likes scotch, she explains she never drinks it. "I know it comes in a bottle and my husband used to drink it," she says.

We've seen the property before and there's not much to it, but I enjoy Joanie's company as she goes through the paces of her tour, not giving us any more information than we received the year before, with no emotional connection to the work of distilling, but she is emblematic of this place, being from here, and being the engine that keeps the commercial aspect of this business running. We pause in the tasting barn and revisit the two *finishes*, meaning whiskies finished in different casks, one sherry and bourbon. They will be blended ultimately, maybe for the release of the ten-year, which used to be the standard by which a distillery was judged until inventories became diminished and distillers started selling younger and younger spirits in the form of named proprietary blends, like the Macallan Ruby, the Ardbeg Uigeadail, or the Laphroaig Cairdeas. Cynics, myself among them, feel these non-age-statement (NAS) whiskies are a way of selling younger inventory, often with added coloring, while commoditizing this idea of prestige, though I have tasted fine NAS whiskies made by reputable producers.

Back in the barn, we enjoy tasting the new make spirit, the clear distillate right from the still, and some of each wood finish. The young spirit has an electric, cereal, heathered flavor, leaving a residue of honey on the palate and a whisper of iodine in the finish. Showing some of that balsa-flavored astringency of young whisky, it is raw and vital, and I can't wait to taste these spirits when they're older—and more than this, I can't wait to try Marko's subsequent bottlings made entirely from his own grain. It's amazing to believe that this will make him the only distiller in all of Scotland who curates every facet of the production, and in so doing, he may actually be saving the category, or at least preserving a connection with its origins.

We finish our morning with Joanie, who shares her memories of the Isle of Lewis from her childhood. "My parents were crofters," she says. *Crofters* were people who worked rented farms. "They made everything themselves. This way of life was only possible because we'd all help each other. We'd go to the other's place and help them and they'd come to ours. Now it's not possible. People don't help each other like that anymore. The island has changed." I ask her if she likes Abhainn Dearg because of the ways in which it is reminiscent of older times. She looks at me without expression. "Oh, I wouldn't know about that. Maybe so." She's not being mean—she's just not interested in that conversation. Things are the way they are, and I agree. As much as one fetishizes the past, we have no choice but to be content in the present. Or not. We fill a box with as many 500-ml bottles of Abhainn Deargh as we can carry. As the whisky is only sold on premise, one must travel to the Isle of Lewis to buy it, so why waste the trip?

I worry Lester is disappointed we didn't get more time with Marko than the brief exchange we enjoyed at our first visit, but to me the distiller's elusiveness seems appropriate. His labor is one of love and is its own reward; people in scotch gossip, and others have criticized Marko for being grumpy, for not being hospitable. One reseller told me he said, "Why the fuck would I sell scotch to you? What would I have to sell for myself?" While the teller of this story affected outrage at Marko's tone, I feel pretty certain from experience that he was simply being direct, not hostile. The lack of veneer is in keeping with the rough-hewn thirty thousand liters of whisky, which Marko doesn't need help selling. In our times at the distillery, we've seen people from all over the globe. The Japanese in particular, Joanie told us, with their love of pure ingredients, come in droves.

A small isthmus connects the Isles of Lewis and Harris, for which we are bound when we head up the far hill out of the tiny valley that houses Abhainn Dearg. The coastline is ablaze with radiant Scottish sunshine that cheers us as we drive with our windows down, breathing the fresh air tinged with salt and grass and the smell of the shit of Highland cattle that line the road in patches, anonymous with long, shaggy hair that obscures all details of their faces. A tiny peninsula catches our attention, spotted with sheep and thrusting into the deepest blue version of the Atlantic I've ever seen. Lester is always up for a walk, so I'm not surprised when he pulls over without a word and we're away toward the ocean on this walkway of green grass, about one hundred yards across and several hundred yards in length. The sheep keep their distance, but one ram stands defiantly in profile against the choppy water in the background, his long woolly coat being blown by the wind. At the edge of the headland, I peer down and see jagged crevices lined with lichen and jutting weeds, at the bottom of which seawater roils, clapping into the steep walls that climb toward me. I gingerly make my way down a steep, rocky descent to the water's edge but stop short, about eight feet above water level, on a broad plateau of rock smoothed by the elements. I stare out over the Atlantic and think to myself, *I am at the world's edge.*

The SWA lists five regions of scotch production in Scotland: Lowland, Highland (which includes the islands), Speyside, Campbeltown, and Islay. Most connected to the industry seem to agree these regions don't mean what they used to, as little or none of the peat, yeast, or grain used today are at all regionally specific; they come often from as far as Eastern Europe. Most of the stylistic decisions a distillery will make have nothing to do with the raw materials but rather with fermentation, distillation, and aging. And none of these factors are tied to the place in which they're performed. In fairness, one aspect that seems to remain tied to region is which waters are used, as the sources for them are generally quite local. Still, the finished product seems largely determined, particularly when caramel is added and the spirits are chill filtered, which most are. Scotch today is not unlike the scientifically driven wines of the height of the California boom, or digital music as compared to analog by the latter's greatest advocate, Neil Young. We are interested in analog spirits, where the collision of wild forces yields unpredictable results.

In the last twenty-five years, companies, particularly the large ones, have used this idea of region to promote their scotch. From DCL's "Ascot Malt Cellar" in 1982, to United Distillers' (now Diageo) "Classic Malts," included in which are Talisker, which the company describes as "powerful, smoky, made by the sea—Talisker is renowned for its maritime character." Also in the collection is Dalwhinnie, "as sweet and accessible as its Highland home is remote," and what has become a peaty caricature of the supposed Islay style, Lagavulin: "The biggest. The most intense. The definitive whisky." These and other smaller companies have drawn on vinous ideas of connoisseurship, where regional appellations like Bordeaux and Burgundy fetch premium prices, just as they hope the historic regionalism and tribalism of Scotland will solicit a similar audience. The reality of scotch is that the main consumers and producers of the last hundred and fifty years have been those of blends, which have relatively little regional identity, as they are built of malts from various regions and a majority of neutral spirit. Much as the patrons who buy cognac from the big houses do, blended scotch consumers rely on blenders to have specific styles of whisky they accomplish perennially, which thus allows the blender to calculate and preserve their house style and enables the consumer to have confidence that their blend of choice will remain the same.

My favorite scotch writer, Charles Maclean, expands upon the topic in his book *Whiskypedia,* asserting that regionalism is not particularly relevant with single malts as well as blends:

> *The truth is that it is not location—terroir—that dictates the style of a whisky. It is tradition ... the style, character and flavor of any malt whisky come from two principal sources: the way it is made and the way it is matured. The way it is made embraces the peating levels in the malt, the way the malt is processed, how long the wash is fermented, the size of the stills and how they are operated, the style of the condenser (traditional worm tub or "shell-and-tube")—above all, the craft of whisky making: how each individual distillery makes its whisky, and has been making it for decades. ... If they choose to, the owner of distillery x (on Islay) can make a "highland style malt" (and they do, see Caol Ila, Ardbeg, Bruichladdich) while distillery y (on Speyside) can produce a smoky "Islay" style (and they do: see BenRiach, Benromach).*

No scotch region has done a better job of marketing and commodifying the regionality of their whisky than the Islay producers, largely thanks to the multinational efforts of Lagavulin, Laphroiag, and Bowmore—which, it is worth noting, are run by Diageo and Beam Suntory, respectively.

Much as I loved the fullest-bodied Zinfandels and Cabernets when I first became interested in wine, I gravitated toward the famous peaty style of Islay. In the last twenty years, I've come to regard both styles as the result of engineering. Nonetheless, I am always excited to return to Islay where I will see one of my favorite independent producers as well as the canonical champions of the briny Islay style: Laphroiag, Lagavulin, Ardbeg. One of our first sightings upon arriving at the Port Ellen ferry landing on Islay is

Diageo's Port Ellen maltings facility, which looks a bit like the Death Star as it looms over the coastline. It is malting and kiln-drying grain, not the devil's work, but it is nevertheless responsible for the homogenization of scotch whisky: the peaty characteristic of most scotches produced in Scotland can be traced to this facility, which relies on the Castle Hill peat bog, three thousand tons of which are harvested a few miles from the maltings.

This trip we are staying in the town of Bowmore, famous for the eponymous distillery that still does 30 percent of its own maltings. Old single casks of Bowmore are some of Lester's all-time favorites, but the commercial blends of late have not excited him; Bowmore was one of the first distilleries we visited together. The town of Bowmore reminds me of Portrush in Northern Ireland, with its three or four roads parallel to the waterfront lined with unremarkable midcentury industrial homes. Walking to our hotel from our parking place some blocks away, we smell peat smoke coming from every chimney on this cold July night. It is an enchanting smell, a fusion of shit, iodine, seaweed, and salt. Tonight is Friday and we arrive at the modest, two-storied hotel, which is painted flat white with navy blue shutters. Seemingly, this place is also one of the few destination nightspots in this tiny town. I feel myself tense, again reminded of Portrush, moving through the bar that is elbow to elbow with shit-faced punters of all ages who seem keen to fight or have intercourse with each other. Only time will tell.

We have a mediocre dinner in the restaurant next door. I have venison with a juniper sauce, which reads much better than the reality: overcooked meat with a thin, watery gravy with hard juniper berries. Lester has an enormous bowl of mussels. The proprietor, a man of about Lester's age, takes a great interest in him. "How 'bout you lads. Good to see you again. Thank you for coming back." He rests his hand on Lester's shoulder. "Remind me where yous is from? Canada?" We've never seen him before, and Lester offers,

"Well, we're from California, but we've never been to this hotel . . . though we do come to Islay sometimes." The owner disappears suddenly and without a word, leaving us to our thoughts and some attempts at shouted conversation over the din from next door. ("Is he the owner?!" I shout conversationally. "What?!") As suddenly as he left, the presumed owner is back, this time with a large, framed photograph that he shows to Lester. He seems uninterested in me. Lester takes it and shows me the photograph of our man wearing a three-piece suit and standing in front of a massive Lincoln Continental with a California license plate. Apparently, he'd lived in California. Judging by the vintage of the car and the evidence of passed time in the man's face, this California tenure had been several decades ago.

"Do you want to see what I drive now?!" he asks, as though this information will really rev our engines. I hear this, but it is easy to pretend I don't as I take an intense interest in my venison. Lester is dragged by the cuff from the dining room and stays away with his new friend for about ten minutes. He looks exasperated upon his return and finishes his meal quickly before we pay the check and retire to our filthy, tiny rooms, which are directly above the bar. We pass a few minutes in my room before turning in, during which Lester explains our host had been a little handsy. "So many touches," he says. In my twenties, I had trouble imagining people in their forties as sexual beings. Now, in my forties, I am certain I will feel every bit as sexually relevant in my seventies as I do now, as did our friend who once drove a Lincoln Continental with his long hair blowing in the wind down Highway 1 forty years ago. Failing to sleep in the two tiny beds pushed together that were advertised as a twin, with the treble-heavy sounds of Eurobeat dance music permeating the floor that separated me from the bar, I feel a moment's pride for Lester that this man took an interest in him. Life is long and every minute of it is rich.

I wake without an alarm at 6:30 the next morning, and lie there worrying the same worries as ever: bankruptcy, irrelevance in my community, prison for tax debt. On a good day, I get to worry about cancer or retirement, so unrelenting is the constant chatter in my brain about small-business concerns, but the full Scottish elevates my spirits, and as the strong, black tea enters my bloodstream, I am enlivened, remembering why I am here. Lester opts for coffee this morning and regrets the gamble. Today is the first day on Islay, and I'm psyched to breathe the amazing air and drive around the island listening to Celtic radio on the BBC, which is going strong as we alight for the Bruichladdich distillery. The short journey will carry us in a semicircle around the heart of the small bay that penetrates to the center of the island of Islay. We are lucky, with three consecutive songs on the Celtic station—haunting and moving, women sing in a percussive yet lilting tongue that really does remind me of the Scandinavian languages. It is blissful having no idea what the singer is saying, yet feeling it full-blast in the chest as the tension I woke with, that I wake with most days, begins to evaporate. I am contented beside my stepfather; with him I am a child and a man at the same time, and feel for some lovely minutes that nothing is wrong. California is asleep and no checks will bounce, no tax collectors will call, no one will email asking me for money I don't have until at least five this afternoon.

We arrive at Bruichladdich, which sits right on the edge of the bay and is painted with the iconic thick, matte white but accented with bright, aquamarine details, a clue as to the unpretentious atmosphere Bruichladdich works hard to maintain. We're five minutes early, and I pass on Lester's invitation to stroll along the water's edge. Instead I watch him as I sit listening to the news in Gaelic, delighting in the utter mystery of the language with the occasional cognate or modern word that I recognize: "Brexit," "Nice." This is the week when the world witnessed a man drive a white truck through a crowd in the jewel of the French Riviera, crushing human life in its path.

Even in a language I don't understand, the news is unbearable. The nationalist decision of the UK to remove itself from its growing European community couples with the endless accounts of sectarian and secular violence to give one the idea that the world is collapsing inward—at least, that's what many would have us believe. I understand why people cling to artisanal goods in these times. Food and drink have a tactile clarity; they are comforting and can tie us to a tradition, a community, an ecosystem. Americans, consumers that we are, take solace in the quality of what we eat and drink now more than we ever did. We show each other photographs of it constantly, hungering for the connectedness of common experience. The story of the small-batch, handmade, grower-producer is comforting to us because it connects us to a rustic past rather than a merciless, unknown future. We want the world to change, but we want it to stay the same, even to regress; food enables us to be nostalgic while always trying something new.

Nowhere is this paradox more apparent than Bruichladdich, which calls itself "the progressive Hebredian distillery" while doing more than almost anyone to champion the antique tropes of barley variety, provenance, terroir, and traceability, arguably the ideas that most interest me applied to the production of sprits. The spirit of the place is emblematized by the optimistic aquamarine color, which the proprietors refer to as "laddie green," that augments the whole distillery, from packaging to barrel heads to the detailing of the white distillery buildings. The myth is that the water stretching out before the distillery was exactly this color the morning the deal was inked for Mark Reynier of Murray McDavid to take over Bruichladdich just before Christmas in 2000.

It is 10:00 and we are crossing the road to visit Bruichladdich again; this will be our second visit. I've asked the favor of a private tour of a very sharp woman named Emily, who works for Rémy Cointreau, the multinational that bought Bruichladdich in 2012 from a small group of investors. Included in the group of investors was the legendary distiller Jim McEwan, who has presided over multiple distilleries for more than fifty years, including Lester's beloved Bowmore in better years. McEwan announced in April that he would retire in July, the very month I am writing this.

Since my last visit to Bruichladdich, I have been conflicted, loving their old, unpeated whiskies and the beautiful Victorian facility but cynical of the brand's pervasive marketing since the purchase of the company in 2000 by a group of private investors, and the expanded production since the subsequent acquisition by Rémy Cointreau in 2012. My hope is to be won over once and for all by the distillery that was one of my favorites for a period.

We are greeted by Raymond, who shakes our hands and leads us energetically toward the interior of the property. He explains that we'll have a private tour with him, and then join a group that's enjoying the cellar's tasting. My hope is that this tour isn't canned, and that we get some access to the unrehearsed side of Raymond. Truly, it is a mixture of both, comprised of humorous anecdotes about the distillery and the charismatic people who work there, but also Ray answers questions freely and honestly, which is refreshing and differentiates him from most distillery tour guides.

The equipment at Bruichladdich is largely from the Victorian era, which the producers believe contributes to the timelessness of the distillates. When we first toured Bruichladdich, it had just been sold to Rémy Cointreau. I was nervous that another independent was being assimilated into a larger company, especially when I heard that they would be doubling production. The reality is Bruichladdich had huge inventories of its famous unpeated Islay malt that the distillery was able to sell to keep afloat while developing an inventory of the new Jim McEwan spirit, before the property was acquired by Rémy Cointreau, which doesn't appear to want to change the identity of Bruichladdich. The old, unpeated whiskies are beautiful, and Raymond concurs that they were sold too cheaply. I can remember buying these old bottlings for a great price, thinking I was falling in love with the new Bruichladdich until I realized I'd been falling in love with the old one while we waited for the McEwan stock to age.

In the fifteen years they've been distilling since the mothballed distillery was resuscitated, they've gone to market with more limited releases than have been seen from any other scotch distillers. "To be a complete collector of Bruichladdich, you'd have to be a fucking billionaire," Raymond jokes, and he is not far from the truth. To wander the gift shop or tasting room at the distillery is to be lost in shelf after shelf of limited releases by Bruichladdich, all of them in the trademark bright packaging that reminds us that this is the progressive Hebridean distillery. This confusion is compounded by the fact that the distillery produces three separate marks: the still unpeated Bruichladdich; the heavily peated Port Charlotte line at 40 parts per million (ppm) of phenols, the molecular compounds that imbue scotch with its peaty quality; and the superheavily peated Octomore line, having accomplished the heights of 258 ppm with an eye toward a never-achieved 310 ppm. So, with Bruichladdich we see the great paradox of the liquor game embodied in spades: innovation concurrent with traditionalism. Bruichladdich grasps at the best of both worlds, relying on science to engineer exaggerated concentrations of peat while taking pride in its Victorian origins and the fine tradition of the unpeated Islay.

Raymond was refreshingly candid about the financial pressures Bruichladdich had endured, from selling old inventory at too low a price for cash flow, to the maltster who'd given them grain on credit for months, to how strapped they were at the point Rémy Cointreau purchased the company. He also gave a priceless demonstration with a vial of E150a, in which he added a drop of it to a three-year-old scotch to create "a twenty-five-year-old scotch." He abstracted the problem with caramel color as effectively as I've ever heard: "They say it doesn't affect flavor. Bollocks. Smell it. If 5 parts per million of phenols dramatically change a whisky's flavor, what's this shite doing?" The three-year in combination with a pin's head of the stuff appeared auspicious and brown, and had that smell: the subtle redolence of warm, flat Coca-Cola. I am confident Bruichladdich does not use the stuff.

Four years further into small business ownership, I feel more compassion for Bruichladdich than I did when they first sold the beautiful, oceanfront property to a French corporation. On that first tour, our host said it was a good thing they'd be doubling production because more people would get work. I was inwardly cynical, thinking if you make twice as many sandwiches in the same amount of time, your sandwiches aren't going to be as good, my favorite metaphor. Some years later, though, the distillery has more than eighty employees. Compare that to some of the Diageo distilleries I've visited, like Lagavulin and Caol Isla, which are largely automated and have fewer than ten employees, leaving them feeling haunted and empty until you get to the command center, where one to a few people are remote-controlling every aspect of the endeavor. This human scarcity was most palpable at Cameronbridge, where we wandered acres of the plant that produces hundreds of millions of liters and saw only six other people, five in the cockpit and one, who seemed to be there for our benefit, in the blending room.

Calories have value, especially when they are liquor, and every distiller has pressures, be they simply surviving or the demands by shareholders for greater performance. I judge far less than I used to. I am comforted that Bruichladdich is surviving and employing as many people on the island as they do, while still playing the dilettante and experimenting with some really neat stuff. They treat scotch like the agricultural product it is, producing site-specific scotches, organically produced scotches, and Islay-specific scotches, among other compelling experiments. At the same time, though, they are on the knife's edge of determined flavors, using science to generate hyperbolically peated whiskies the likes of which the world has never known. This contradiction confounds a little, and with the recent departure of their patriarch distiller, one fears the distillery is in danger of being top-heavy and rudderless. But you must root for Bruichladdich, with its warm personnel and sense of adventure.

So, Bruichladdich regains its rank as an emotional favorite, though it also remains an enigma. We repeat the rhythm of our first visit to Islay five years ago when we traveled from the anticipated Bruichladdich to a new distillery, Kilchoman, which takes us fourteen minutes to reach. Traveling east, we pass the occasional peat farm, evident by the wall of cleanly exposed earth where segments of peat have been harvested. The roads are long and lined by abundant, boggy meadows of multicolored grasses, from dried and red to vibrant green to almost blue when compared with the dome of a silvery-blue sky decorated with plaster-white cumulus clouds that seem painted. We stop first at the ancient settlement of Kilchoman, with the simple ruin of a church that was built in the 1820s replacing a medieval church, of which no evidence remains. The most striking evidence of the site's ancient origins is the large Kilchoman cross. Almost eight feet in height and three feet across, it was carved in the fourteenth or fifteenth century and, with its carved figures and ornaments miraculously unmolested by lichen, is a great example of the Iona school. This cross adorns the Kilchoman whisky label. Benefiting from the ever-changing Scottish weather, we are suddenly in the midst of a crisp, perfectly clear day. Machir Bay, for which one of Kilchoman's scotches is named, spreads out before us, and we stroll the grounds looking at tombstones and taking deep draughts of nourishing Scottish air. I pause at a tombstone that commemorates the life of a wife and mother of five children, all of whom died in childbirth. I foolishly take a photograph of the stone; like many of us in the twenty-first century, I don't know what else to do in the face of something really moving.

My wife and I are trying to have a baby and have known only abbreviated pregnancies, which are challenging enough, but they draw into stark relief what matters, and to my wife and me what matters is each other. The prospect of having a child is forced into the context of success or failure, which puts tremendous pressure on a woman: what if, ultimately, it doesn't happen the "natural" way? Then adoption becomes the only option, and what child should be forced to enter a family as "the only option"? For this reason, we decided to adopt before exhausting our options; this child will be something we've chosen actively, rather than something for which we've settled. The process of applying for adoption has taken about six months and has entailed home visits, psychiatric evaluations, sensitivity training, and workshops where we encountered couples who felt they'd failed, weeping at the experience of countless miscarriages or the inability to conceive. The culmination of the process was to write a long letter to prospective mothers who will have the freedom to choose the parents of their unborn child. This agency champions open adoption, which begins with the premise that the birth parents and adoptive parents will know each other. This alarmed my mother, who imagined genetic grandparents stealing her grandchild. Katherine, my wife, worked for weeks on the letter, writing from a place of great vulnerability and nervousness. The resulting letter was a miracle, in which she managed to depict her and me as passionate, warm people who love cooking for friends, dancing, traveling, and who enjoy rich careers. She described our extended families, the culture into which the child would be invited, with some detail, but neglected to mention my mother explicitly. This morning I received a text from Katherine, explaining that my mother had called to share her disappointment at not being mentioned properly in the letter. My mother felt she couldn't share copies of the letter with people in her community—a strategy recommended by the agency to get the letter shared as far and wide as possible—as a letter that didn't mention her would seem strange to her friends. Understandable on one level, but in my current regressive state, I am stewing a little bit about this as we arrive at Kilchoman.

For me, one of the chief draws at Kilchoman is its humble cafeteria. I have a bowl of cullen skink, a Scottish chowder I order often, made from smoked haddock, potatoes, onion, and milk, and a cheese-and-pickle sandwich on thick, white bread. I share a big pot of tea and milk with Lester, who is having a ham and cheese roll. I study his mouth as he chews, wondering if he really eats loudly or if I'm just being an asshole. More and more, I'm assuming it's the latter. "My mom called Katherine," I say.

Lester looks up from his sandwich. "That's nice," he offers.

"Apparently, she's upset she wasn't properly mentioned."

Lester's forehead wrinkles and he turns up one side of his mouth. He seems to know just what I'm about to say and interrupts me. "Shit, she did? I'm sorry."

I am startled that quite suddenly my throat begins to close and my eyes become glassy, and I am again watching myself overreact. "What the fuck is she thinking," I begin.

Lester puts his hand flat on top of my hand and says, "She just wants to be a part of it."

"I understand," I say, "but what right does a woman with five children have to doubt a woman who has been trying for years to get pregnant? Imagine. Every month when her period comes ... She maintains a great attitude ... But I can see how hard it is for her, and then her mother-in-law calls her to question her because she's not properly mentioned in an adoption letter?"

A few tears roll down Lester's cheeks, some disappearing into his frosty beard, some beading on its surface like on waxed cotton. "I'm sorry," he says. "I'm really sorry. That's terrible." I have seen Lester cry two other times. The first was when I was eleven or twelve, watching *E.T.* Overwhelmed myself by the image of the harmless extraterrestrial, mistreated by humanity, being resuscitated with defibrillator paddles that caused his delicate torso to convulse, I turned to see Lester's tears reflecting the celluloid light. I was comforted that he felt for E.T. the way I did. The second time was when his father died.

I'm a little dried up myself, and have cried very little since I could grow my own beard; in fact, I didn't even cry when Les died. But now, too much water has accumulated at the bases of my eyes, and I feel tears escape and travel down my own cheeks. I am only moderately embarrassed that we both are crying quietly and holding hands across the table. With my churlishness, I have been avoiding authentic feelings with the one person who has time for all that is weighing on me: the constant fear of failure; the infertility; the possibility that the tax man will lock me up; the sense that I'm an impostor, a loser. "Thank you for your patience with me," I say. "I'm sorry I act so childishly. I appreciate you giving me the latitude you do." I know this has not been about my mother. She and I have long forgiven each other. I am a boy in a 6-foot, 8-inch man's body.

"Of course," Lester says. "We do that for each other." We sit looking at each other for a moment. My sinuses, usually blocked, are uncharacteristically open and empower me to take several deep, slow breaths. I take my hand back and sit still a moment longer. We smile wordlessly at each other and then we begin again to eat in silence. We've always enjoyed eating together.

After lunch, we are emboldened for another tour of Kilchoman. It's one of our favorite distilleries, one of the six independent distilleries in Scotland—the only on Islay—and a true family affair, run by Anthony Wills with the help of, among others, his wife, Kathy, and his three sons: George, Peter, and James. We've enjoyed the hospitality of one of the sons, James, in the past, and today we will be given a rather dour tour by the patron of the family and distillery. Anthony Wills is tall and youthful for having three adult sons. In the relatively small community of small, independent distilleries in Scotland, he has a reputation as not a bad sort but someone who does not suffer fools gladly. When I ask him to what extent this venture is ideologically motivated, he looks at me quietly for what seems like minutes, during which I wonder if he knows I was crying in his cafeteria a half hour ago and is disgusted. "Well, this is a business," he says. "No amount of good feeling or idealism will do us much good if this does not succeed."

I ask this clumsy question because Kilchoman is an inspiring project. The first new distillery on Islay in 120 years, its proprietors call it their "farm distillery," which does not feel like posturing. Already releasing bottlings that are made exclusively from Islay grain and ratcheting up their own growth of base materials, this small producer is one of only a handful who boast their own malting floor, which currently does not produce enough for all their production but nonetheless speaks to their commitment to a handmade spirit. From the malt floor to the kiln to their second hand mill to the mash tuns from which they feed their cattle with the spent remains of the grain to their small copper stills and the filling and bottling that are done by hand on the premises, the Kilchoman distillery compromises little. I admire that Anthony sees Kilchoman as a business, not a think piece.

As he walks us through his project, he softens a bit, growing a bit warmer—in part, I like to think, because we are enthusiasts, and, after that first one, our questions are not asinine. Though I think I may have lost ground when I ask about Francis at Daftmill: "It seems like you have a lot in common with Francis. Both of you are passionate about similar things . . ."

He doesn't let me finish. "Well, some of us need to actually earn some money."

I've subsequently read in an interview on Scotchwhisky.com that Anthony put everything he had into Kilchoman:

I risked a huge amount when I started because I put all my money in, all of it, and more. It concentrates the mind hugely when you do that and we never raised anything close to what we needed because no one was interested in investing in something that was so high risk.

I knew no one had built a distillery on Islay for 120 years but I didn't really do any research; if I had I wouldn't have bloody done it. If I'd spoken with my accountant he'd have said I was mad and forget it because it's not a model that anyone's going to invest in, and he would have been right. It took me four years to raise the initial funds because none of the financial houses would look at it with a barge pole.

I am grateful to Anthony for this language because it encapsulates my own experience better than I ever could. What those outside these businesses can never quantify is the crushing effect of financial anxiety. For this reason, I do dub Anthony and others like him a hero. He insists on doing something the right way despite overwhelming evidence that it may not be financially viable, and out of this passion comes a spirit that is artfully made and is enjoying global acclaim. I wish Kilchoman continued viability.

In my passenger's seat on the left side of our Volvo, I study Machir Bay as Lester drives us back down the hill. The scenery is almost comically beautiful, with its undulating grass, and volatile sky that has now transformed into a shocking blue, the white caps articulated against the slate-blue bay. A good distillery like Kilchoman leaves me feeling peaceful, reassured, optimistic, and we are bound for another such property, Springbank, which coincidentally is the distillery of which Kilchoman most reminds me. Springbank is another of the independents and the Bob Dylan of distilleries, forever relevant, soulful and uncompromising, and most of all, producing substantive whisky. Like Kilchoman, Springbank malts, ferments, distills, bottles, and ages on its premises in Campbeltown, once one of the main producing regions of scotch. In the nineteenth century, there were twenty-eight distilleries in Campbeltown; now there are three. Unlike Kilchoman, who began producing in 2005, Springbank has been operating as an independent distiller since 1828. The facility is a Victorian wonderland, with museum piece after museum piece of perfectly tarnished and worn equipment that is decades, if not more than a century, old. The facility is covered with dirt, clutter, and handwritten notes posted on walls in which senior staff members chastise anonymous irresponsible personnel: "* EMPTY DUST BAG AFTER EACH GRINDING * IF YOU CAN'T BE BOTHERED DON'T WORRY SOME OTHER *MUG* WILL GET IT *"

Springbank is a very human operation. From the uninhibited chatter at the diversely staffed bottling line, to the crew surrounding the mash tun working to get the spout that feeds the wash into the grand cast-iron vessel open, to the students of the whisky school who participate at each juncture of production, the distillery is warm and alive. The students are an international group of all sorts: wholesalers, retailers, enthusiasts, distillers. They stay on the premises for a week at a time, taking advantage of Springbank's facilities and expert instruction from the distillery managers.

So Springbank is a lovely place, and those who work there are quick to credit this quality to Mr. Wright, the patriarch of the fifth generation of the Mitchell family, which has been owner and operator of Springbank since its inception. Mr. Wright is loved by his employees and that affection is reciprocated in a number of ways. His first goal is to employ a person rather than rely on machines, which explains the scores of employees where other companies staff in the single digits. To avoid a boom-and-bust economy, he is conservative in production, making the same amount of whisky each year even when the market could accommodate more. He has also created a trust that governs the distillery, ensuring it will not be liquidated after his death. Sale of the distillery would have to be approved by all of its employees. This holism seems modern or progressive in the United States, but in Campbeltown this kind of humanity seems timeless and routine. At the end of our tour, we are lucky enough to try new make spirit. Springbank is one of our favorites: vibrant, lightly peated, with qualities of apricot and other golden fruit. Of course, our opinion of the spirit is subjective, informed by the compelling context that the greater distillery embodies. I am not interested in how I would evaluate the Springbank in a blind tasting. Every spirit has its story, and I include it in my evaluation, just as I do with human beings.

Mark Watt is the person we know best in Campbeltown. He is the steward of the barrel room for Cadenhead's, the merchant-bottling facet of the Springbank Distillery. In addition to producing their own whisky from scratch with their own maltings, they also buy casks of whisky from other producers or brokers and bottle them under the name Cadenhead's, a firm that Mr. Wright of Springbank bought some years ago. Watt is responsible for several warehouses of inventory of single casks of whisky bought from all over Scotland, as well as other single-cask spirits. He decides what spirits to buy, in what casks to age them, when to move them from their casks, and when to sell them. The company insists that spirits are never sold before they are perfectly ready. As we've learned in other regions, guarding inventory is one of the arts of survival in this high-attrition industry. No one honors their inventory more than Cadenhead's. And speaking for Lester and myself, two of our finest afternoons in Scotland were these passed in the barrel rooms of Cadenhead's with Mark Watt.

Unlike the last time we hung out, today Mark greets us in a suit. He is in his midthirties, tall with workman's shoulders and rosy cheeks. He wears studious large-framed glasses and a narrow tie. He looks a mixture of lumberjack, professor, and boarding school student, and puts us immediately at ease, greeting us like old friends. "All right, then," he says. "Hasn't been so long. How are you?" Entertaining us is his job, but, as he tells us each time, he loves his job. We are sheltered by a classic, clear and blue Scottish afternoon as we walk from the Cadenhead's shop to Mark's domain at the barrel house, which is a sprawling, low-roofed affair with thriving mold on every surface and hundreds of barrels all from different distilleries—107 in total, we've learned in the past.

"I think after visiting these other industrial distilleries," Lester says, "I was more appreciative of how *inconvenient* things are here at Springbank."

Mark has definitely heard it all before, and his answers are at the ready but never sound rehearsed. I've heard him say the same jokes three times over the last few years and I only enjoy them more.

"If we can find a difficult way of doing something, we'll do it," he says. "I know myself when I started working here, you're like Jesus, ehm, you could do this better, you could do that better, but if you change anything, you change what Springbank is." Mark pulls from a box a couple of small, stemless, tulip-shaped tasting glasses. "Here are your glasses. You can keep these."

"Oh, wonderful," Lester says sincerely. He is in heaven here. For both of us, this is the high point of our trip.

"For me, warehouses are probably the best part of a distillery. . . . Like, the stillhouse and everything is great but . . . and that's what annoys me when you go 'round distilleries that don't let you into warehouses or they have a fake warehouse. And it's just like . . . it's just not the same. The smells. And the . . ." He stops speaking for a moment, looks at his feet, and looks at us briefly with a smile as though he may have gone too far. Not for us Californians. He's only just begun.

"We'll start Glenrothes, Speyside," he says. "This is a 1989 Glenrothes. So, twenty-six or twenty-seven years old. Now there's water kicking about there if you want water. I'm not going to tell you how to drink whisky. Ah, shit, you go to different people's tastings. Some people tell you to add water. Some people tell you not. Some people hold it like this." He suspends the glass pretentiously in his palm, like a snifter. "Some people don't. It's just . . . you know. Drink it the way you like it." These last words he abbreviates with a couple of sharp, loud blows on either side of the bunghole of the first cask we're sampling. The bung is loosened sufficiently to allow him to release it by hand and slide in the whisky thief, a long metal tube with a small hole at one end that he covers with his thumb before extracting the tube with liquid trapped in its interior, like tasting a drink with a straw.

"Last year we had a really good Fettercairn," Lester remembers aloud nostalgically.

"It's still here," Mark says. He doesn't miss a beat. "Yeah. So '89 Glenrothes, twenty-seven-year-old, 53.1 percent." Tasting these barrels at natural proof is such a treat. They have been hand-selected to survive autonomously rather than being blended with other barrels or neutral spirit. They are elite because of the character of this particular portion of spirit or this particular cask or the unique synergy between the two. Also, they are not chill filtered. Right on time, Mark gives us his familiar caveat about the process:

"Chill filtering I just think is the most ridiculous thing in the world," he says. "I always say people who chill-filter whisky should be shot because you're murdering the whisky. If you chill-filter the likes of this, half the body is gone and it's the mouthfeel and that chewiness and the finish that's different. It's stripping the body out of the whisky, which is not good."

Having heard the answer before, Lester advances the conversation politely, "Is that happening a lot in Scotland with the single malts?"

"Yeah most. Ninety-five percent of all single malts are chill filtered. I was going to say unless it says it's not chill filtered on the label it will be, but then at Cadenhead's we forgot to actually put it on the label . . . we've taken it for granted for so long. I don't know what you call it in the United States, but here you have full-fat milk and skimmed milk, and skimmed milk is like colored water." Lester laughs heartily and warmly.

Mark's job is to liberate barrels that would otherwise endure a sad end, stripped of their character, blended, and cast into an ocean of mediocre whisky. "Shall we move to Isla? A wee Bowmore and then a Caol Ila?" The metal thief in his hand, he walks past Lester and me toward a fungus-covered wall behind us where rest the two Islay scotches.

Returning to a favorite topic of mine, I urge Mark on. "I asked you this last time," I say, "but I don't remember the answer. With all that's happening and whisky production quadrupling, is there really good whisky to be had from all distilleries?

"I would say that increasing production is not necessarily a bad thing," he says. "I would say that there's a chance that whisky is becoming more homogenized. The quality is probably much more consistent than in days of yore, but the quality is much more driven by yields. You look at Springbank, it's got the low wash at 4 or 5 percent and the long fermentation times. (The "low wash" is the beer that will eventually get distilled into scotch; many distillers produce beer with as high an ABV as possible, as this yields more alcohol per run, and therefore more profitable runs.) "I think this is going to be the problem because maybe three, four, five years ago a huge increase in production happened with most distilleries, not Springbank of course—not just the building of new stills, but a lot of them are like right, let's cut the fermentation time to forty-eight hours and we'll make as much as we can in this short period of time. That's got to change the distillery character, and I think it's going to be interesting. A lot of these distillers used to be fermenting for seventy-two hours and now are forty-eight. Why? Well, they say it doesn't matter. If it didn't matter, why were you doing it before? If it didn't matter, every distillery would ferment for the shortest time possible. I'm trying to keep track of which distillery has changed and when, so that in ten years, when I'm bottling stuff, I can say, 'This is from before there was short fermentation.' People under-estimate fermentation. It's building the final flavor." At moments like this, Mark raises his small glass as though making a toast, gripping it by its stubby base so as not to mar the tulip-shaped body of the glass. "You then take that flavor and you distill it to make it more concentrated. I understand yield being important, but for Springbank it doesn't matter. We're getting 100,000 liters a year. So whether we get 400 liters per ton or 420 doesn't make a huge difference. If you are Caol Ila or Glenlivet, though, and you're making 12 million liters, an extra 20 liters per ton makes a huge difference to your final outcome. Another thing is that there's a lot more whisky being filled in crap wood because casks are getting used more and more. I have seen a lot of younger stuff we've been buying that looks like it hasn't even seen a cask because the wood has just been filled until it's nothing."

Just offering the slightest nudge, I ask, "This must mean more coloring and flavoring?"

He fills his lungs quickly through his mouth and continues. "Coloring I can understand, because the big guys want consistency. If you go to the shop one day and you buy Coca-Cola, it's the color of Coca-Cola. You go back the next day and it's the color of Fanta. You're like, 'What's going on here?' Same if you go and buy your whisky and one day it's really dark and the next day it's light. But when people add loads of caramel to make it look darker and make it look older and charge you more? That's ridiculous. That's why in Germany, Denmark, and Norway, legally, you have to put on the label if caramel's been added. And I think that should be law worldwide."

Mark is always very reasonable, slow to tear down his peers. "At Springbank, we are lucky. We don't need to be consistent. We don't go, 'This would look nice with coloring in it.' People who add coloring to the whisky will tell you it doesn't change the flavor. It does."

I couldn't agree more.

"It might improve the flavor of some whiskies to be honest." Lester laughs again, happy and in his element. "Forty parts per million peat makes a difference, but forty parts per million caramel doesn't? It makes a difference."

"And all the big guys are adding color now?"

Mark smiles and waits a beat, his cheeks rosier with each dram: ". . . Yeah."

We talk into the afternoon, lamenting the proliferation of non-age-statement whiskies that are prohibitively expensive and comprised of young, incomplete malts with the addition of caramel. We hear how the Chinese and Indian markets are not what people hoped they would be. We enjoy stories of Mark's childhood where he grew up, literally, at the Macallan distillery, the son of employees of the famous producer.

I am not irritated in the least as Lester asks questions and enjoys the many diverse drams. We have broken through again, and the rest of the trip will be sweet.

If you eliminate all the scotches that are chill-filtered and augmented with caramel and outsource their malting, you are left with a number of distilleries you can count on one hand, and Springbank is the elder statesman of these. Skippered elegantly by its patron Mr. Wright, who has ensured this property will never be liquidated or sold without the consent of its employees who idolize him, Springbank is the archetype of single malt scotch, and its sister project, Cadenhead's, is the same for merchant bottlers. At my bars, I sell Springbank, Kilchoman, and some Cadenhead's cask bottlings, nothing else. As Mark puts it, "What you have to remember is that we're whisky geeks, and if you look at the industry as a whole, we're irrelevant. Several years ago, the exports of scotch whisky reached one billion bottles, for a turnover of five billion pounds. So, the average price of an exported bottle of whisky was five pounds. It shows you how most of the industry is cheap, nasty, rotgut whisky. That we'll never drink, thankfully."

Our time in Campbeltown, in particular our audience with Mark, has provided a pleasing coda to these trips to Scotland. Springbank embodies the idealism and fervor of the younger, independent distilleries, while exemplifying the priorities that allow a company to stay viable and relevant for close to two hundred years. Given its recent trajectory, one can scarcely imagine the state of scotch in two hundred more years.

Yesterday was the first anniversary of Les Senior's death. I called Lester, his son, from the 101 South on my way from San Francisco to visit Patty, Les Senior's widow and one of my favorite people, in her home in Foster City. I said I was thinking of him and remembering that night a year ago when we sat with Les as he left us. My voice caught and I couldn't speak any longer. My wife, Katherine, was sitting in the car beside me listening to Lester on speakerphone. I could see tears on her cheeks. My mother was with Lester, listening to us. Lester said, "I'm really glad you called." Katherine and I share that the adoption agency to which we gave fifteen thousand dollars and eighteen months of our lives is filing for bankruptcy, forcing us to start anew, optimistically. "Oh shit," my mother says. "Oh shit," Lester says.

When Lester and I left Scotland a couple months before, we'd stopped at the duty-free store and joked with each other about the overpriced bottles of scotch on display. "My goodness," Lester remarked, gaining my attention. I studied him a moment. He was standing back a couple of feet from a shelf featuring a number of caramel-colored, overpriced, and extravagant bottles of non-age-description whiskies. Each one was in an absurd limited edition case that opened in some unique way, like a box Indiana Jones might outsmart to gain a priceless artifact. His wicking wool socks emerged from snugly tied hiking boots. He wore hiking shorts, now quite familiar to me, pale tan with many full pockets; prepared to the very end, he would visit me again at my seat on the flight home with the sliced cheese and pepperoni he bought at the market the night before. He wore a navy pocket T-shirt under a Lands' End chamois shirt, along the front of which rested the strings that guarded his glasses. As I consider his sugar-dusted afro and full beard, he turns to me and shakes his head, smiling amusedly as only he can.

PART FOUR

A CATEGORY OF HUMAN EXPERIENCE
IS BECOMING EXTINCT
AND IT IS CAUSE FOR CELEBRATION

Chapter Nine

OAXACA, PART I

A STOP ON THE HIPPIE HIGHWAY

Oaxaca reminds me of my favorite scene from Fellini's *Roma*, in which a collection of municipal workers are digging a train tunnel beneath the city's surface. The progress of the dig is stopped by a wall. The foreman calls for the "cutter," a large drill deployed to penetrate the wall. The drill's futuristic whirring provides soundtrack as the viewer is treated to images of what's on the other side: an ancient Roman apartment decorated with immaculate frescoes, vivid in color and appearing untouched by time. The monotonous sound of the drill does not relent as we move back and forth between the ancient chamber and the action on the other side of the wall. In the scarce light of the sealed room, the camera jumps from image to image, colorful portraits of straight-faced Romans who seem like fugitives, frightened they will be discovered after centuries of privacy. From within the catacomb, we watch the drills progress, creating an aperture that allows a circular shaft of light to penetrate. The end of the cutter's whirring coincides exactly with our awareness of a new noise, that of a continuous gust of wind howling through the opening between the two eras. People climb through the opening and explore the archaic interior, marveling at the preserved relics and abundant frescoes while, uninterrupted, the moaning sound of the wind persists and disconcerts until we watch the surface of one of the frescoes begins to deteriorate.

A worker cries out to the foreman from behind her dust mask, "The frescoes are fading! It's the air from outside! The fresh air is destroying the frescoes! Oh no! How awful!" The corruption of the frescoes accelerates and we are helpless, watching them all disintegrate.

This archetypal moment, when the so-called developed world encounters the older one, is upon us in the state of Oaxaca and other more rural provinces in Mexico, and though its drama unfolds much more gradually than Fellini's, it is multiplied by the number of North Americans captivated by mezcals created by tiny producers who are often subsistence farmers distilling in a more primitive fashion than most anyone, relying on ancient technique at every stage of the process.

At their best, these spirits are truly agricultural ones, produced from indigenous farmed or even wild agaves, using technologies unchanged for centuries. The most affordable mezcals are generally made from *espadín*, which is the most broadly cultivated type of agave; it is the same strain used in the production of tequila. The most prized mezcals, though, are produced from wild agave, *los silvestres*, which can take decades to mature. The rarity of these *silvestres* is a large part of their appeal, and while more and more of these wild strains are being domesticated, at least for now, we still have access to spirits made from truly wild plants. Much is made of the disappearance of *los silvestres*. The fact is the ideal of mezcal made entirely by hand from wild agave is not a sustainable one. The current market could only be supplied by cultivated material, which explains the more and more frequent deception of mezcals that claim to be 100 percent *silvestres* but are made from domesticated agave, most often the affordable *espadín* with a bit of the wild spirit integrated, with their always magical-sounding names: *tobaziche, tobalá, tepeztate, cuishe, madrecuixe, barril, tripón,* and *jabalí.*

For the spirits enthusiast tired of base materials stripped of any provenance—molasses, corn, rye, barley, and so on that is bought and sold on the open market—this source material is thrilling. We become like archaeologists working to authenticate these primeval spirits. Compare this to modern Scotland, where the origin of the grains is secondary to the malting, a process that happens centrally irrespective of region—and scotch is considered by many to be the most contemplative of all spirits.

I cannot consider Oaxaca and the mezcal trade without perceiving it through the prism of my time in Guatemala, where I arrived at a more nuanced opinion of Latin America and how my country and I relate to it. My time there informs all the time I spend in South and Central America.

I moved to Guatemala when I was thirty-five, at the tail end of a nervous breakdown, in a last effort to escape the service industry. I'd fled hospitality once before, in my twenties, when I took advantage of a friendship from school to work at Oracle Corporation. I lasted two years until I was fired by a supervisor who was twenty-two; I was about to turn twenty-nine. I returned to bartending and worked three to six days a week for the next seven years, rewarding myself every single day with a joint before bed, where I'd watch a French film on my laptop and eat granola. Two of my relationships failed, and when I was dumped the second time, I woke up to the excruciatingly small world I inhabited, where my king-size bed occupied almost the entirety of my studio apartment, literally, leaving room in the two-foot margin that surrounded the mattress on the floor for nothing more than a bedside table.

My adolescence had lasted twenty years, and I worried I was too late to claim a real, adult life. The pain was so acute that all I could do was put down the weed—I have not been drunk or stoned since—and see an analyst five days a week for the next year, during which time I mourned for every blown relationship and every squandered moment of the previous fifteen years. A great, raw pain occupied the front of my body, emanating from my solar plexus, which abated as slowly as I could possibly bear. If it had taken an instant longer to ease, I was sure I would have died. The pain seemed to have a half-life of a couple months, and as it dissipated, exponentially in reverse, I grew more and more positive that I needed to leave the service industry. I investigated my options on the then-youthful Internet and decided the world of nonprofits and NGOs (non-governmental organizations) could redeem me.

I found an organization in Guatemala and filled in its application. Strangely, I was invited to join them. I gave three months' notice and prepared to move to Central America where, when I arrived, I felt only worse. The organization placed me in a small village of their construction about a half hour from the center of the capital. Guatemala City is a city that begs you to accept versions of the Christian myth because it is damned, boasting at that time almost twenty murders a week and truly biblical afflictions like the spontaneous opening of enormous sinkholes that swallowed citizens and architecture. The house to which I was assigned was made of cinder blocks, supporting a flat, corrugated metal roof that rattled percussively in the hard rains of the wet season. The doors were cast iron with a couple of inches clearance at their base and head, guaranteeing access to every form of Central American insect and arachnid, including my terror animal, the tarantula, one of which came to occupy the drain of the rain tank–fed, cold-water sink in the bathroom. One morning, I had concluded brushing my teeth when I turned on the faucet. As the first drops of water disappeared down the black drain, an eight-inch, hairy beast emerged, improbably, from the same opening that was about one-eighth its size. I was grateful that I screamed in a masculine octave, and that I was alone in the place. I did what my peaceful older brother had taught me and grabbed a bowl, with which I covered the enormous spider, a creature that felt more like a mammal when I felt its weight against the construction paper I'd slid beneath the bowl. I tossed animal, bowl, and paper as far as I could, over the miniature banana tree into the ravine behind the house.

In addition to the legions of insects, lizards, and occasional rodents that inhabited every surface of the insecure building, I lived with two humans. The first of these was Chris, an Australian guy my age who had been the lone occupant of the home for quite a while and had taken the liberty of hanging a heavy bag in the center of what we called the living room. My first afternoon in New Hope Village, as the NGO had christened it, Chris made a point of working out with the heavy bag in an aggressive manner that assured me he'd be fine if it was me, not the donated bag which he'd appropriated from the children of the village, suspended from the I-beam rafter. He molested his cushion opponent cruelly, rattling it with forearm blows and manly shin kicks while occasionally making expressive eye contact with me until I looked away submissively. "You know Russell Crowe is a mate of mine," he offered in one of our first and only conversations.

"Oh, that's cool!" I said. "I like . . ."

"We were in his first film together," he interrupted confidently. Coincidentally, Chris kept with him a copy of *Romper Stomper* on DVD, which he allowed me to watch, verifying that indeed Chris did appear briefly in what he assured me was an Australian cult classic that marked Russell Crowe's debut.

Whatever small hope of burgeoning friendship I maintained was shattered during my second week in Guatemala when Chris threatened violence overtly. "I hear you're trying to take out my lady, mate?" Chris had introduced this woman to me as his girlfriend only the week before; a few days later, I ran into her on the street in Antigua, the nearby town that housed the project's headquarters, where we spent weekends with amenities like Wi-Fi and hot water. She rented a home in town, and we discussed noncommittally the possibility of a dinner at her place with Chris and some other volunteers. We traded numbers and I didn't think about it until Chris confronted me. "You and me have a real problem now, mate," he said.

We never fought, and fortunately Chris would be gone in a month, failing to complete his committed two years so he might travel with said girlfriend, leaving me with the other resident of the home, Katherine, who had arrived in Guatemala the night before I did, and would eventually become my wife. I woke early after my first night in my cinder-block room and lay awake in bed on my back, my inter-laced fingers providing a cradle for my head. The night before, Chris had collected me at the airport and informed me Katherine arrived earlier the same day, but she was in bed by the time we arrived home (which means we've literally lived together since before we met). I heard her voice, deep and confident, before I saw her face.

My curiosity drove me from bed, around the corner toward the small kitchen, where I first saw my wife, from behind, bent over, looking for the soy milk in the small refrigerator we shared. Old-fashioned red gym shorts with white piping stretched to contain her attractive, broad bottom, and I was pleased to see her legs were unshaven. She also wore a vintage gray gym shirt that I would see said BRECK in bold black letters across the chest as she turned to face me with the soy milk in her hand. Katherine has raven-colored hair with dark eyes beneath thick, black, expressive eyebrows that augment her immaculately formed nose, which is long and decisive and adds a vulnerable charm to her smile and clean laughter, which keeps me alive still, many years later. We shook hands. "Does the soy milk mean you're a vegetarian?" I asked. How lucky that I was in the midst of my vegetarian period at that moment we met, from which we were sharing meals, shopping together, smelling each other's shit on the toilet paper we weren't allowed to flush down the primitive toilet and tossed in the bin. We enjoyed a domestic partnership before we became lovers, and that foundation yielded a strong, passionate marriage.

From New Hope Village, we would walk to the neighboring village, Las Brisas, where a woman sold fruits and vegetables from a dirt-floor shack attached to her family's one-room home. We'd stop at the tortilla woman's house on the way back so they'd be warm when we'd reach our cinder-block home. There we'd finish yesterday's guacamole with the warm corn tortillas while we cooked, generally making the same simple dinner of black beans and rice with pico de gallo and the guacamole made from the abundant Guatemalan avocados—rounder than those we generally see in California, with sweet, buttery flesh—that we ate year-round. If we were able to find a nice melon or *piña* (pineapple), we'd cut it up for dessert, deftly, as we'd butcher hundreds of each by the end of our time in Guatemala.

It's tempting to stop at this first impression of rural Guatemala as an agrarian place where we lived close to the land, buying locally grown ingredients, but the reality is that these women from whom we bought produce and tortillas had two jobs: traveling an hour by chicken bus to and from the city where they bought industrially grown masa, fruits, and vegetables that they carried back to our towns and then selling the wares to locals. While these vendors had to fetch their own merchandise, ironically, the wholesalers of candy, soda, and salty snack foods that comprise most calories consumed in these villages would deliver to the tiny *tiendas*, in trucks guarded by *ayudantes* carrying shotguns. This underscored another disillusioning aspect of where we were quartered: the looming possibility of bodily harm in this rural area, where gunshots were heard almost daily, indicating acts of celebration and, at times, tremendous violence. Murders within walking distance were not uncommon, including Las Brisas. We happened upon numerous homicide crime scenes, including one that was particularly ghastly, in which

a government car had been severely perforated by automatic gunfire. Countless shell casings surrounded the vehicle, which housed
three victims whose blood decorated what remained of the car's
windows. The government official, who'd been killed for working
to mitigate drug traffic, his daughter, and his driver were covered
with tarpaulins. Katherine was forbidden by the NGO from walking
or taking a jog on the road outside of New Hope Village. More than
half of the volunteers we knew in the country of Guatemala were
robbed, generally at gunpoint, in this time when we were supposed
to be helping the Guatemalans.

Quickly I came to appreciate the hubris of the agenda that
justified my presence in Central America. Katherine and I were
assisting with community development in New Hope Village, which
initially was a collaboration between Common Hope and Habitat
for Humanity. Habitat built the rows of cinder-block homes that
surrounded the school our organization funded, in addition to some
administrative buildings where we did our work. After Habitat left
the area, our group administered what were called "sweat-equity
mortgages." Those accepted for the program would pay for their
homes over time with hours of work, which could be contributed in
the form of cleaning, building, teaching, or attendance at the town
meetings organized by our group. At these meetings, we worked,
abstractly, to foster a notion of community while enforcing the rules
of the town imposed by our organization, like the limit to the number of family members citizens of New Hope Village were allowed
to house. We created programs we hoped would benefit the village,
like recycling, shared childcare, or the election of town officials.
The residents of the town who attended generally sat in silence,
unresponsive to our patronizing questions and mediocre Spanish.
They were there because it meant they got a cinder-block house.

As someone who often opts for the next elevator rather than ride
with other passengers, I began to wonder what I could offer in this

context. Furthermore, how could North Americans with their fragmented, disintegrating communities be of assistance? Fortunately, the director found other work for me. I was thirty-five, while none of the other volunteers were older than twenty-three or could drive a manual transmission. This left me uniquely qualified to be the project driver. My duties included airport runs, shopping, and moving bodies, tools, and supplies from New Hope to the project headquarters in Antigua. Among the human cargo were prospective donors visiting from the United States. They arrived mostly from Minnesota, the locus of the NGO's domestic headquarters. So, I was often driving a van full of midwesterners from New Hope to Antigua or the other direction.

What I realized about NGOs is that they are primarily fundraising organizations. As with any company, the first order of business is generating revenue; how the money is appropriated is almost secondary. Transporting prospective and previous donors gave me a view of the sausage being made. The group wanted to get the donors in front of as many children as possible: while they study, while they play, while they dance, while they draw, frankly, because beautiful children loosen the purse strings. The other must for a brigade a *brigada*, as tour groups were called, was to spend an afternoon with Tono, who headed up his own NGO called, appropriately, Ecotono. I would translate for Tono as we drove the *brigada* around the more rural parts of Guatemala. There they'd encounter a less picturesque poverty in villages—if you could call them such—where no running water or electricity existed and full families lived in lean-tos of salvaged plywood and unsecured cinder block. Children had more access to soda sold in four-liter bottles, their chief source of calories, than to potable water. The shantytowns were encircled by a perimeter of human waste that corresponded to the distance people were willing to walk to relieve themselves.

Tono was macho in the best sense of the word. He wore cowboy boots and tight denim pants that accentuated his package, with a braided leather belt that fastened around his waist, which was slim but not feminine, a perfect girth that showed he was not vain and enjoyed a good feed. His shirt was always tucked in and usually of the cowboy style, with the snapping buttons, or khaki with abundant pockets, like those worn by wildlife photographers. He wore a tightly groomed beard and short-cropped hair. Children loved him. He would squat on his heels to speak to them, holding his cowboy hat in his hands. He earnestly asked them how they were doing and nodded gravely like a doctor as they answered. Tono had two simple agendas: to get children to eat real food, not junk food, and to provide a simple water-free toilet he'd designed for communities and schools. Tono liked to talk about toilets, returning generally to his key statistic, which is the truth that all of humankind cannot have a flushable toilet; we simply do not have enough water. This convenience, which most of us take for granted, is a key indicator of the entitlement of the "developed" world. With food, Tono's strategy was a simple, two-pronged one: teaching families how to grow their own fruits and vegetables in the fertile Guatemalan landscape, and removing fast food from the schools. This second ambition proved a dangerous one. As I've mentioned, the purveyance of fast food was militarized with the shotgun-wielding security and now death threats, administered to Tono and his wife at their home. Tono remained unflappable and continues in his clear purpose today

I admired Ecotono's efficiency. The organization's only overhead was the pickup truck that conveyed Tono and his two assistants around the countryside. His agenda was manageable and he worked in the communities of his youth, which he had left only to go to college. When I contrasted Ecotono to New Hope Village, I felt embarrassment. We were successful fund-raisers; like a lot of NGOs, we sold self-esteem to our donor population, which was also the commodity we sought as volunteers and underpaid social workers. I am positive after my time in the sector that the work of NGOs is selfish, motivated by the desire to feel better about ourselves, which is also to say that there is no such thing as true selflessness. The best way to live may be by helping others, but I must be honest about the impetus that drove me in this work.

Common Hope had money to burn, which we did by constructing large buildings that loomed over the village, below which was the school, quite grand by Guatemalan standards, and the full-size, covered basketball court that abutted it, a stipulation of one of our more generous donors. The children generally used the facility to play indoor soccer. I think it's always valuable for disparate cultures to come together, and we provided valuable resources, but they were ultimately controlled by our organization, not by the Guatemalans we claimed to be empowering. Moreover, as I traveled and worked more in the area, I saw how NGOs acted as a knife's edge of colonization, providing its employees a base from which they could research and buy real estate, more often than not for personal, sincere reasons: to raise a family, to create a life in the area, to work in a local trade like coffee or chocolate.

This population of NGO workers merged nicely with the progressive, artistic migration from North America, people who reminded me of my hippy family members who moved from the East Coast to California, to Oregon, to Washington State, and to Alaska along the "hippie highway," drawn by lower costs of living farther afield. The motivation seems similar for quite a few gringos I've seen settle in the Mayan parts of Mexico and Guatemala. Who wouldn't want to buy a spread of land by Lake Atitlan and play guitar with the youthful guests at your bed and breakfast, which is staffed by the local population for comparatively low wages? These people are not evil (I'm not sure that anyone is), but when one group uses the strength of its home nation's economy to secure an advantageous position in a weaker one, they are participating in colonialism—just as I am participating in gentrification when I lease a property in the Mission neighborhood of San Francisco, because it has more affordable rent and its population is growing more fashionable and affluent in perfect synchronicity with the financial risk of my entrepreneurism. These dynamics are unavoidable, I think, and largely determined by forces greater than us. Clearly, human history is one of shifting populations that displace others to help improve their own circumstances. Generally, those with the resources to travel and penetrate other cultures are intrinsically more powerful than the cultures they penetrate. This imbalance was more evident when it was maintained with weapons and violence rather than stronger currencies or the accumulation of liquid capital.

Fortunately, this book is not a rigorous historical or economic text but a memoir, which affords me the freedom to generalize this way and to extrapolate grandly from small amounts of anecdotal evidence. But these are the thoughts and memories that inform my impressions of mezcal, Oaxaca, and the gringos who operate there; and these are the reasons I believe, while it is forgivable and to be expected, those participating in this economy of advantage are obligated to perform some amount of introspection regarding this colonial relationship. What disappoints me is the general sentiment on the part of the merchant mezcal bottlers that they are performing human aid. In reality, the arrangement is more complicated than that. They are benefiting greatly from the authority they enjoy, authority intrinsic to the market, and the producers they intend to support have historically been relegated to their inferior positions, in part at least, by these colonial relationships between nations and their citizens. So, while you're telling me of how children are going to college for the first time in a family's history because of your trade, also acknowledge that you are enjoying a remarkable quality of life, traveling freely around the Americas with a greater liberty and affluence than those you pay to perform hard physical work, whose names may not even be on the bottle you designed.

Much has been made of the rules of nomenclature of mezcal. As with every appellation, the body that protects the product often harms the category as well. The chief complaint is that it costs a producer several thousand dollars to receive the designation of mezcal. Impoverished producers, many of whom follow all the rules of the appellation but cannot afford the fee are relegated to the designation of *aguardiente de agave*, basically a declassified mezcal.

Also excluded is a whole category of *palenques*, or distilleries, that use a primitive column still, rather than double distillation as prescribed by the body that certifies. It's worth noting that many of the world's great spirits are single-distilled, for example, armagnac, which is once-distilled in a small column, whereas cognac is twice-distilled in a pot still. The world is missing out on these single-distilled agave spirits, which I have experienced at Mezcaloteca, the famous agave tasting room in the town of Oaxaca owned by Sylvia Philion and her partner, Marco Ochoa.

There, and in *palenques* in Oaxaca, you are invited to imagine how Armagnac, Cognac, and Scotland, the world's other great regions of production, may have been at one time littered with small, subsisting distillers who drew on a more specific lot of ingredients—the water, the grapes, the peat, the barley, all within arm's reach—and how they relied on cultures of yeast unique to that very spot, and handmade stills imparting their own particular qualities to the finished spirit. So, in Oaxaca, one becomes anxious, wondering if these truly singular *palenques* will soon disappear, like Fellini's frescoes, as the developing world further penetrates the region, increasing demand and altering production to accommodate the exponentially growing global market for this special spirit, leaving a more industrial, consolidated distilling landscape, along the lines of what we now see in tequila. And demand is increasing for mezcal, exponentially.

This demand has been cultivated by a number of merchant bottlers who, like the rest of us, have been captivated by these rare producers. One such merchant is Judah Kuper, who launched a label called Vago. Judah was, by his own description, a bit of a lost soul who was traveling the world surfing. He was staying on the coast near Oaxaca when he had an accident that required urgent medical care and a visit to the hospital, where Judah fell fast in love with one of the people administering his care and married her. As it happens, this woman's father distilled mezcal that provoked a reaction in Judah equivalent to that inspired by his wife. Ever since, he has been spreading the gospel, initially bottling his father-in-law's spirit, and then some others, and selling it abroad. Charles, Craig, and I enjoyed the good part of an evening with Judah at his tasting room in Oaxaca, where he has the spirits he sells in addition to a collection of mezcals ample enough to qualify him as a true zealot. Judah is good company and completely unpretentious in his enthusiasm about these spirits. He showed an interest in Charles's work as an importer, and had questions about other spirits and how their production and trade might relate to his corner of the world.

Jonathan Barbieri is an artist who also fell in love with the area. He began the brand Pierde Almas and has grown it in my market to the point where it's handled by one of the largest distributors in the Bay Area, and has gone so far as to produce a gin with a mezcal base.

To continue to speak anecdotally, a number of entrepreneurs traffic mezcals between Mexico and the rest of the world, working to grab some market share. The bartenders at Bar Agricole joke that for a time someone was stopping in each week who was an artist who lived in central Mexico, or who had gone to USC and grew up in Mexico City, or who had gone to USC and roomed with a guy who grew up in Mexico City, and were selling this mezcal to help a humble master distiller. All the bottles have earnest, indigenous designs and words, and are adorned with paper composed of the repurposed refuse from the distillation process. These merchants often act as ambassadors to the indigenous culture as well as sales-people of a luxury good, performing a complicated brokerage, and I find it easy to be cynical. But at the heart of it all are some raw and beautiful spirits.

Perhaps the most famous of these ambassadors is Ron Cooper, with whom I tasted about fifteen years ago, though I'm sure he wouldn't recall that. Ron is an artist from New Mexico who fell in love with that Mayan part of the world. His Del Maguey label has done more to popularize mezcal in the United States than any other influence. We sat and tasted some of his spirits, which were wild and fascinating, as was he when I met him. He insisted the spirit be consumed from a *copita*, a shallow earthenware cup of about a one-ounce capacity that looks like a tiny terra-cotta flower-pot underliner, an inch and a quarter across. He was a wonderful ambassador, harnessing the mystical nature of spirits and honor-ing the context from which he'd pulled them. We sold some of the spirits, in *copita*, over the bar at the Slanted Door, but guests were slow to catch on and we lacked the bandwidth to promote it suit-ably amid the barrage of orders for cosmopolitans and mojitos we endured then. A few years later, I would feature one of the *espadíns* in a drink that became popular at another bar and we sold gallons of mezcal, though mixing it with other ingredients didn't do justice to the vegetal, consuming aspect of the spirit, which, when of a certain quality, probably is best served on its own. Still, we were pleased to sell so much mezcal, and, subsequently, Del Maguey would release a more affordable one (called Vida) intended for use in cocktails.

Ron Cooper really created a blueprint for how to buy mezcal in one market and sell it in another, which a number of subsequent oper-ators have followed, wittingly or not. From my limited perspective,

I would guess that Cooper believes he is being copied and it does not please him. To visit his properties and producers is impossible without signing nondisclosure agreements that stipulate developing trade relationships with anyone in his cadre is actionable.

On another of my visits to Oaxaca, I had the pleasure of bringing my friend Charles Neal, who, as you may recall, speaks Spanish with an imperious Castilian accent and is comically biased toward the Old World spirits he imports. We were the guest of the Iniciativa de Mezcal, a young government organization created to empower mezcal producers to maintain dominion over the export and distribution of their sprits. Throughout our time with the Iniciativa, we perceived what was often a subtext and occasionally a direct current of criticism toward Ron Cooper and the trade relationships he's engendered in the area. Their agenda was clear and sympathetic toward the local producer. Their goal was to empower these distillers to distribute directly without a controlling third party.

This trip was somewhat ill-conceived. Charles managed to offend the Inciativia by consistently calling mezcal "tequila" in front of them, and late into one of our dinners, in response to a passive-aggressive comment about Del Maguey, he good-naturedly argued that the Iniciativa should build a statue of Ron Cooper in the town center and kiss its feet every morning. So, we were never invited back by the Iniciativa. That said, I haven't given up entirely on the possibility of bringing in a mezcal directly with Charles's help, though he is reluctant because I always owe him money. Furthermore, I want to better understand the market, which is a topic of much heated discussion these days in our trade. For these reasons, I keep returning to the area, and on this trip I am excited to take a closer look at Del Maguey, largely for anthropological reasons, an opportunity to further contemplate the relationships between North and South.

The morning that Gabe, the Del Maguey employee who lives here in Oaxaca and has kindly agreed to give me a tour of some distilleries, is scheduled to pick me up, Mexico smells wonderful. A great deal of rain fell during the night, and standing out front waiting for my ride, I appreciate the smells of diesel exhaust, bread baking, coffee, and petrichor. The late summer sun enjoys that perfect clarity that follows a heavy rain. Looking down the street, to the left and then the right, I mark the satisfying, symmetrical architecture of the colonial avenue, lined by stucco homes and businesses, washed in lovely matte colors: tangerine, jade, saffron, russet. Gabe's new Jeep SUV materializes from around a corner two blocks down the road and approaches, traversing the vivid townscape. Reggaeton plays and the warm interior of Gabe's new vehicle is reassuring. Free of Oaxaca City, our first stop is a, if not *the*, central facility for Del Maguey bottling, labeling, and distribution. The construction is somewhat humble in scope and reminds me of a number of nonprofits I've visited in Latin America: simple but distinct from most buildings of the area with its clean and well-developed environs. I follow Gabe around the facility, taking in the five-cent tour. In one warehouse, the shape of a Quonset hut or airplane hangar, I find stacked tens of shrink-wrapped pallets holding hundreds of the indicatory green bottles in which all Del Maguey mezcals are bottled. Nearby are stacked capacious plastic containers, each holding a different Del Maguey mezcal. Upstairs is another enormous room with a thatched roof, clean concrete floor, and hundreds of degrees of view of the surrounding valley through glass windows that make the large, newly built room feel even more airy. All that is housed here are scores of bound bundles of the Del Maguey inscribed boxes that will shepherd the filled bottles around the world. On the other side of the great room is a long, narrow table with hundreds of the "Vida" label laid out, ready to be adhered to the full, green bottles. Vida is the comparatively affordable *espadín* intended to be used in mixed drinks. Moving through a courtyard and a couple of small, brick buildings with the same simple, pleasing design that allows in an abundance of fresh air and natural light, Gabe and I greet a handful of workers at various stations en route to a small office, where he pauses at a desktop computer to print my nondisclosure agreement.

I wait for ten minutes or so while he fiddles with the printer, returns to the PC, then moves back to the printer. I don't mind submitting to Latin American time and breathe a bit while I look around. On the desk over here is a register with meticulously handwritten accounts of how much of each type of mezcal has been bottled and on which day. Over here is a gilt-framed banner, exclaiming in Spanish that "mezcal with water is not mezcal," referring to the fact that these artisanal producers do not dilute, further testimony to the uncompromising nature of their spirits. I think this piece is an original by Ron Cooper. We'll see a number of them throughout. The whole time I'm on the premises I feel a little as though I'm trespassing, maybe in part because I'm being asked to fill out a nondisclosure agreement (NDA).

From my detached perspective, Ron Cooper feels a little like the cool guy in high school who resents you for learning to enjoy the Smiths or Black Flag after he did, but rather than keep the music to himself, Ron is actively trying to sell the stuff to you while retaining some kind of authorship. No one likes having their ideas stolen, and I respect that many have visited his operations with an eye toward replicating them and, I suppose, ultimately supplanting Del Maguey, intentionally or not. But, honestly, no one has ever asked me to sign an NDA, not in Normandy, not in Gascony, not in Japan, not in Jamaica, not in San Sebastián, not in Denver, not in Belize, not in Guatemala, not in Arandas, not in Martinique, not in Scotland, not in Ireland, not in Cognac—not even in Cuba. If Ron is simply protective of his business, I am less sympathetic; we all have to compete in this market, and we can rely on our strength as operators and benefit from sharing, just as we have benefited from those who share with us. To open a bar or restaurant is to watch your best ideas be appropriated within months, weeks, even days. We are all building on each other's efforts and most of us fail, which *is* the service industry, which *is* the luxury goods industry. I empathize with the fear and anxiety, but I do not admire it or feel proud of the ways in which I emulate it. I think of Springbank and how they opened their doors to new distillers like Kilchoman, and of my friends the Leopold brothers, who are an open book. I think of my friend Lance Winters, owner of St. George Spirits, and how his shop has been an open house for people interested in his craft. This trade is too lonely not to share.

I am less judgmental of the impulse to protect the craft; I think all of us are nervous about what will happen to mezcal. We've seen the spirit of every great producing region subjugated to the marketplace. Scotch, armagnac, calvados, cognac—mezcal allows us to fantasize about what they might have been, unmolested and produced simply as their own reward. But then, if the mezcals had stayed that way, none of us would have tasted them. If it weren't for Hennessy or Cooper, who would know about brandy and mezcal? And one can hardly fault the great thirst that develops for these spirits, just as one could hardly fault those who hope to profit from quenching it. Every facility you visit in Oaxaca affords you a glimpse of some modernization, be it an awning over a roasting pit or a chipper in place of a prehistoric tool that crippled its handler. Like Fellini's subterranean murals or the aboriginal cultures of New Guinea, their contact with a curious, greater world has catalyzed a change that cannot be stemmed.

I believe that mezcal will evolve and change, and that we occupy a sweet moment when we can taste the distant past in some of these spirits whose production doesn't require anything beyond manual technology: wild vegetation roasted in the earth and pulverized by hand, fermented in animal hides or open tanks handmade from wood or stone with no inoculation of commercial yeast, distilled in pottery. Yet to taste these spirits is to participate in their abolishment. I salute Silvia Philion, owner of Mezcaloteca in central Oaxaca, who has preserved a demijohn of every lot she's bought of mezcal in the last decade. As she attests and easily proves, resting the spirit in glass can improve it greatly, but also these spirits are worthy of conservation as surreal artifacts: clear and identical in their corked receptacles, but infinite in their variety and individual aspect. Perhaps tasting them in a hundred years will resemble a comparison of contemporary bourbon with its bonded ancestors, made from a different caliber of grain on an entirely different scale.

Gabe gives up on the printer and warns me I'll need to sign the NDA later before guiding me toward the heart of the matter, the tasting room, which is pleasantly cluttered. Along one wall is a small set of shelves laden with plastic bottles of various sizes and shapes, presumably containing samples of Del Maguey's own producers' spirits or those made by others. A large cask rests on the floor—an experiment in cask finishes that will probably never be more than a novelty, as these mezcals don't need this kind of augmentation. Another set of shelves is wedged full with rolls of Del Maguey labels for its multitudinous offerings. The labels, like all of the outfit, are lovely examples of design. The deep, ubiquitous green bottles are decorated with the now-famous illustrations by Ken Price, who has not been to Oaxaca but manages to conjure the mood, palate, and topics that resonate with everyone who touches the spirit, from the indigenous people of the area who are said to love the label to the international community that buys and drinks the spirits. Truly, the whole venture is masterfully curated, which substantiates Cooper's description of Del Maguey as his "ongoing sixteen-year art project, bringing transformative Spirit out of Oaxaca to the world," which seems at once charming and hubristic. The comfortable tasting room is adorned with some of Ron's original art as well as a faux gilt frame containing an icon to the Virgin of Juquila, a saint with appeal to both Catholics and nonpracticing indigenous people alike. The Virgin is mounted on a woven mat on the wall behind the low table holding all the different spirits Gabe will avail me of this morning. This table is literally an altar, with lit candles and a less ceremonious tablecloth emblazoned with bright, varied still lifes of tropical fruit, a charming scene.

I work my way through at least a dozen mezcals, rarer offerings by Del Maguey as well as samples of producers they are contemplating distributing, some of which are from hundreds of miles away. The flavors are a spectrum of greens and yellows, from the deepest most vegetal green pepper or asparagus to the brightest, filigree moments of citric acidity; the cacophonous, microbial flavors of wild yeast and the microscopic ecosystem that flourishes in the fermenting environment and survive the act of distillation; and traveling back in time further to the fundamental flavors of wood smoke and earth that informed the caramelizing sugars from the piña of this bizarre relative of the asparagus plant. To taste this spirit in its most basal, wild form is a deeply meditative experience.

After I taste through the altar at Del Maguey, Gabe invites me to join him in visiting a couple of the producers whose spirits they bottle and sell. We stop en route to the first distillery in a small village for enormous quesadillas from a stand in the street. The young lady pulls segments of a rubbery, coiled white cheese and lays them on the large flour tortilla like pieces of rope that slowly soften and settle on the tortilla, which is heated on a piece of sheet metal, before being covered with mushrooms, chicken or beef, and a choice of green or red sauce, then folded deftly so we can eat them by hand. The meal satisfies and I am in good cheer riding in Gabe's Jeep for the rest of the way to the village of San Balthazar Chichicapa, which rests in the Central Valley at an elevation of about 7,000 feet.

We are here to meet Faustino García Vasquez, who presides over this distillate of *espadín* that Ron Cooper has been selling as long as he's been in business. Faustino greets us at the metal door that allows passage through the metal walls that surround his compound: about 10,000 square feet of earth floor surrounded by high metal walls. What is clearly the roasting pit rests under a modern canopy in a style of construction that reminds me of the buildings we just left at the Del Maguey bottling facility. Faustino, a small and lean man, is wearing a cowboy hat, shirt, and boots with dark blue jeans. His eyes are hard and glossy, giving them a gemlike appearance. He is diffident to say the least, never speaking really unless first spoken to by one of us or his wife, who is sitting nearby, though not exactly a part of the gathering for the duration of our stay. She wears a skirt with sandals and a men's untucked work shirt. Her skin is creased with what looks to me like worry, though I may be projecting. We are led to a simple card table in the middle of the facility, which is basically outdoors. A concrete slab occupies one corner of the compound where the stills live, though at the moment they are disassembled, the copper tops locked away somewhere when not in use so they won't be stolen. We receive no real tour, but the whole operation is visible from our seats, which are folding chairs at the simple table. As Gabe asks him how they are enjoying the new awning built for them, Faustino grabs a bot-tle of mezcal without a label and puts glasses in front of us while agreeing politely that the cover makes a pleasant difference. What follows is a two-hour drinking session that really isn't of particular interest to me. Gabe's Spanish is great and Faustino is a lovely guy, but I just sit and watch him drink himself into gentle oblivion while Gabe, the driver, matches his efforts.

Faustino's *chichicapa*, named after the town in which he makes the mezcal, is an archetypal *espadín*, well worth experiencing. We'd just missed the exhumation of freshly roasted *piñas* (the bulb of the agave plant) that lay, still steaming and smoking, alongside the crater where the agave had been roasting, covered in earth for four to five days. Now that I'm in my midforties, drinking away an afternoon is much less interesting than it used to be, particularly when the Central Valley of Oaxaca is sprawling around us. I am here for work, to learn, and Don Faustino is relaxing after his work, so our agendas are not exactly simpatico. Don Faustino's wife chimes in amicably every twenty minutes or so from her perch across the dirt floor of the fortress, and his son arrives after about an hour with his own two sons, whom I enjoy watching play hide-and-seek around the facility. They hide beneath a rusted old bed frame and mattress in one corner.

So we walked to the card table when we arrived, and now, two hours later, we are walking away from the card table toward the door where Don Faustino welcomed us. As he shows us from his structure, he invites us to his grandchild's baptism, for which they will be slaughtering twelve goats later in the week. This invitation is one I am sad not to be able to accept.

On our way to Minero, we stop for another quick meal of chicken soup and freshwater shrimp. It's a great outdoor café in the middle of nowhere, and I remain particularly grateful to Gabe for his hospitality. He is clearly an interesting guy of great substance. He has worked extensively abroad, which gives him that rootless, expatriate quality that I find appealing, particularly when mixed with his history as a very successful baseball player, which contributes to his approachable, decidedly unpretentious personality. He is from New Mexico, which gave him entrée with Mr. Cooper, particularly when combined with his Spanish language ability and history of working in NGOs. Gabe's official job title was "sustainability expert," a title with literal and figurative connotations that are never fully explained to me.

It is afternoon when we arrive in Santa Catarina Minas and, more specifically, the *palenque* of Luís Carlos Vasquez, where we find the maestro well into his afternoon rest. He is robust and short, wearing a wide-brimmed sun hat, a glossy soccer jersey, and new blue jeans. His moustache is silver and well groomed, like many moustaches I've seen in black-and-white photos. Here, no mention is even *made* of looking at the distillery. My presence here seems secondary to Gabe, who is happy to see these friends of his; I am tagging along on a social visit, which is fair enough, as I haven't been a great client of Del Maguey. Immediately, another lightweight table is pulled out and glasses are set on the table with another two unlabeled bottles. I sit down with Gabe, Luís, Luís's son, a young woman I believe is Luís's second wife, and their young son, who is probably four years old. What ensues is another drinking session, during which a couple of themes recur. First is a photo Luís shows to those present of himself passed out drunk on the floor at a recent party. Arms and legs akimbo, face flat on the concrete floor, in the photo Luís looks like he should be surrounded by a chalk outline. Second is Luís's fascination with a little windup drummer doll that belongs to the child; more specifically, the drummer is an anthropomorphized centipede and periodically Luís winds it up and delights at the figurine's action as it moves its head to the left and right while drumming with its left arm, right arm, left arm, and right arm in rapid succession. In a flurry of glances, Luís makes eye contact with everyone at the table, opening his mouth wide and laughing manically. My sense of time is dissipating but, seemingly, this drill is repeated every ten minutes or so.

Luís pours *copita* after *copita* while I sit and pay as much attention as I can—but the countryside is beautiful in this late afternoon and I came to learn about this place. I keep getting up, pretending to use the bathroom or make a phone call. I stroll around the grounds, finding first a goat pen filled with healthy, white-faced animals with otherwise black coats. I watch them jump and bump heads and am reminded of their handsome cousins at Brasserie Lebbe. The four-year-old arrives not long after me with a ball, and we toss it back and forth a couple of times, neither of us catching the other's toss, before the young one manages to throw the ball onto the roof of the goat's pen. He is even-headed and processes the loss of the ball maturely before wandering off in search of other stimuli. The hillside is impossibly lush, clad in a pelt of long, thick, turgid grass, still moist from the day's periodic rains. Flowering trees surround the simple bungalow where Luís lives that abuts the dirt road by which we arrived. Neighbors periodically walk by carrying bundles, and, as they pass, they shout greetings and jokes to Luís, who is clearly well liked in this community.

I return to the table and sit for as long as possible while Gabe, Luís, and the others chatter away in that circuitous fashion that can be very boring if you are not drunk. Our hosts have put some nuts tossed in oil and chile on the table, which are very welcome. I occupy my chair restlessly for another fifteen minutes that feels like an hour and get up again, this time to actually urinate in the outhouse, which does not have a door that closes but is structured to block any direct line of vision to its occupant.

I stand ready to pee with my penis in my right hand and look down and to the right to see the four-year-old who has appeared silently and is watching the action expectantly, eyes trained at my genitals. *I need to get this kid out of here*, I think, or *I will be lynched for child molestation.* Then I reconsider, deciding that maybe this anxiety is the result of living in the litigious country of California, leading me to my next thought that I need to relax. This is perfectly natural, and these earthy folk are probably not inhibited like I am. Doubtless, they are comfortable watching each other do something as natural as go to the bathroom. I seem unable to urinate, though, with this little spectator. Perfectly timed with this last thought, the four-year-old asks simply, "*No viene?*" At forty-seven, I'm old enough to be nervous about the onset of difficulties with urination, something a four-year-old probably can't imagine. Defensively, I form sentences in Spanish in my mind. *I don't have a problem. I just can't do it with you staring at me!* By the time I've finished the internal conversation, the child is thankfully gone. I strain to hear over the sound of my healthy stream what is being said at the outdoor table where the family sits drinking, which is still within earshot. I brace myself for the sound of the child explaining that the tall gringo has shown him his penis. Fortunately, this did not transpire.

I take the opportunity to wander more around the grounds, the sounds of laughter dissipating into the background as I leave the table behind. Across the dirt road, I see fermentation tanks silhouetted by the early evening sky that is burnished with shades of pink and pale, pale blue. The familiar smell is comforting as I approach the full wood tanks, which have a thick, caked cap showing that fermentation has been going on for some days. Here they often ferment for more than three weeks, giving the environment every opportunity to seep into the liquid that will be distilled. Presumably in this period of time, the fermentation will naturally end, as the percentage of alcohol rises until the yeast that produces the alcohol can no longer survive; in this toxic atmosphere, its appetite for sugar has created a kind of suicide. Even after the fermentation is ceased, the invisible organisms that thrive in this fertile hillside will infiltrate and inform the flavor of this solution and the rare distillate it will become. Minero by Del Maguey was one of the first mezcals I really came to love, and I wish this visit felt more significant. Beyond the fermenting tanks, I see the woven bamboo walls of what I hope is the locus of the stills. I take a few steps up a steep muddy incline and gain purchase on a stone threshold of the doorway that opens into the stillroom. The low evening sun thrusts through openings in the bamboo walls, forming shafts that frame the two clay stills in a picturesque light. There is no evidence of technology from the Iron Age or later.

My reverie is interrupted by Luís, who seems to have realized I am no longer at the table. He stumbles from the other side of the road and takes me on a perfunctory tour of the infrastructure, pausing many times to say decisively, "The old ways are the best ways," or, "We work in the primitive manner here." I don't disagree with him; it's a beautiful facility and a beautiful spirit. Soon we are back in Gabe's Jeep, heading down the dirt hill toward the highway that will convey me back to Oaxaca, where Gabe drops me as he found me that morning, in front of my rental home.

As Gabe drives away, I wish I'd been better company for him. I know what it is like to live down here. These were his friends he visited today, and he wanted to connect and socialize. I don't blame him and because of his generosity, giving me full access to his community today, I will always think well of him—and of Del Maguey for employing him. I suppose Gabe reminds me of myself at his age, when I'd decided to work in Guatemala where, ultimately, I couldn't find meaning or make a living in NGOs, hoping to change another culture in which I was not expert. Gabe's job in the private sector seems cleaner, somehow, than mine was in the public, but I imagine both of us were drawn south by a desire to touch something simpler than whatever it is that's going on up here, north of the border.

I suppose a similar desire must have taken hold of Ron Cooper, who found solace in Mexico and who, as this book goes to press, has just sold controlling interest of his sixteen-year work of art, Del Maguey, to the multinational Pernod-Ricard for millions of dollars.

Chapter Ten

OAXACA, PART II

PINCHE TEACHERS

I have returned to Oaxaca most recently in September 2016 with my friend Jay Palmer, popularized in my account of our frustrating trip to Cuba, and Chris Moreno, one of my senior bartenders who has yet to visit any distilleries outside the United States. I am excited about our chemistry. Both Jay and Chris are mellow, sensible guys who have Mexican parents and are passionate about spirits. For these reasons, I've decided we are destined to have a great trip. I had planned the trip initially with Jay, who joins me on an early-morning flight that has two legs and lands us in Mexico City, or DF (*Distrito Federal*), as the fashionably bicultural call it. I have success renting a car in DF and driving to Oaxaca, which is a long drive but affords us a better understanding of the terrain between the two indigenous hubs: one Aztec and one Mayan; one sprawling and urban, the other a better preserved colonial jewel with its original Spanish grid of streets and effective zoning that limits the height of its buildings and maintains its more parochial charm. Also, about halfway there you encounter Puebla, which has its own historic cuisine and at least one great, old-school restaurant with many dishes prepared tableside, including a plate comprised of cactus grubs that are flambéed in mezcal right before you.

Unfortunately, Jay and I won't be hitting Puebla in time to eat anywhere. A drive that should take less than five hours lasts more than nine, beginning with a rush-hour drive to Jay's favorite DF taquería. This takes hours but eventually yields some remarkable tacos, which we are encouraged to dress ourselves from the abundant buffet of toppings. We adorn our tacos with grilled onions, *nopales*, radishes, and colored salsas. The organism of traffic has its own biology on Mexican highways, urging you ever forward. The car, or more often semi in front of you, will signal with the left blinker that you should go for it, and you do, opening the throttle full, displaying utter faith in this other driver as you move blindly into what could be oncoming traffic. The customs of Mexico are not exactly like Guatemala, where I drove daily for a year. In Guatemala, you enjoy a kind of peaceful anarchy with no lines, no lanes, and no direction. Traffic moves more slowly and people are gentle as you move into what seem like impenetrable roads, packed with other vehicles that magically part for you like water pierced by a dive. Honking is an affable form of communication, inviting you to enter a lane or pass, or thanking you for your concession of the right of way. In Mexico, there is a mania; everyone urges each other on madly and plays chicken constantly, entering the lane of oncoming traffic that has no choice but to move aside, allowing passage.

Between DF and Oaxaca this night, we feel very much in sync with our Renault Duster, an unimpressive crossover (what we call a car that looks like an SUV but has none of the horsepower, or off-road capability of a real SUV). Our beginnings with the Duster are promising; while the night traffic is moving, we devour miles of rural highway, pulled forward, passing and being passed as Jay curates the music. Our progress is stopped, though, at about 2:00 a.m. when we encounter another round of traffic, which culminates in an hour or so with flaming roadblocks choking the main highway into Oaxaca.

I am not qualified to describe the history of the teachers' strikes in the Oaxaca area, but I can attest that they have continued intermittently for decades and these teachers are adept at complicating daily life. More than once on this visit, we would jokingly raise our fists and cry out, "*Pinche* teachers!" mocking the stereotypically meek profession and their ironic ability to fuck things up when you're trying to get around Oaxaca. By the time Jay and I penetrate the *periférico* of Oaxaca, by way of secondary and tertiary roads, and begin moving through a gauntlet of traffic lights punctuating dark, vacant city blocks at about five in the morning, we are exhausted. Jay is fast asleep and I have no business being on the road as I creep along at about five miles per hour, drifting in and out of sleep until Jay and I wake up at the same time, stopped in the middle of a block where we've been fast asleep for an unknown period of time. We are in a light industrial suburb of Oaxaca lined with auto body and tire shops, all made of the inescapable cinder block. A hundred yards ahead I can see the flashing red traffic light. Inexplicably we both laugh, and I'm restored enough to get us to the home we're renting for the next four days near the center of the old town. It's becoming light as we go to bed. I text Chris, who's on his flight, that we will not be at the airport to pick him up and he should find his own way to the house. I feel a little shitty because this is Chris's first trip to Mexico and he has seemed a little nervous about it, but Chris eventually arrives at the house, and Jay and I get some sleep.

We unite a few hours later in the modern living room of the home we are renting, feeling stoked, and step out to walk the town and find some breakfast before driving to the municipality of Matatlán, outside of town, to check out a couple of distilleries. At its full height, the early-autumn sun shines immaculately in a uniformly clear and powder-blue sky, casting a light that seems to penetrate every corner and cranny. The town is fully open and brilliant, which allows us to enjoy the bold, solid colors that clad the century-old buildings in rows: rusty browns, deep persimmon oranges, pale lurid blues. This quality of light matches the sensation I enjoy in my chest, an open freedom; I woke without worry today, a rarity. I am eager to find some fresh fruit and strong coffee as we head toward the cathedral. Jay is already in his element, nodding warmly, wishing passersby an early good afternoon. Chris is more diffident. Though of Mexican extraction, he doesn't speak Spanish, is shy, and when he does so, he speaks quietly in a warm, friendly mumble. He looks down a little as he walks, hiding soft, brown eyes. Like Jay, Chris is very handsome, with coarse, wavy hair that is just beginning to thin and impressive forearms and shoulders, made strong by his trade. I buy some pineapple with chile from a vendor whose old cart rests on two wagon wheels with two wood stumps that keep the cart still. Jay gets some sliced mango in a plastic bag. I start what would be a running joke with Chris. "Hey, don't freak out. These people are just as scared of you as you are of them." Jay laughs with a wide mouth and wide eyes. He wears a ball cap that is just a little too small and makes his delicate good looks and light beard seem a little more timeless. "I've done a lot of pretty rugged traveling," I continue. "At first, you're shitting your pants, but you have to dive in, go for it, breathe it in. This is *piña con chile*." I extend the bag toward Chris. "Put it in your mouth, bro. Start living." In character, Chris reaches tentatively and touches the bag with the tips of his fingers before taking a small piece of pineapple, littered with chile, and placing it calmly between his lips. "Sensuous, no?" I say. Chris closes his eyes. "Oh, yes," he says.

We walk back to the house and free the Duster from its enclosure beside our Oaxaca home. The fruit and coffee have held us for the first hour of the day, but we decide we'll have a little lunch at a place Jay's girlfriend recommended. We park a block from the restaurant, which is rustic yet sophisticated, selling dishes made from masa comprising heirloom strains of corn, a meal both delicious and enlightening and an excellent example of one of the world's great cuisines. Arriving at the car after our quick lunch, Chris photographs the Duster from behind, a photo he'll share with us later with great nostalgia. We mount up to drive the long, straight road toward Matatlán. Before we can clear the city's limits, though, we encounter roadblocks constructed by the still-protesting teachers. "*Pinche* teachers!" we joke to each other.

Eventually, we are able to navigate the blockades that stop progress on all of the main streets out of town by zigging and zagging on secondary roads until we are back on the main highway but on the right side of the protestors, heading toward Matatlán, first passing the Árbol del Tule about six miles out of town. The tree, estimated to be twelve hundred to three thousand years old, has the thickest trunk in the world, which withstands an abundance of branches and leaves that make this tree seem like its own universe. We vow to stop on the way back so Chris can take a closer look. Elementary students give you tours of the tree, pointing out trompe l'oeil in the body of the tree: an elephant here, an old woman there.

"Chris," I say, "that tree will blow your mind."

Calmly, Chris says, "I bet it will."

The road through Matatlán is lined with the shitty, cinderblock, single-story construction ubiquitous to Central America and Mexico. The floor of the valley is flat, baked, and uninspiring, but dust rises, acting as a filter for the hard geometry of the triangular hills that constitute a horizon of earthy greens of varying pallor, like something rendered by Georgia O'Keeffe. As you travel farther from Oaxaca, evidence of the mezcal industry becomes apparent. Old wood-paneled trucks, laden with manicured *piñas,* pass you in either direction. Fields of agave with its thrusting, pale-green, turgid blades are visible all around us and *palenques* begin to appear and recur with greater frequency until we are at the region's heart.

The first distillery we visit is El Rey de Zapoteco in the town of Santiago Matatlán, the self-described "world capital" of mezcal, which is more a sequence of businesses than a village—five or six restaurants, distilleries, and shops that interrupt the joyless progress of the highway. El Rey is one large room visible from the street through a pair of grand archways. In the single quarter, you see quickly the steps of artisanal mezcal production, including the plants themselves in the background behind the *palenque.*

A circular trough, created by a rounded wall of concrete at its center and exterior, constitutes a pathway for the old *tejona* that will grind the roast agave prepared in the subterranean roasting pits at the back of the facility. The *tejona* is connected by a thick wood pole to a withered horse, which is almost comical in its chronic exhaustion. This animal is a slave and you almost expect it to sigh to you, "*Ay, dios.*" As the horse circles the trough, he drives the shaft that causes the *tejona* to rotate, crushing all in its path and forcing the unctuous nectar from the roast *piña* that will ferment and be distilled into mezcal. Four shallow wood fermentation tanks stand open at the center of the room. A protective mesh over them keeps out larger life-forms but not the ambient yeast and microbial life that make the roiling ferment particularly pungent and leads to a lovely high-ester spirit that dominates the palate and captures the imagination. The distillation transpires in two tiny copper stills at the facility's front. Both are clad in concrete and a single arm joins each to its respective copper condenser, which rests, submerged in water, in open concrete tanks. The stills are unattended, and I pass the fingers of my right hand beneath the spigot that produces the clear, fresh distillate. I touch it to my lips and tongue before passing the glass to Chris, inviting him to do the same; he does and raises his eyebrows expressively. This flavor is unlike any other, comprising opposites: fruit and vegetable, sweet and savory, salty and quenching.

"See, it's not bad," I say rhetorically. Chris never doubted it would be good.

Chris smiles humbly. "It's great."

I explain, "Charles is bringing in some of their *espadín* for us to bottle under our own label. And to place this in context, this setup is more rustic and simple than anything we'll ever see in France or Scotland." Jay kneels down and tastes the new make from the still as well. This experience is primordial, tasting what the alchemists accomplished in their efforts to produce an elixir that imparts immortality. Distillates do not engender immortality, but they are enchanting simply in their concentration of flavor and aroma, setting aside their intoxicating qualities. Jay nods and smiles at each of us. With these flavors coating our tongues, the roofs of our mouths, we have arrived.

I am proud to see Chris pleased at our first stop, and it is a good first stop. In the spartan tasting room, we try a few of their *silvestres*: a *tobala*, a *barril* and a *tobaziche*. I have stopped trying to categorize the *silvestres*. I used to work to catalog their flavors, looking for descriptors that characterize a *tobala*, the way the flavor of blood might indicate Sangiovese. I was disabused of this practice by a woman who helps run In Situ, a *mezcaloteca* with encyclopedic inventory. I'd ordered samples of three *coyotes* and was laboring over them to find what characteristics unified them. I asked her opinion and she set me straight. "Tasting is private," she said. "Gringos try too hard to make sense of mezcal. It is a mystical experience. Each taste is entirely different, and the point is to experience this flavor now, not to relate it to other flavors or other experiences. Tasting is private. It is interior. It is not intellectual." I agree with her. These flavors and aromas are transcendentally intense. They can free us from categories—from time and space.

We sit still a moment in the Duster outside of El Rey Zapoteco. "Let's check out one more for today," I suggest. "Let's look at something shitty. Chris, you choose one." I start the car and pull cautiously onto the two-lane highway, turning back toward Oaxaca.

"Which one, Chris?" I am driving slowly, allowing Chris to study the few other *palenques* that line the road.

"Let's go to that one that says '*amor*,'" he says. Ahead on the left is a distillery I now know is called El Mal de Amor. I slow to almost a stop and signal left. I am turning in that direction when I hear my passengers gasp, just as I become aware of a presence on my left that slams into the front quarter panel of our Duster, hurling it toward the right shoulder. I watch the four-wheeled vehicle that struck us at a tremendous velocity skid with absolutely no traction tens of yards onward. The scene, still completely surreal at this point, reminds me of playing with Matchbox cars as a child, forcing them over jumps and rooting for them to land on their wheels. The other vehicle rocks to the left, rising high up on those two wheels and then to the right, tilting up on those two wheels, all the while hurtling forward with great speed. I desperately want it to land on its wheels. It veers right, then left, then right again, each time tipping a little less than the previous until it comes to rest.

Having been in too many accidents in my time, I know I should try to piece it together. My left leg is bleeding, but I am otherwise unharmed. I ask the other two if they are okay, and they are physically fine, though visibly shaken and pale, their dark pupils dilated in the afternoon light. I take a breath and review the logistics. I had attempted to turn left across an oncoming lane of traffic and another car struck me from behind, meaning they had tried to pass me on the left as I was turning. That familiar, sickening feeling of car accident grips me by my intestine. This can't have happened. Can we back up and redo this one? The car seems to still be running as I pull it the rest of the way onto the right shoulder. The left front wheel is impinged by some bent metal, but we could make a run for it. I am sure it's not my fault, though, and the truth that other people are involved in the accident brings me a little more into the reality of the moment.

I step from our Duster and move toward the other vehicle, which appears to be some kind of minivan, white and still, in a jackknifed position, blocking both lanes of traffic about a hundred feet from where our car came to rest. I hear the others exiting the Duster behind me. I begin counting the men who emerge from the minivan that struck us: one, two, three, four, five . . . I lose count and turn my attention to two men walking much faster than the others right toward us. One is in a glossy, rust-colored two-piece tracksuit and moves with great purpose. Struggling to keep up, the other man is short, with short legs, wearing a loose-fitting white windbreaker bearing a logo over his heart that I cannot read. "Is everyone okay?" I ask, truly concerned.

"What the fuck are you doing, you fucking idiot!!!" chastises the man heading the pack in his tracksuit. He wears clean, white trainers and his head is quite ovoid, with thick, short-cropped hair and a moustache. His eyebrows are coarse and dark, and his skull looks formidable and thick. I assume this furious man is the other driver and his reaction changes things immediately. I feel all empathy drain out through the soles of my feet.

"What the fuck am *I* doing?! What the fuck are *you* doing?! I had completely stopped and was turning left. And you passed on the fucking left!" Within an instant, everyone is yelling. The second in line is an average middle-aged man with a full belly and a white, collared shirt decorated with understated linear patterns. He wears a beard, glasses, and a fanny pack. He seems composed, like a professor or particularly accomplished high school English teacher.

Jay joins in. His Spanish is very good. "My friend, you were going more than a hundred kilometers per hour." Another of the men from the minivan, small, with a bright-red hooded sweatshirt and blue jeans, shouts that in Mexico we pass on the left when someone signals with the left directional. I cringe inwardly because I know this to be true. I also know that what they have done is technically illegal. And later, after this is all over, I will check traffic law and Reddit threads and TripAdvisor threads many times to confirm this. I also know that in serious accidents both parties will be thrown in jail in Mexico while culpability is decided. I am only beginning to realize that this is already a shitty situation and everyone is shouting.

"Okay, okay, okay!" the small man in the white windbreaker cautions. "Thank God, we are all uninjured."

"Yes," I say, "Thank God." The mention of God seems to calm everyone considerably. I will invoke him many times in the next few hours. I explain that we have insurance and that I will call the company. I notice that my motor functions are impaired. My hands are shaking. I have a hard time working the telephone and I struggle to think clearly. Okay. Where is the rental agreement? I find the rental agreement and feel the act of reading Spanish become like wading neck-deep through honey. Okay. I find a phone number. Now how to dial it. I turn toward Jay and Chris in the backseat to ask for a reminder about country codes and municipal codes and see they are both very pale. They are very far away. I turn back to my phone and remember the international assist feature, one I've used hundreds of times. I dial successfully only to learn this number is out of order. Right, I'm in Mexico. I find another number and dial it. This is a wrong number, but it is someone at Budget, nonetheless, who is able to give me the number of someone who can help. I reach a human being at this number and explain to her what's happened; she passes me to another individual in the office, and I am comforted by the familiar sensation of frustration with telephones and bureaucracies, particularly those of the lower Americas.

For the next thirty minutes, seated in the driver's seat of the Renault Duster, I'm on the phone with a few different people at the Budget offices. In the midst of the call, the municipal police arrive. I explain to them I'm speaking with the rental company and they say that's fine, no need to hang up; they take my driver's license and I watch them collect that of the other driver in his tracksuit. I am relieved these officers are municipal, not Federales who are legendary for improvised acts of justice that benefit them. I have been extorted by Federales in DF. On that occasion, Charles sat behind me in the car, coaching me. "Act like you don't speak a word of Spanish," he said. "What are you doing?! . . . Oh! . . . stop! . . . shit!" I continued to speak Spanish with the Federales, doing my best to ignore Charles. They fined us for an "illegal turn" and encouraged us to pay them right away. By some coincidence, the amount of the fine equaled exactly the total of the cash in my wallet, a combination of US and Mexican currency.

My call culminates in a conversation with the insurance adjuster for Budget, who says he'll be on the scene in forty-five minutes. He's just leaving Oaxaca City now. Naively, I am heartened that we are less than an hour from a solution.

Two other cars have arrived on the scene while I was on the phone. Both SUVs, I notice more clearly now that one had parked directly behind our little Duster and the other parallel parked directly in front, leaving only inches of clearance on either side of our vehicle. Details are sinking in, but I have a strange faith that this scenario has a floor we're standing on. The bureaucracies we're relying on will sustain us, will resolve this, I think. Budget, their insurance. Time is undulating, passing quickly, then slowly, then quickly again like the cars that speed by on the highway intermittently. They pass at tremendous speeds, causing our Renault, just clear of them on the shoulder, to shudder and rock from the displacement of air. I look closely at my watch, a Panerai I'd bought as a gift for myself to celebrate the opening of the second bar, and notice that I am still quite foggy. I muster great focus to ascertain for myself how long we have been here since the accident. Two hours. How long have we been waiting for the insurance adjuster? Already an hour.

As I instinctively look toward the group of Mexicans, I keep involuntarily performing unappealing mathematics. Three of us, and now ten of them. One of them is a woman. I internally accuse myself of sexism for forming this distinction, and then realize I am out of my depth if I am auditing my internal identity politics. I notice that a couple of the men have collected long, thick sticks from what appears to be a fire pit attached to the *palenque* across the street.

The woman approaches the bonnet of the car, against which I am resting. My legs have become strangely elastic in the last few hours. "Where are you from?" she asks, good-naturedly. She is likely my age. Her unruly hair, touched with gray, is tied back in a kerchief. Her eyes are pale brown and she has an attractive, tired quality to her. "California. San Francisco," I finally answer. "What are you guys doing in the country?" I ask. She smiles and answers, "Well, we're teachers, we've been organizing for the strikes . . ."

She is interrupted by the angry one in the red hoodie. "Hey! Get the fuck away from there! These aren't our friends!" She makes eye contact apologetically and moves away from the front of the car, only to be replaced by red sweatshirt and the thick-skulled driver who demands hotly, "Look, motherfucker, how are we going to fix this? You've totally fucked up our van." I realize, privately, that probably no one present owns their van. It appears to be a government vehicle.

"Look, the insurance adjuster is coming," I say.

The driver interrupts, "Fuck that. I don't believe that." I take out the phone. "Okay, I'll call him. You can talk to him." Each time I speak, they look at me incredulously. I imagine it is a combination of my mediocre Spanish and my northern faith that other people are going to help us. As I dial the adjuster, I notice the light is beginning to dim. It's 7:00 p.m. An elderly couple are sitting on the porch of their home about forty yards up a gentle slope from our scene on the roadside. They seem at peace, enjoying the show.

I consider how it would go if we shut ourselves in the interior of their home. Then what?

I have the adjuster on the telephone and pass it to the driver, who puts it against his left ear, against his thick skull. I look over his shoulder at the group of men and the woman. Now one of them is holding a large flashlight. Another holds a tire iron.

"Jay, can you call Budget?" I say. "Explain to them what's going on and that we really need some assistance." I am speaking in an exaggerated, measured tone, as though I am perfectly in control of my faculties and the situation. I give Jay the number and realize I should have had him on the phone much sooner. His Spanish is much better than mine. The driver in his red, shiny tracksuit turns his attention toward me again. Without words, he passes me back my phone. "Did he say he was coming?" The driver doesn't answer and walks back to his group. I hit the green telephone icon on my screen to redial the adjuster. He answers immediately. "Look," I begin without greeting him. "How far are you now?"

He is nonplussed and calm. "Just leaving Oaxaca. I should be there in forty-five minutes."

I hear myself raise my voice. "You said that more than an hour ago! If you aren't here soon, we are going to have problems!"

He does not sound worried. "Is there somewhere you can wait?" he says.

As I convince him of the danger, I am growing more convinced myself. "We're in the middle of nowhere," I say. "There's nowhere to go."

The adjuster is silent a moment. "Okay, hang tight, I'll be there in forty-five minutes." He hangs up before I can complain—just in time for me to hear Jay finish making the same explanation to someone at the Budget office, though in much more eloquent Spanish. I walk away from the front of the Duster, putting it between me and the white van and its passengers. "What did they say?" I ask Jay.

"She said we can leave the car if we have somewhere to go," he says, looking tired and expressionless. I sit with that information for a moment. Peripherally, I notice movement up the hill and turn my attention to the elderly couple, who are moving inside—not unlike the cliché of residents leaving the porch in an Old West town before a gunfight. Now it is almost dark.

I start a morbid calculus in my mind. *Okay, nine against three. I am physically larger by at least seventy-five pounds than everyone there. I could go after one of the guys with the sticks. The stick wouldn't hurt that much. But the flashlight. Or the tire iron!*

I am interrupted by the small one in the red hoodie, standing at a safe distance, who actually throws his head back and sticks out his chest. "I've had enough of this bullshit! How are you going to make this right?!"

The small man in the white windbreaker, who'd earlier shared the belief that the most important thing was that we were all fine, approaches me from my right.

"Look, man, these guys are pissed," he says. "I am keeping them calm, but there is only so much I can do. You need to decide how you're going to make this right."

The small man looks up at me paternally. His graying hair is parted on the side, his oversized white windbreaker hangs from his narrow shoulders. Raised by educators, I am disconcerted to find myself in a bizarro universe where teachers are marauders. In this reality, is Lester menacing young travelers with a tire iron? Is my father, professorial in the tweed, elbow-patched jackets of my childhood, somewhere robbing the disadvantaged with blunt instruments found on the side of the road?

The mathematics remains the same. Except for the driver with his thick head, each of these teachers is entirely unimposing, but collectively they have become an armed gang. Two of the men are on Jay, pinning him to the front of the Duster.

"Enough of this shit! What are you going to do to make this right?" I can't tell who is speaking at this time. To arrive at this point has taken long hours, but in this moment it feels as though this has all happened quite suddenly. Straining my eyes in the darkness to make out who is speaking, I am confronted with the truth that in Mexico, as in Guatemala when I lived there years before, there is no net. No police or justice system will evaluate this evening's outcome. Whatever transpires will be resolved in the eyes of the law; how strange that I was relieved when the municipal police left.

Jay is confident in his reply. His Spanish seems to improve under duress. "Guys, there's nothing we can do. We don't have the money to fix your van. We will wait for the insurance. There's nothing else to do." He speaks quietly and directly, as though he is as disheartened by his truth as the others.

"Where are you from, man?" the driver questions.

Jay answers, strangely defiant, telling his story by way of introduction, as I've read done in fantasy novels or melodramatic accounts of American Indians. "I am Jay," he says. "I am from California, but my family is from Michoacán."

The driver looks at Jay with the same thick furrowed brows he has shown me. Suddenly someone cries out. It is Red Hoodie. "Enough of this bullshit!" He splits the two Mexican men that blocked Jay from leaving his place at the front of the Duster and punches Jay. The blow glances off of his right cheek and the sound of the partially landing blow is a thick slap, embodying all that is mediocre and stultifying about violence between humans.

"Whoa! Whoa!! Whoa!" I move around to the front of the Duster holding both of my palms out front at waist height, perpendicular to the ground. "Enough! We can figure this out! Thank God none of us were hurt more!" This crowd has lost interest in being relieved no one was hurt in the accident.

With the first blow struck, we have reached a point of no turning back, but also this act of violence is attended by a certain catharsis. The group seems sated for the moment. Jay runs back behind the car and across traffic toward the opposite side of the road. I am worried he'll be struck in the dark by someone passing on the highway, but he makes it across and stands, looking side to side with his arms swinging alternately at his sides in a posture of vigilance.

"Give me some fucking space!" Jay shouts, holding his left arm straight out with his hand flat, like he's conducting traffic. It is almost dark now, and I am most aware of Jay by his white T-shirt and the whites of his eyes, which are open very wide.

Chris, who has been very quiet and still, asks me a very pertinent question. "Thad, what are we going to do? I mean . . ." He pauses. I can't tell if he is unusually calm or completely detached. "What should we do? I don't understand what we're supposed to do."

I wonder inwardly what is going to happen to Chris on this first distillery trip of his. "Shit, man," I offer. "I really don't know. I think this is what we have to do. Hold tight." The reality is now inescapable. I grow aware of someone touching my left arm gently. It is the peacemaker in the white windbreaker. "Brother. You need to make a decision right now. Money or violence?"

Without facing him, I ask, "What do you want me to do? We don't have enough money to fix your van."

"Well, how much money do you have?"

I think I have about a hundred dollars in pesos in my wallet. "Not enough. Not much," I say. I am irritated now. It seems like they want us to perform this robbery for them. Why don't they just ask us for all our money and get on with it? In part, because they are not unified completely.

"Okay, enough," the professor in the fanny pack says. He squints his eyes, suddenly looking a little like Eli Wallach engaged in a triangular standoff at the end of *The Good, the Bad and the Ugly.* "If you don't make this right, we are going to fucking burn this thing."

Another voice emerges from the darkness behind him: "Yes, burn it!"

Another voice, emanating from a man I can't see, reasons, "It's not their car. It's a rental." No one really responds to this observation, and all of us feel a strange relief when the professor smashes the windshield, or attempts to, with his board he too had collected from the fire pit. Spiderwebs form on the shatter-resistant glass, and Chris and I take a few steps backward, toward Jay. Now the three of us have formed our own small front. In the peace after the first blow struck against the Duster, we strategize as well as we're able to in our current state. Who can we call? Gabe! Jay has his number and moves a little farther from the crowd to make his phone call as Chris and I watch the next scene unfold slowly. One of the other fellows holding a tire iron and wearing a T-shirt with a picture of someone who, in the poor light, looks like Lionel Richie, comes from behind the professor to strike the passenger side window, which, with a clean crashing sound, disappears into countless, uniformly small pieces of shattered glass. His group makes an involuntary "oh" sound, like spectators at a sporting event. Now a third man mounts the hood of the Duster with a large, wood pole that he seems scarcely able to wield. He manages to raise it over his head and bring it down on the roof of the car with his limited, full force coupled with that of gravity, changing the shape of the roof but hardly leaving the satisfying dent for which he'd hoped. Chris, Jay, and I watch the man with the tire iron move systematically around the car, shattering each window and taking some amount of anger out on each panel. The man with thick eyebrows and skull, who was driving the van, waits until the back window with its threads of defrosting wire is ruined, then opens the hatch and rifles through the back compartment until he uncovers the spare tire and tire-changing kit, which he appropriates and moves toward the white van where he stows it in the back of the vehicle. The professor is bent over, showing the world his butt crack as he rips out the stereo.

Jay, Chris, and I are now surrounded by a horseshoe-shaped crew of six men, all with weapons; I notice now that one man has an L-shaped single-size socket wrench, presumably from our tire-changing kit. Another man brandishes a large folding knife, trained in the direction of the three of us with the blade facing upward to match the palm that holds it, like something out of *West Side Story*. God, I am exhausted—are we at last building to a climax? Though unified in appearance, the six men closing in around us are still a collection of individuals. "Give me your watch," one of them says to Jay, who gives no indication that he's heard the request. I take that opportunity to unfasten my Panerai and let it fall into the darkness of the long grass at my feet. Again, each of the men are undaunting when considered independently, but together I don't see any way to overcome them—particularly now, with the blade in play, when my greatest concern would be someone getting stabbed in a skirmish. Not that I'm an ass-kicker who just needs the right angle; this is just what you find yourself thinking in this situation.

As I walk slowly and cautiously backward, I can see clearly over the heads of the men who are marching us very slowly farther into the taller grass behind us. The scene beyond them continues to unfold. Two men remain engaged with the Duster and use a wooden beam and a boulder as a lever and fulcrum system to raise up the right side of the car before removing its wheels and letting it rest again on bricks they've slid under the naked hubs. The white van is running, and someone, presumably the woman with whom I was not allowed to speak, is waiting in the driver's seat. Okay, almost to the end. I am standing in a posture that resembles what I was taught to maintain when I played defense in basketball: legs spread, knees flexed, bent slightly forward at the waist with both my palms open and facing forward at chest level. Jay and Chris are moving backward a little less slowly than I, and they disappear from peripheral vision. I know that Chris is between Jay and me, a little closer to and behind me. My supercriminal beseeches me one more time. "You can stop this from happening, my friend." His touch is clammy, now on my bicep. Something happens. I sense a commotion to the right and behind me. Angry hoodie has circled around, behind Jay and punched him hard in the back of the head at the base of the skull. Jay pulls him to the ground as he falls, and the two of them grapple in the dirt. I am blocked by four of the men and their primitive weapons. I want to get over to Jay and help, but he springs up suddenly and is wild-eyed and shouting, "Calm down! Calm down!!" Chris is nearer to me, and there are now five or six men with arms closing in on us, and Jay is surrounded by his own cohort.

Everyone in their group is shouting, "Give us your fucking phones and watches!" I see them pushing Jay, but no one is touching me. I take out my wallet and pass the contents to the man nearest me as Chris is doing the same. I can't see what is happening with Jay, but it looks like he is being pushed backward by his assailants. The men who have Chris's and my money run away, and I can't reach Jay before his robbers are gone as well. We watch them climb clumsily and rapidly into their van, the wheels spinning in the gravel as they escape; we can hear the sliding door close and panicked voices. "Let's go! Let's go!" The other SUVs that had joined the event late pull out in pursuit.

Then the night is very quiet. The three of us are standing in the darkness. On the opposite side of the road, the sad Renault Duster rests demolished on blocks. The elderly couple in the house on the hill reemerge and resume their seats on the porch. We take a physical inventory, and no one is cut or badly harmed. Jay is the only one who's received blows. As the adrenaline wanes, he will be in more pain, but for now we are all whole, blessedly. I am looking for my watch in the grass as we debrief each other. We all have our phones, but they took Jay's watch, a gift from his grandfather, with far more value to him than the watch I am retrieving bears for me. The net fiscal damage seems to be the equivalent of about two hundred US dollars. The duration of the robbery was close to five hours. Now it's approaching 9:00 p.m. We wait in the bushes, avoiding Federales, until someone arrives. The first is the adjuster in his khaki trousers and white collared shirt, holding a clipboard, four hours late, who could not be less impressed. We take a seat and wait in his car and watch while he circles the Duster, making notes on his clipboard. After I've filled out a couple of forms, we are free to go. When pressed if this is common, we are not surprised to hear him answer it is. We said we thought they were teachers, and the adjuster just shakes his head in the affirmative, without words. *Pinche* teachers.

We are waiting for our ride a few more minutes while the adjuster circles the remains of the Duster, making notes of the specific blows and damage, an autopsy. I turn to Jay and Chris: "I'm really glad I could share this with you, guys."

Before long, our hero Gabe arrives to convey us back to Oaxaca, to our rental home near the town center. The ride back is subdued; strangely we don't talk much about the robbery but speak instead about the industry and common acquaintances in our small world. The destroyed car—our poor Duster—seemed explanation enough. Like the adjuster, Gabe is not shocked to learn what has happened. He leaves us at our place with a few recommendations of where to eat and an agreement that we will try to hook up in the next couple of days. For all the disillusionment I feel with humanity at the outcome of the encounter with the teachers disguised as brigands, I am encouraged by Gabe's generosity of spirit, driving to retrieve strangers from a complicated and violent scenario.

It is not even 10:00 p.m. when Jay, Chris, and I are back inside, standing in the atrium of our house. We look at each other for a moment, then exchange hugs in a round-robin: Jay and me; Chris and Jay; Chris and me. "I hope I don't sound patronizing when I say I'm proud of you two," I hear myself say. "You behaved really admirably."

We are still vibrating and opt for a bit of a night out, which begins on the roof of La Mezcalarita, where we taste a number of *silvestres* from their extensive list and smoke three Montecristo No. 2s. The coruscant aromas and flavors of the *maguey*, the agave, fire our senses and our confidence, and we are renewed in our adventure, positive we want to see our trip to its scheduled end. Our stomachs are tight, and food will not appeal to us for a couple of hours. We are like hunters after the kill, telling the story to each other, again and again. Each time one of us recalls another detail, another perspective. I have read of repetition compulsion and this seems like its healthiest manifestation, repeating the event in story form until we have a grasp of what has happened, and whenever the three of us see each other again, we are telling the story anew, with words or silently with no language at all.

We spill from La Mezcalaria ravenous and cheerful. Jay has asked the bartender where to go for tacos, and he guides us there through the safe, cobbled streets. At the taquería, Jay and I eat fifteen *al pastor* (barbecued pork) each. Chris has eight. Jay is ebullient and tips the chef, calling him "captain." His joy is infectious, and Chris and I, with our comparatively subdued personalities, follow suit, wishing everyone "*buen provecho*" ("bon appétit") as we leave the restaurant and head home.

Walking the rest of the way home, we consider the plan of renting another car early in the morning to carry ourselves back to Minas, where we'll be meeting some other producers. We agree we don't feel much like driving again after the events of the early evening, which now seems like a month ago. We agree we'll hire a driver, and wish each other good night on our way to our rooms like family members who have lived together for years.

The following morning is bright and clear, and as we walk through the town to have some breakfast and coffee before hiring a driver, we notice consciously for the first time that we really are the only gringos around. Looking back over the last couple days, we remember that the bars, cafés and restaurants where we've spent time have all been empty. I've been peripherally aware of the teachers' strikes for more than ten years, even avoiding a road trip from Guatemala to Oaxaca once because of them, but I think only today have I come to fully appreciate why people consider these protesting teachers dangerous. I will learn that many people—including journalists, teachers, and police—have died this year in the conflicts triggered by the massive protests.

Fed and coffeed, we bargain with a taxi driver named Ismael, who will carry us around for the day for less than we would have paid for a second rental car. Again, we navigate the teachers' blockades and find the main highway past the grand old tree, through the flat valley back toward Santa Catarina Minas, where our first stop will be to visit Eduardo Angeles, or Lalo, as he asks to be called. We've been here before but we struggle to find the *palenque,* though everyone knows Lalo, who was once the mayor of the town, and we need only ask passersby, "Where's Lalo's place?" Each person gets us a few blocks closer, with directions that even Ismael, a native Oaxacan, seems to struggle to understand.

I have met few characters in distilling more charismatic than Lalo. He greets us with a machete in his hand, a prop that seems to underscore a dramatic and beautiful scar across his left cheek, adulterating an otherwise perfectly symmetrical, classically handsome face with broad cheekbones, a pronounced chin, and polished, artful dark eyes that always seem about to shed tears.

Immediately, Lalo pulls us into the sensual experiences associated with distilling.

The agave plant is a relative of the asparagus. Its bulb, what we call the *piña*, is the heart of mezcal. Lalo buries his *piñas* in a roasting pit, with hot coals, cooking the sugars gradually over several days. These subterranean ovens compare favorably with the steam-powered autoclaves used to produce most tequilas in the north, which yield a more neutral flavor, as there is no earth or wood smoke to infiltrate the agave. Expert producers, like Lalo, will put a layer of *espadín*, the cultivated, more common variety of agave, closest to the coals, shielding the subsequent, more valuable layer of *silvestres*, wild agave, from the heat and smoke. We kneel and touch the mounded earth of the roasting pit with open palms, feeling the heat from within.

Lalo moves us to the covered slab where the roast agave is pulverized for fermentation. I notice a wood chipper where once there was none. Without being asked, Lalo makes the observation, "The people who feel most passionately about using a large stick to smash the *piñas* are not the people who do it. I have workers with shattered forearms. Young men who are weak before they are old." When he says something like this, Lalo pauses, often rubbing his right cheek, the one without the scar, with the open fingers of his right hand, as though evaluating the quality of his shave.

In the more traditional of the *palenques,* the liquids are generally extracted from the roast agave in one of two ways. The first is by *tejona*, a large stone mill wheel that is affixed to a thick post, anchored to a centerpiece, and pulled by a donkey. The other means of extraction is to place the roast material in a narrow stone trough and then batter the agave with a long, fifty-pound club with a particularly thick, bulbous head. Generally, most of the labor is in lifting the tool; gravity assists in its descent and ensuing impact with the meat, causing rivulets of unctuous brown juice to flow toward hand-made receptacles. While the human scale of this work appeals to the Luddite in me, I must defer to our host when he says it harms the workers.

Lalo waits a beat and smiles before hurling the blade of the machete he holds into the meat of a *tobaziche piña* while holding fast to the handle. The blade's momentum is stopped about a foot into the heart of the roast flesh before he withdraws it gracefully and buries it again, creating a V-shaped segment of *piña,* which he secures with the tip of the machete and moves to his left hand. With the machete under his arm, he segregates stringy segments of the agave heart and passes them around. He takes some himself and puts it in his mouth. We follow his example and enjoy, simultaneously, the reedy, fibrous quality of the flesh and the sweet liquid that our chewing forces from the vegetal filaments. This experience of the base material is always so satisfying, not only because of the familiar and amazing flavors of the rivulets that travel between the teeth, beneath the tongue, down the back of the throat, imparting acid, sugar, savory, and bitter flavors in unison, but also because touching and tasting the material places it in the context of the production process and ensures traceability and quality.

We diligently chew the rugged cud left behind long after its juices are beginning to be digested until, following Lalo's example, we toss the spent agave into one of the shallow wood fermenting tanks: more microbial life.

The most yearned-for mezcals are fermented in open tanks of weathered wood, leather, or even animal organs. Where most of the distillers in the world hasten fermentation with yeast inoculations, these fermentations begin naturally, as yeasts living around the distillery eat the sugars of the roast agave. Little effort is made to keep the fermentation equipment and process particularly clean. Microbial life—from the rustic fermentation vessels, from the air around the *palenque,* from the animals and children that frequent the distillery and put their fingers in the sweet ferment—is invited into the process. Like great cheese, great spirits can be the progeny of these microscopic colonies.

Fermentation at my favorite distilleries will yield a thick, filthy foam at the top of the tank, so concentrated near the end of the long fermentation cycle that you can rest a glass on top of it without it sinking. Lalo sticks crucifixes in his ferment, as if they are mountains he's climbed. When asked why, he replies simply, "*Soy Catolico.*"

From fermentation, we move into the lower slab, where the tiny hand-built stills are chugging away. Lalo squats by the still and interrupts the flow of the clear, new make spirit with half a dried gourd, which he fills a third of the way before tasting it there on his haunches with closed eyes. He stands effortlessly from his deep squat and hands the gourd to Jay with a wordless nod. We stand in silence and enjoy the telepathy enjoyed by tasting together. No language is necessary as we are each consumed by exactly the same psychedelic taste sensation—heady stuff. We move into the grand field above the *palenque,* where Lalo shows us different *piñas* of different strains, different ages, and illustrates the difference between plants that were planted in different epochs, wet or dry. Lalo is passionate about agriculture, explaining that really there are no true *silvestres*, only *cultivados.* The plants advertised as wild are always cultivated. He believes in the agaves of this region and is committed to their conservation, to which end he maintains an enormous greenhouse that serves also as a museum of strains of agave and the history of the region. He addresses each agave as an individual, drawing attention to the difference in its fronds, altitude, and girth.

I am sorry that we've had a large breakfast when he asks if we'd like to eat. The last visit we had a memorable meal with his workers. In a cinder-block shed with a corrugated metal roof, Lalo held court at a large table around which everyone was equitably

seated: laborers, distillers, and a few tradespeople in addition to
Lalo's family and us. A matriarch in the corner used a pot-bellied,
wood-burning stove to heat large flour tortillas that were folded
into quarters and served to us alongside golden mounds of scram-
bled eggs. Two dried gourd halves held red and green sauces, and
we were all given large chipped bowls of Oaxacan hot chocolate. I
couldn't finish a plate without it being refilled, begging ultimately
for them to stop.

Today, though, we will get a snack. After our agricultural tour,
we walk back down to the stills, where one of Lalo's workers is
preparing fresh, wild fruit for their *pechuga*, which is a famous
style of mezcal produced for special occasions. The spirit is infused
with ingredients connoting opulence: fresh fruit, dried fruit, cured
meats. Each distiller has a proprietary style. Lalo explains that his
pechuga is made only with wild fruits from the vicinity of Santa
Catarina. We eat small, yellow bananas with firm, pleasing flesh and
striking acidity; Lalo also passes around slices of a midget pineapple,
only about six inches in height and three inches in diameter. As is
often the case, the smaller version of this fruit has a particularly
concentrated flavor.

We finish the visit in Lalo's home, tasting a multitude of his
distillates, which he sells under two labels. Domestically, he has
his own mark, Mezcal Lalocura, but internationally he uses the
Sacaparablas Mezcal Aresanal label that is not so widely distributed but is maintained by a friend who handles the headache of
export. His spirits are among the finest we'll taste, and his company
matches. Before we've been at the table long, he gives us each a
tall, cold glass of *jamaica*, or hibiscus tea, sweetened with a little
sugar. It's a hot, sunny day, and we appreciate the hydration. Here
we have enjoyed a holism in Lalo's approach that I did not see with
Del Maguey's distillers who, while lovely, felt disembodied by comparison, disconnected from any greater context, local or global. Lalo

takes a great interest in our work—in particular, what the market is like in San Francisco. He asks what our clients pay for various spirits and takes great interest in the answers. He is quite free in his criticism of gringos who buy and resell mezcal down here. He says, without hesitation, that these merchant bottlers are extorting the producers. Our talk is full of laughter and comfortable silences. We are sad to leave, but we are going to visit Lalo's sister, which lessens the sadness of saying good-bye.

Graciela Angeles Carreño, sister of Lalo, lives just down the road from her brother, where she operates Real Minero, a renowned owner-operated distillery that does its own bottling and distribution. Again, we navigate not by GPS with Ismael, who enjoyed a nice long nap in his yellow cab while we passed time with Lalo, but by voice, asking the children we pass exactly where we can find Graciela's place across the basketball court as she said we should. We find the basketball court and see a long, metal wall with a couple of locked doors on either side of a large simple rendering of the Real Minero logo, with its silhouette of an earthenware jug and charming all-caps block letters that look like the script of a warm-hearted architect. We are at an impasse, standing equidistant between two doors, when an officer of some kind standing with a friend by the basketball court asks if we were looking for Graciela. He directs us to the door on the right, where we enter and wander into a kind of courtyard with laundry hanging and a small house with white plaster walls. We can hear women and children within, and I immediately feel intrusive.

Tentatively, we walk toward the origin of those voices and sounds, leaning forward and craning our necks around the corner to see within. Chris is ahead of me and is greeted by a woman I can't see, who asks us to wait a moment. We do. Before a minute has passed, a vital, small man emerges, smiling beneath a cowboy hat with a creased brim. Like Luís Carlos, he wears a well-manicured silver moustache and a cowboy shirt of a pale grid pattern with a snap front. His cowboy boots are weathered but clean, and his powder-blue, faded denim pants are creased like a boy's whose mother did his washing. In general, he looks like fresh, clean laundry, a match for the linens and clothes drying in the breezy sunlight. This is Graciela and Lalo's father. He makes friendly eye contact with each of us and invites us to follow him a few meters to a pickup truck. We climb into the back and remain standing, steadying ourselves with the large metal rack affixed to the bed. We drive only a short way until arriving at another black metal barrier that lines the road, this time decorated only with the words *Mezcal Real Minero* written in the same appealing font. Papa Carreño swings open the metal gate, and hops back in the driver's seat to bring us to the other side of the metal boundary, which was obscuring from us a paradise of thick grass, palms, flowering trees, and an abundance of agaves of various extractions, shapes, and sizes. As with Lalo, this tour begins with and prioritizes agriculture. In between descriptions of various *piñas*, he jokes with us that his daughters do not let him drink anymore. It's been years. He is of a similar age and appearance to Luís from yesterday, but he feels engaged and curious and his excitement is infectious.

In the midst of our enjoyment of her father's company, Graciela arrives, heralded by the slam of an iron door that penetrates the same wall as the gate by which we entered. She is all about business, shaking each of our hands firmly and repeating each of our names to herself and to us to be sure she has them correct. She will use them through the tour, earnestly at first but then later in a more intimate, joking manner. As she is beautiful, with thick, unruly hair parted in the center and held fast at the nape of her neck, I imagine we all wish she would cross the line toward flirtation, but she will not. Instead, she pokes fun at us. Describing the process of distillation quite clinically, she finishes and with feigned somber interest asks, "Don't you agree, Chris?" who seems to miss the Spanish. I don't know why this is funny, but it is. Graciela stands still a moment with an indulgent gaze aimed toward Chris, who is a perfectly impassive straight man.

We enjoy the peaceful afternoon, being guided about by Graciela in her form-fitting blue jeans tucked into work boots and a loose women's work shirt with a white flower pattern on a navy backdrop. At one point, she insists that I stand an enormous *largo piña* upright and position myself beside it, feigning profound curiosity as to which object may be taller. The tour is great fun not only because the large artisanal facility is well maintained and produces great spirits that we are fortunate enough to taste at various stages of production, but also because of the visit's tone. Professional but warm, she tells us a bit more about the family. Her father has no formal education, but out of his seven children, five of them went to university. I ask her why Lalo left to distill on his own and she answers impenetrably, "I believe this is what Eduardo prefers."

On these trips to Oaxaca, I am left contemplating what is the greater context that mezcal will come to occupy. These are savage beauties compared to the other spirits I traffic, but mezcal is being brought indoors. Its ascension to a greater scale is inescapable, but what I would hope for is that it is presided over by the likes of the Carreños, with their passion for agriculture and their ancestry that connects them to the provenance of these spirits. They advocate for the advancement of the category but also for their families and their village; the two are inseparable: from Lalo, once mayor of Santa Catarina, whose facility is crawling with children and affectionate relatives and will take us to meet his neighbor, who produces a tiny amount of mezcal fermented in leather and insists we buy it from the man at the price he sets—a far cry from asking us to sign a nondisclosure agreement—to Graciela who now invites us into the tasting parlor at Real Minero. We taste five or six spirits of her choosing. Each label is marked with a decisive color, which I note and ask her, for example, why is it the blend of *espadín*, *largo*, *tripon* (one of my favorites), and *barril* (another of them) bears a label that has a rusty, bloody color. I am delighted when she replies that tasting mezcal makes her think of colors. Oh, how I agree. This sanguine, clay color is what's conjured when she tastes this mixture. I'm sure I am impressionable, but I do concur with her choice of color.

We enjoy the cool, late afternoon light, occupied by the dirt and pollen of this fertile property, as it penetrates the high windows to the tasting room. I am pleased with my company and feel an easing of the chronic tension between my shoulder blades that I only become aware of by its passing. "Well, Graciela," I say. "What am I looking for in this *arroqueño*?"

Graciela turns the corners of her mouth up slightly, and replies flatly, "Well, Tadeo, I can't speak to what you're looking for, but I can tell you what you might find."

Chapter Eleven

KENTUCKY

THE RARE OLD MOUNTAIN DEW

To take a tour of an American whiskey distillery in Kentucky is almost inevitably to be immersed in apocryphal horseshit, which is only appropriate, as bourbon is our nation's "native spirit," as decreed by Congress in 1964. We are the nation of apocryphal horseshit, and at no point is this more apparent than the day I most recently arrive in Kentucky, on November 8, 2016. I am joined by Chris and Craig, who arrive on a red-eye an hour after I've arrived on a red-eye of my own, leaving me time to go grab the car: a beige, new-model Cadillac. My last rental car was the Renault Duster we left dead on the side of the road in Oaxaca, and I notice I'm a little jumpy as I leave the rental lot. But what car could surpass a modern Cadillac in its adequacy for a fresh tour of bourbon distilleries?

I collect Craig and Chris from the curb at the Louisville International Airport, and we're off to our first appointment of the trip at Four Roses Distillery. I've put in the necessary legwork speaking with brand ambassadors and distributors about each of our visits to arrange more personal and informative tours than we'd get if we just walked in off the street. To be fair, I should say that we do not sell these brands at our restaurants, which explains why we likely will receive little in the way of special treatment, though we are expected at each of our stops.

When we opened Bar Agricole in 2010, we had no bourbon on our list, which was poor timing because Americans had probably never been more obsessed with bourbon and we were certainly receiving orders for it. As is now clear, I am most interested in spirits with clear agricultural origins, and until relatively recently it was practically impossible to find a consistent supply of American whiskey that wasn't built from commodity-grade grain bought on the open market. The same is true of most scotch, we recently learned. Further cementing the identity of bourbon as the native spirit of the United States, and our lack of enthusiasm for it, is the truth that this whiskey is a by-product of corn subsidized by 1.5 billion dollars in Kentucky alone in the last twenty years. A number of great books and films about corn in the United States already exist. I will leave my hat out of that ring, but I also assume most readers have, at this point, developed a weariness of North American corn, which has infiltrated every corner of our diet in the form of industrial sweeteners, empty calories, and feed for the excess of protein bred in the United States that destroys the environment and saps us of water. Worth mentioning is that domestic whiskey producers are starting to rely more on non-GMO grains, largely due to the European Union's restrictions of products made from these scientifically modified crops.

Bourbon is a paradox. At once the most obsessed-over spirit, with bottles like Pappy Van Winkle's twenty-year selling for thousands of dollars, it is also a pretty industrial, unremarkable spirit compared to a number we have already tasted on our journey together. For the three thousand dollars a twenty-year-old bottle of bourbon fetches, I could fill your shelves with thirty grower-producer, wild-fermented, cask-strength, unfiltered bottles of spirit that blow your mind. When opening Bar Agricole, we wanted to put our money where our mouths are and we stocked only one American whiskey made by our friends at Leopold Bros., who operate one of my favorite

US distilleries. Its aroma and flavor were grain-forward with fruity cereal notes, but it was aged in used oak (regulations specify that bourbon must be aged in newly charred, unused American oak), so it was not representative of the sweet, vanillin, caramel richness that consumers expect from American whiskey, especially bourbon. Certain guests were consistently disappointed with our American whiskey, wishing it had more "body," which really means "sweetness." This chagrin was particularly frustrating to us as the Leopolds' whiskey was, understandably, more expensive given its small production and attention to provenance.

So after a year of disappointed guests, Eric and I conceded and headed to Kentucky to choose, from our perspective, the best of the worst. Our attitude was certainly a little arrogant, though informed by years of waiting on predominantly men with an imagined connoisseurship for American whiskey, which, when I'm at my most cynical, tastes like grain vodka blasted with caramel. What happened on that first trip? We met Jimmy Russell, head distiller of many years at Wild Turkey, and were won over by his charm. Wild Turkey, for reasons I'll explain later, became the one straight bourbon to join Leopold Bros.' American whiskey, if you must know.

Of late, though, I have a restored appreciation for American whiskey for three primary reasons. First, bourbon and rye are proper appellations, meaning clear requisites of production exist to which producers must adhere for their product to be labeled *bourbon* or *rye*. In particular, to be labeled as bourbon or rye, the whiskey's composition, or "mash bill," must adhere to certain ratios (that is, bourbon must be distilled from a mash bill of 51 percent of corn or more, rye from 51 percent rye). It must be put in the barrel at an ABV below 62.5 percent, which ensures it will retain some of the character of the grain from which it is made. Remember that the higher the percentage of alcohol in the distillate as it comes off the still, the more neutral, perhaps less interesting, it will taste.

Bourbon barrels must be new American oak, which means that charred wood sugar informs the smell, flavor, and color of these whiskies. Arguably, bourbon *is* a real agricultural spirit, just one that prioritizes the flavors of its cooperage over those of its base materials. Really, the enjoyment of bourbon is the appreciation of American oak. In this way, bourbon is not unlike cognac, which is distilled to a fairly high ABV and aged, then blended. Bourbon and rye may be blended, but straight bourbon and straight rye do not allow for augmentation with caramel coloring or flavoring, ingredients that are virtually ubiquitous in cognac and often yield one of those spirits that taste like flat Coca-Cola. The term "straight" is important, though; if it's not on the label, the whiskies might have additives. In fact, every other aged spirit in the world allows added caramel coloring or flavoring, so straight bourbon and rye are where we find the truest categorical representation of barrel aging, one of the most-prized characteristics in the spirit world. That genuineness alone is reason to respect these straight American whiskies. Sadly, though, to find other genuine qualities in bourbon can be difficult.

Four Roses Distillery is an hour due east of the airport, and we drive along straight, flat roads that penetrate the fertile Kentucky countryside. Not surprisingly, Craig, who tastefully and obsessively curates music at both of the bars in San Francisco, has prepared a playlist for our travels, which begins with Bill Monroe, Kentucky's son and progenitor of bluegrass music. We are silent, listening to "Six White Horses" while the thick, shaggy Kentucky grass stretches out all around us beneath an outspread November sky shot through with cumulus clouds. Every mile or so we pass beneath a concrete overpass, moving slowly through a large grid of rural highways at a pace that matches the melancholic soundtrack.

Were you there when they crucified my Lord?
Were you there when they crucified my Lord?

Oh, sometimes it causes me to tremble, tremble, tremble.
Were you there when they crucified my Lord?
Were you there when they nailed him to the cross?
Were you there when they nailed him to the cross?
Oh, sometimes it causes me to tremble, tremble, tremble.
Were you there when they nailed him to the cross?

This song holds special meaning for me and triggers my own reverie. Lester, my stepfather, is a bluegrass guitarist, though he doesn't play much anymore. When he and I were much younger, he played bluegrass every Tuesday night with a colleague of my mother's named John Robinson, who played the mandolin and would prepare himself for these sessions with a skinny, wrinkled joint.

I remember clearly their rehearsals of "Were You There?" When they arrived at the chorus and sang, "*Sometimes it causes me to tremble . . .*" they would trade the word "tremble" back and forth, each singer performing the word at a higher octave than the previous. Neither could sing in a falsetto, but it was John who would sing the final "tremble" in his highest voice, which would crack at times and cause the two of them to laugh. At the age of seven, I was a serious audience. Songs like "Knoxville Girl," which depicts a man who kills and drags his lover around by her hair beside the river, or devout gospel numbers that promised hell to those who do not practice Christianity, frightened me. More than once, after John had left, I asked Lester if we were going to hell and he would promise that we weren't.

Many credit Irish immigrants with the introduction of distilling to the United States. Similarly, the influence of the British Isles can be found in the musical history of the Southeast, from the use of similar instruments like banjo, fiddle, and guitar to the prevalence of traditional music, evinced by the famous Lomax field recordings of old English folk songs in Appalachia. Lester and John would try their hands at some Irish folk music as well. Most significant for me was the old tune "The Rare Old Mountain Dew," an ode to distillation that I'm sure is in part to blame for the wanderings that have become this book:

Let grasses grow and waters flow
In a free and easy way,
But give me enough of the fine old stuff
That's made near Galway Bay,
And policemen all from Donegal,
Sligo and Leitrim too,
Oh, we'll give them the slip and we'll take a sip
Of the rare old Mountain Dew
At the foot of the hill there's a neat little still,
Where the smoke curls up to the sky,
By the smoke and the smell you can plainly tell
That there's poitin brewin' nearby.
It fills the air with all dew rare,
And betwixt both me and you,
When home you stroll, you can take a bowl,
Or a bucket of the Mountain Dew
Now learned men who use the pen,
Have wrote your praises high
Of the sweet poitin from Ireland green,
Distilled from wheat and rye.
Throw away with your pills, it'll cure all ills,
Of Pagan, Christian or Jew,
So take off your coat and grease your throat
With the rare old Mountain Dew.

While I am not expert enough to prove it, I believe, sadly, we are becoming less and less connected to this kind of folk music that spans hundreds of years and that survived great migrations and cultural collisions. I love the tones of the mandolin, fiddle, and acoustic guitar, and their organic quality reminds me of the kind of distilling I like most, a folk distilling if you will, that inseminates spirits with the trappings of a certain place and time. These flavors are primary and analog. Just as I wonder how an American living in rural Appalachia learns and sings "The Ballad of Matty Groves" on homemade instruments, I imagine how spirits must have tasted, borne of different subcultures distilled in their respective pockets of settled land.

If you will pardon more amateur anthropology, this confluence of flavor and song has another parallel: that of jazz and the mixed drink. Distillation starts with agriculture and is historically rural. But the mixed drink's identity is urban. More specifically, in the trade hubs of the late eighteenth, nineteenth, and early twentieth centuries, cultures collided in cities like New Orleans, New York, Chicago, and San Francisco. Bottled spirits with their near-infinite shelf life arrived courtesy of evolving shipping and train technology, which shrunk the world and granted access to suites of ingredients never before available from around the globe: fresh fruit from the Americas, cordials from Europe, herbs and tinctures from the East. The *cocktail*, which by its earliest definition is a simple mixture of a spirit with a bitter and sweetening agent, took hold in these newly cosmopolitan parts of the United States. As the luxury goods market evolved and more products became available, the cocktail gave way to "improved cocktails," which were a new category that allowed for variations and combinations beyond just spirit-bitter-sweet. Instead of adding some raw sugar syrup and gentian bitters to whiskey (a traditional "cocktail"), you might see combined a spirit, maraschino cordial from Yugoslavia, sweet Italian vermouth, and amaro (an "improved cocktail").

The evolution of the mixed drink is traceable to these cultural nerve centers, where the first great bartenders combined the ingredients they now had on hand in the more-thirsty social climate of a young United States. Simultaneously, the collision of these cultures manifested in their music. European training and virtuosity converged with folk and improvisational traditions and begat a new form, jazz. One version of the story is the country became more diverse; immigrants enjoyed bittered slings while delighting to Dixieland. Many books have been written about mixed drinks, and about jazz, but I digress to encourage the reader to contemplate the production of spirits and their mixture both as art forms, or at least a true craft

Imagine if jazz had been abolished at its onset—an act of cultural murder, of course, but also a gesture of division when multitudinous cultures and ethnicities were truly integrating in one art. This is what happened with the ratification of Prohibition in 1920: the art form of the mixed drink was censored. While many prohibitionists were sincere in their desire to protect the bodies and souls of Americans from the degradation of drink, fear of the mélange of flavors, people, and sounds in the new American city doubtless contributed to other, more prejudiced politics.

Prohibition lasted thirteen years, long enough to see the great bartenders of the United States leave for Paris and London, and to eradicate the fledgling tradition of licensed US distilling. Upon repeal of the Eighteenth Amendment, the US spirits market came aboveground again. But the industry was collectivized and conglomerated by the likes of the Canadian giant Seagram Company, which capitalized on its status as the largest legal distiller in North America to develop and own the US market. Seagram's introduced their famous line of blended whiskies to the US market, starting in 1933 at the end of Prohibition when they were poised and ready to capture the newly opened American market with their ample stores of aged whiskies, ultimately becoming the first company to sell a million cases of any spirit.

Before Prohibition, many small distilleries thrived across the country. But after repeal, and for the rest of the twentieth century, the production of spirits was increasingly industrialized and consolidated as the industry grew larger and larger in scale. Nowhere is this more true than in Kentucky and Indiana, where the American whiskey trade is dominated by a few huge distillers that you can count on one hand.

Consolidation is what we're planning to see on this trip as we continue across Kentucky on a calm November day. The cool country air is immune to the naked sun that washes the landscape. Trump signs mark the abundant and famous grass. I am optimistic about the election tonight, and looking forward to enjoying a large cigar and talking about American whiskey, about which I am less optimistic, while we watch the returns come in. Ironically, I will be surprised on both the election and whiskey fronts.

Our strange, late-model Cadillac, trading on its grand American reputation just as bourbon does, gets us to Lawrenceburg with an hour to spare, so we consult our list of barbecue places. The most convenient today is called Staxx, not far from Four Roses. Staxx's building and ephemera are adorned with a jolly, anthropomorphized pig that seems to celebrate his own evisceration, a recurring strategy of decoration I find unsettling at times. We order a half-pound each of pulled pork, brisket, and smoked sausages; for sides, we order pickles, coleslaw, green beans, and potato salad. We agree that the barbecue is tasty, and discuss what we're hoping to accomplish in Kentucky. No one's expectations are high, but we are here to meet bourbon on its own terms. Chris's only other distillery trip was to Oaxaca, so he is swinging rapidly to the other end of the spectrum here in the United States. Craig finishes strong, mopping up the last of each of our plates of barbecue; he has a tremendous appetite and metabolism.

We are received warmly at Four Roses and are diverted to our tour guide. Big operations like this have a tiered system of tours and we, as insiders, will get a good off-the-shelf tour but won't gain access to much that is authentic. We watch a promo film that is full of floral language like "golden ripe corn," "flavorful rye," "full bodied," "consistently smooth mellow taste," and "exquisitely smooth." We learn that three-quarters of a million bushels of grain are used by Four Roses each year; that's 26,400,000 liters. This kind of information alone always causes me to lose interest, betraying my prejudice against spirits of this scale. The agricultural component is unremarkable, composed mostly of subsidized, commodity-grade grain. We endure the rest of the video, which gives a layperson's description of the history and production, walking us through a rudimentary description of fermentation, distillation, and aging. After the video, we are led on a walk around the grounds by Clark, who is collegiately dressed in a navy sweater and white shirt with exposed collar. Clark treats us to a rehearsed tour, complete with historic anecdotes delivered hurriedly in a good-natured monotone, beginning with the obligatory origin story: the name of the place is in honor of the corsage worn by the distillery founder's beloved to signal that her answer to his marriage proposal was yes.

Seagram bought Four Roses in the mid-1900s, growing its scale mightily and simultaneously limiting its distribution exclusively to overseas. This was due to the sudden shift in the domestic market away from brown to clear spirits, coinciding, of course, with the introduction of vodka to the US market. Vodka was the ultimate post-Prohibition spirit: easy to produce and, due to its neutrality, a fine marriage with any highball component.

In 2002, Four Roses was reintroduced to the domestic market by Kirin Brewery. Kirin had purchased the brand from Diageo, which had acquired it from Vivendi, which had first bought Seagram. We follow Clark along a paved road overlooking the facility, a mission-style warehouse complex painted the brand's trademark yellow, which looks more like a dreary, faded mustard in this late-afternoon light. Clark explains that Kirin is working to double production here from thirteen thousand gallons a day to twenty-six to thirty thousand a day, or ten million gallons a year, produced now by two enormous column stills.

This tour is not the worst we've had. Our guy is friendly and efficient and has us convinced he doesn't hate his job, but we do not see any aspect of the production process during the tour. Chris and Craig look how I feel: tired from the day of travel, but persevering through those fading hours that separate daylight from night. Our category of tour entitles us to taste three different Four Roses products of our own choosing. One nice thing about Four Roses is that it generally produces and bottles whiskies only under the Four Roses label. This already differentiates it from several of the largest distillers, which sell countless whiskies with different labels in order to give the impression that each comes from a unique distillery, when really a few large factories are making the great majority of the American whiskey sold. Also interesting is that Four Roses has five different yeast strains and two different mash bills, making for ten unique whiskies that they bottle here.

I taste their Yellow Label, which is the proprietary blend of all of ten whiskies, but it is bottled at 40 percent and chill filtered, like pretty much all American whiskey. As I've said, I'm not a fan of nonfat milk and I remain critical of chill-filtered spirits that have been divested of the fats and oils that give the spirit its character. Bottled at 40 percent, the Yellow Label doesn't taste much of grain but delivers the familiar trappings of barrel aging: vanillin, caramel, baking spice. I graduate to two of their cask bottlings, which are each pulled from single barrels of one of the ten varieties of whiskey. Blessedly, they are not chill filtered and are bottled at a higher ABV. Though they do not defy the stereotype of bourbon, the higher proof and unfiltered quality make them more interesting. Again, to be a connoisseur of bourbon is to be someone who enjoys the flavors of burnt oak, which are definitely crowd pleasing. We are also allowed to pick a bottle from the gift shop to take home, in addition to an item of memorabilia, or *swag*, which was a nice gesture. I pick a bottle of the Yellow Label, which I'll end up selling at Bar Agricole to a party that wants bourbon drinks, and a bright yellow Four Roses T-shirt.

Over the next two days, we eat a lot of barbecue and taste a great deal of bourbon, and we notice an interplay between these two facets of Kentucky gastronomy. Neither insists on a particularly high standard of agriculture for their animals or grain, respectively, which makes sense because the core ingredients are secondary to the satisfying, rich flavors of sugar and wood smoke. I enjoy bourbon just as I enjoy barbecue, but I am not interested in appreciating them as a connoisseur. The difference is that barbecue remains unpretentious for the most part, but bourbon has gone off the rails with people paying hundreds, if not thousands, of dollars for simple, column distillate with no real sense of place, hammered with charred oak then chill filtered.

We visit Jim Beam, whose entire tour aspires to appear sepia toned, with its portraits of ancestors and inescapable old-timeyness. Owned by the Japanese multinational Suntory, Beam produces more than twenty whiskies that come from the same large column still, including their "small batch bourbon collection" that includes Booker's, Baker's, Basil Hayden's, and Knob Creek. The Jim Beam Harvest Collection sounds interesting, featuring six bourbons augmented with particular grains: triticale, high rye, six-row barley, soft red wheat, brown rice, and whole rolled oat. A line like this seems to cater to some population that is interested in agriculture, but I'm reluctant to get too excited by these offerings from a company that also sells cinnamon, apple, maple, and honey liqueurs as well as the recent Devil's Cut, which is an extraction of the whiskey trapped in an empty barrel's staves mixed with young bourbon. Our friend Mark at Cadenhead's was shocked recently to see that a scotch he was finishing in a bourbon barrel was getting no benefit from the cask. Upon closer inspection, he realized this barrel was one that had been used for a project like the Devil's Cut; all residual flavor had been stripped from the staves. Jim Beam is not the only distillery practicing these tricks. Since bourbon cannot be called bourbon unless it is aged in new oak, distilleries are left with an abundance of barrels they can't use again. These barrels are sold around the world and are a primary source of casks to age all kinds of spirits.

We visit Heaven Hill, or at least their tourist center, whose waiting room features the ubiquitous series of monochromatic portraits and vintage anecdotes convincing us that we have arrived at the cradle of American whiskey. And in a way we have, though not as this historic exhibit would have us believe. Heaven Hill holds about one and a half million barrels of bourbon, which, when combined with Jim Beam's inventory, equals half of the bourbon in the world. Our tour guide is Clancy, who actually does seem of these parts, though a little weathered in his stovepipe dungarees and Heaven Hill polo, at least two sizes too large, which is tucked into the margin of a belt pulled so taut it seems to endanger his spine and kidneys. His coarse, graying hair is parted carefully but is otherwise messy, with cowlicks standing out in the back. He speaks with a warm and ambling diction, stressing right away the fact that his company is "family owned," a distinction I've seen others stress but does not, in itself, really mean anything. I find large producers usually emphasize this detail in hopes that it makes the company more approachable, like our strategically hired host who grew up only a few miles from this tourist center. Presumably, a family-owned company wouldn't take marching orders from stockholders, but I see little evidence of them operating like a company whose primary focus is anything but making money. Clancy sticks to his memorized material with rigid intensity, straining a little to stay on script, which undermines his precisely timed jokes. "Heaven Hill is happy to be number two to Jim Beam and take it easy," he says, turning up the corners of his mouth in what would be a smile were it not for the look of detached horror in his eyes that are focused on nothing in particular. Craig laughs politely, leaning forward in Clancy's direction, in a posture of deference. Chris looks on, stone-faced.

Heaven Hill is the sixth largest producer of spirits in the world, Clancy tells us proudly. They manufacture more than one hundred bourbons and twelve hundred other products, which run from HPNOTIQ, the famous electric-blue cognac-based tropical fruit cordial, to Fulton's Harvest Pumpkin Pie Cream Liqueur to the grand, continental, fortified wine Dubonnet.

Watch out for the European classics. We learned on a previous trip that Wild Turkey bottled Campari, now cloyingly sweet and dubiously colored, at their distillery for years. We avoid Campari at all costs, which may not help our cause in the numerous awards they've been sponsoring of late. Heaven Hill's whiskey portfolio contains scores of differently named whiskies, including Pikesville, Larceny, Old Fitzgerald, Rittenhouse, and J.T.S. Brown. Each of these is marketed like an ancient American classic, with distressed labels and provocative origin story. While we are not shown the behemoth of a distillery, we do get to walk through a couple of the enormous rickhouses that stand out like barracks in the otherwise pastoral scene of low trees and bushy meadow. The interior of the rickhouse seems like a dark hatchery with its rows upon rows of casks. The spirit introduced to these charred vessels, themselves more expensive than the unaged spirit, is simply a means to extract the sweet caramel from the scorched interior of the barrel. Bourbon is basically sweet oak juice.

Many of you may say you don't drink your whiskey from the likes of these distilleries. Odds are, though, that you do, even if you're not aware of it, because small, new distilleries are struggling to survive, given that they must accumulate inventory. While they try to do so, they will generally sell "white dog" or new make spirit hastily aged in small casks that give the whiskey a reedy, astringent flavor. Or they simply sell bourbon made by other distillers. The company that furnishes perhaps the most of this secret, resold whiskey is produced not in Kentucky but Indiana at the factory distillery once owned by Seagram, but now the property of the food ingredient corporation Midwest Grain Products, or MGP. In addition to food-grade industrial alcohol used in solvents, antiseptics, and fungicides, they sell American whiskies that are often marketed as craft or artisanal. Angel's Envy, Bulleit Rye, Filibuster, George Dickel Rye, High West, James E. Pepper, Redemption, Smooth Ambler, and Templeton Rye have all come from MGP and have been sold by the likes of Diageo as buried treasure. Unsurprisingly, they all taste like bourbon, which means they all taste like new American oak, just like all the rest. I've been to all these producers and the similarities far outweigh the differences among their bottlings. While they trade on the hominess of this region, the spirits could be made anywhere, and indeed are made anywhere, with grains from around the world. However, in fairness, they are casked in white oak, which must be grown in the United States.

As a small-business person, I have some empathy for the smaller producers that rely on third-party factory production to get going—to brave years of no revenue in order to develop an inventory is a challenge. But it's not impossible.

We take our buttermilk-colored Cadillac through acres more of flat, fertile pasture to visit Wild Turkey, home to Jimmy Russell, who's been the distiller there for many decades and who now is lucky enough to collaborate with Matthew McConaughey in the marketing of his whiskies. In the past, we've been fortunate to be received by Russell himself. He is mischievous and charming as he disparages his competitors, suggesting with a wink that they might not use grain of the same quality as Turkey, or they might distill to a higher alcohol by volume, rendering spirit with less character than Jimmy's. We chose to sell Wild Turkey for years for a few reasons. First, they make one rye and one bourbon, and sell them under their own name with little fanfare. All of their offerings total about ten labels that make no deceitful effort to appear antiquated and rustic. They were among the first to commit to using non-GMO grain. The spirits are produced on a large scale, of course, but the transaction feels clean. Like an affordable gin or rum, bourbon may not be a single cask from the Camut brothers in Normandy, but it has its value and we generally feel our guests deserve to order it. Furthermore, it is appropriate in cocktails that call for the simple, archetypal flavor of American oak and little else.

Today we are not greeted by Jimmy Russell. Instead, we're grouped with an existing tour, perhaps because we no longer sell Wild Turkey. Our guide is a woman named Susan, who wears a branded windbreaker with chinos and conveys us in a van from stop to stop. We take a cursory look at each stage of the process: a sampling of the grains, the fermentation tanks, the enormous column still, the Spartan rickhouses with their legions of imprisoned, drowning oak barrels. Susan delivers her jokes earnestly and efficiently.

We split from the group before the tasting room and make our way to the Willet property, a smaller distillery that has been distilling long enough to begin selling its own distillate, though a majority of what they sell is still bought from another distillery, the identity of which they won't share. That these companies can simply sell whiskey from another producer is such clear evidence that this category is more to do with cooperage than who makes it and from what. All of these whiskies are basically interchangeable, which is why one distiller can sell so many whiskies under so many labels. The workaday, traditional composition of bourbon should generate a simple, unpretentious marketplace; instead it is the most deceitful, frustrating category I can imagine. This handful of producers flood the market with innumerous, fictitious brands to a seemingly endless demand, and very few smaller distilleries are able to get a foothold in an arena dominated by titans with unlimited inventory who can price small producers out of the market.

But what is the appetite this duplicitous marketing satisfies? I assure you I'm hungry for it, too—but what *is* it? For years, I've been fascinated by the encyclopedic field recordings of Alan Lomax. In the 1940s, '50s, and '60s, he collected and recorded thousands of folk songs from all around the world, including, of course, the United States. When I listen to these recordings I feel nourished by these unadorned analog songs, songs that sound dusty and covered with pollen and could only have been sung on the ground where Lomax recorded them by now long-dead performers. Cowboy songs, prison spirituals, early American ballads, the first calypso ever recorded—the list goes on. Of course, I cannot ask all of the spirits I taste to have the *authenticity*, to use a complicated word, of a Welsh balladeer singing an ancient song a cappella in the early twentieth century. But I am pissed at the companies that duplicitously promise that experience to their consumers.

A couple of days later, after dropping Craig and Chris at the airport, I drive around rural Kentucky. It's a snapping, cold, sunny day, and I pause the Cadillac at various junctures, photographing scenes that I find beautiful: an enormous tree at the peak of its autumn transition; a simple, old, symmetrical barn made of whitewashed planks that support a sturdy, peaked roof. I stop at a general store that sells it all, from dresses to baked beans. Its diversity of inventory rivals that of Walmart or Target and none of it is made here, but the store is independent, which only makes me thirstier, thirsty for what bourbon promises and doesn't deliver. Thirsty, too, for what politicians promise and don't deliver—but their promises are ones of tone and inference, not substance.

Today, in this shitty store in the middle of rural Kentucky, I am far from home, but I feel connected to a choice we all want to make: for something that is not bullshit. This political year I didn't see a choice that could really satisfy my thirst for credibility, and in Kentucky, I don't see the liquid equivalent. But thankfully, I will soon be on my way to Colorado to visit my friend Todd Leopold.

A week later, I land in Denver. Todd greets me in his tasting room in tan, loose-fitting Carhartt coveralls. His thick, strawberry-blond hair and beard are surrendering to the frost of middle age. He is strong and ursine, and I give him a big hug before sitting at the rough plank table in his tasting room. The Leopold Bros.' distillery is in a light industrial mall not fifteen minutes from the airport, an unlikely setting for one of the most trustworthy distillers I've encountered in the United States, if not the whole world. The other Leopold brother is Scott, who is the financial officer that every visionary like Todd should be lucky enough to have. The brothers' relationship is a strong one, built on a fierce, mutual respect. When you speak to one, he will insist that it is the other who is responsible for the business's success.

If you taste the American whiskey of Leopold Bros., you will be stunned by the flavors of grain and yeast—earthy, living flavors—that augment rather than surrender to the pleasantries of charred oak. In sourcing, malting, and fermenting, Leopold Bros., value the provenance and quality of their grown base material more than most distillers I've encountered.

Recently, Todd took an improbable risk in commissioning Vendome, a copper works in Louisville, to build a three-chamber copper rye still, the likes of which no one living has seen. Vendome is a steampunk's dream, building by hand Victorian technology that often looks as if it came from Jules Verne's imagination. Todd's research led him to believe that this obsolete still had once been the standard and is the ideal machine to make rye. I am sworn to some secrecy on this, but this still essentially extracts the qualities of the grain in three different ways, yielding a multitude of flavors, almost like tasting in another *dimension* when combined with the other aspects of Todd's unimpeachable production. All he had to go on were old drawings that he actually believed were wrong, but he nevertheless moved forward with the still. I find this leap so moving. Todd and Scott, without whose financial management Todd agrees this would never have been possible, risked their careers on a machine that might never have worked. A true family operation, these brothers who were just achieving a certain amount of security in a marketplace that destroys small, independent producers or buys them, risked it all to save American whiskey, or at least make some beautiful rye whiskey. I can assure you, the three-chamber still works. The resulting spirit has an added dimension of flavor that left me winded, believing I'd never really tasted rye whiskey before. Sadly, we all must wait a few years while the brothers wisely accumulate the inventory necessary to launch a viable mark.

Todd shows me around the still, which looks like a nineteenth-century time machine. He does not resort to canned jokes or mythologizing, and treats me with enough respect to try to explain the science of the contraption exactly and how it yields a spirit that actually tastes different. The sincerity of this tour leaves me feeling well fed, and we sit again at the long table in the tasting room and talk shop, speaking frankly of the anxiety that producing these spirits and selling them can yield. It is a risky business, and I am heartened by the integrity and brashness with which the Leopold brothers operate. Todd is doing his own malting now, allowing him to make more complicated mash bills while supporting local brewers to whom he sells his maltings. While too many US distillers go to great lengths to sanitize every aspect of production, Todd actually celebrates microbial life and encourages its growth at key junctures because he knows it deepens the spirits. He has clarified to me that much of this life comes on the husks of the grain and must be treated delicately so that it enriches the fermentation. Excitedly, Todd shares with me that he is about to start experimenting with spontaneous fermentation, meaning he will rely on the natural yeasts that thrive in his distillery which have their own identity rather than inoculations of off-the-shelf yeast. Wild fermentation has led to some of the most beautiful spirits I've tasted, particularly in Oaxaca. He is traveling backward through time in a real way, not pretending, and in so doing will let us taste what our forebears tasted rather than alienating us with lifeless, stripped spirits produced in greater and greater quantities. Twice I have flown to Denver simply to talk to Todd; this is how encouraging and inspiring I find him.

Fortunately, I don't always need to travel so far to find this kind of inspiration. Lance Winters and his wife, Ellie, are the distillers behind St. George Spirits in the San Francisco Bay Area. Along with Leopold Bros., they are one of the only domestic distilleries I know that remain both independent and relevant.

For the first time, this year we host an event at Bar Agricole—fifty dollars all you can eat and drink—to celebrate our friendship with St. George. Arrogantly, Bar Agricole has been boycotting the distributor Lance uses because they handle a number of large brands we can't stand. But the loneliness of being right is not as satisfying as doing business with people you love. In our discussion in Denver, Todd characterized Lance and himself accurately: "Lance is bold and passionate. He says, 'I'm going to make an agave spirit. I'm going to make an aperitivo. I'm going to make an agricole rum.' Then he does it. Boom. Me, I'm obsessive. I have to study and consider for months, if not years, being sure it's historically accurate and correct." Todd is right. When he recreated an authentic maraschino cherry cordial, he made countless versions, communicated with the Croatian government, left no stone unturned. It was when he launched the maraschino at Bar Agricole that he and Lance met. Similarly, when he made his aperitivo, an alternative to Campari, he made multiple passes and took more than a year. Lance's seemed to spring fully formed from his skull. Try them both. Both are wonderful, and the distillers' styles are borne out in the juice: the Leopold Bros.' is bright, delicate, and articulate, while Lance's is bold and decisively dark by comparison.

From the agricole-style rums and agave, to single runs of whiskey, to one of the first real and enduring absinthes of the domestic market, to the beautiful pear *eau de vies* that got the house started years ago, St. George continues to impress and to inspire me. A true dilettante, Lance moves around but the quality is always there. He is lithe and handsome, balding with short-cropped hair almost exactly the same color as Todd Leopold's, now that I consider it. He looks and is ex-military, mellowed out by his time as a parent, husband, and small businessman. He prowls his beautiful, copper distillery in Alameda with a panoramic view of San Francisco across the bay, working at times with an unlit cigar in his mouth.

At the St. George's party at Bar Agricole in December, Lance and I catch up as St. George employees mingle with fans of their work who had bought tickets to drink the spirits and eat grilled chicken on a warm, winter San Francisco night. We speak, too, about the anxiety of small business ownership and the risk of independence in an industry that is so dominated by large interests. At the end of the day, we are all just trying to make payroll and pay our taxes. We have parties like this more to honor friendship than to make money. Lance jokes with me that I am too serious, and he is right. I am happy, though, that I turned the negative of avoiding a distributor into the positive of supporting something beautiful: Lance makes beautiful things. It is January; a new year has started and we are all back at it, scrambling to survive, but I am sustained by friendships like these with Todd and Lance. As I am by Joe at Copper & Kings in Kentucky, who named his stills after three women on my favorite Bob Dylan record (*Desire*), and plays music in his rickhouse to influence his American oak aging barrels of domestic brandy. As I am by Robert Dawson at Manulele Distillers in Hawaii, home of Kō Hana Agricole Rum, who is as much a conservationist as he is distiller, protecting tens of varieties of heirloom Hawaiian sugarcane. As I am by my connection with all the characters I've described in this book and others I haven't, be they freethinking or traditional in the finest sense. As I was by Eric when we stood beside the still at Dudognon last year and he said beautifully, "That's why they call them spirits. They are freed to the heavens in the form of vapor, an escaped essence, only to be recaptured and brought back to earth."

On January 20, 2017, Inauguration Day, I'm on a plane to France with Charles, Craig, Jay, and Eric. We'll tell jokes and taste those farmstead spirits that are like apples and dirt and grapes because they are made from apples and dirt and grapes. Just like last year and next year, if we're lucky, Charles will break my balls, smirking and squinting like Warren Oates, because I take sixty days to pay him and we will eat cheeses that smell like grass and shit.

Then I will keep traveling toward what I adore, in the direction of what causes the heart to open, which is what I would hope for us all. I pray we all find buoyancy in whatever time we are living, that we encounter meaning and love in our work so it sustains us, does not deplete us, and empowers us to infect those around us with a contagious optimism, because we all are only human; we all are just trying to make payroll and pay taxes, and we all are deserving of some luxury.

ACKNOWLEDGMENTS

It felt like cheating with all the help I got:

Thank you Kitty for convincing me I had something to say. This experience has been wonderful and I owe it all to you.

Thank you Emily for helping me to write the book I wanted. A dream come true. Every writer should be lucky enough to work with someone like you.

Thank you Margaret. You are a remarkable teacher and an amazing poet.

Thank you David and Windy. I've never done anything like this and you have been so kind and helpful. And patient.

Angelina, Emma, and Martin. It took a long time but we ended up with something lovely. Thanks for sticking with it.

To Ten Speed Press and to my investors, thank you for taking a real financial risk in support of what's fleeting and beautiful.

Thank you Andreas and Eric.

Thank you Greg, Seth, Chris, Kristi, Lauren, and Julia, who kept their eyes on the shop.

To my two fathers, Tom and Lester, thank you for your unique contributions to this project and to my life.

To my two mothers, Candy and Mary-Kay, thank you. I love you both.

To my last two parents, Tim and Bonnie. Thank you for everything.

Thank you to all the people who work in the F&B business, from those I've known for decades to those whose paths only briefly crossed mine. We are all insane but we love it.

ABOUT THE AUTHOR

THAD VOGLER is the owner of Trou Normand, Obispo, and the James Beard Award–winning Bar Agricole in San Francisco. For nearly two decades, he worked to design, open, and manage the bars at more than twenty top Bay Area venues. In 2011, Vogler was named one of *Forbes* magazine's most interesting people. A global authority on craft spirits, he is consulted regularly by national and global press including the *New York Times*, *Der Spiegel*, the *Washington Post*, *Sunset*, *Bon Appetit*, and the *Wall Street Journal*. He has worked with numerous world-famous restaurateurs including Alice Waters, Charles Phan, and Francis Ford Coppola.